ADVANCED OSINT STRATEGIES

ONLINE INVESTIGATIONS AND INTELLIGENCE GATHERING

4 BOOKS IN 1

I0011295

BOOK 1
FOUNDATIONS OF OSINT MASTERY: A BEGINNER'S GUIDE

BOOK 2
NAVIGATING THE DIGITAL SHADOWS: INTERMEDIATE OSINT TECHNIQUES

BOOK 3
ADVANCED OSINT ARSENAL: EXPERT-LEVEL INTELLIGENCE GATHERING

BOOK 4
MASTERING OSINT INVESTIGATIONS: CUTTING-EDGE STRATEGIES AND TOOLS

ROB BOTWRIGHT

Published by Rob Botwright
Library of Congress Cataloging-in-Publication Data
ISBN 978-1-83938-647-3
Cover design by Rizzo

Disclaimer

The contents of this book are based on extensive research and the best available historical sources. However, the author and publisher make no claims, promises, or guarantees about the accuracy, completeness, or adequacy of the information contained herein. The information in this book is provided on an "as is" basis, and the author and publisher disclaim any and all liability for any errors, omissions, or inaccuracies in the information or for any actions taken in reliance on such information. The opinions and views expressed in this book are those of the author and do not necessarily reflect the official policy or position of any organization or individual mentioned in this book. Any reference to specific people, places, or events is intended only to provide historical context and is not intended to defame or malign any group, individual, or entity. The information in this book is intended for educational and entertainment purposes only. It is not intended to be a substitute for professional advice or judgment. Readers are encouraged to conduct their own research and to seek professional advice where appropriate. Every effort has been made to obtain necessary permissions and acknowledgments for all images and other copyrighted material used in this book. Any errors or omissions in this regard are unintentional, and the author and publisher will correct them in future editions.

BOOK 1 - FOUNDATIONS OF OSINT MASTERY: A BEGINNER'S GUIDE

BOOK 2 - NAVIGATING THE DIGITAL SHADOWS: INTERMEDIATE OSINT TECHNIQUES

BOOK 3 - ADVANCED OSINT ARSENAL: EXPERT-LEVEL INTELLIGENCE GATHERING

BOOK 4 - MASTERING OSINT INVESTIGATIONS: CUTTING-EDGE STRATEGIES AND TOOLS

Introduction

Welcome to "Advanced OSINT Strategies: Online Investigations and Intelligence Gathering." In an age dominated by digital information, the art of open-source intelligence (OSINT) has become an indispensable tool for individuals, organizations, and governments seeking to make informed decisions, uncover hidden truths, and protect their interests in the vast expanse of the internet.

This comprehensive book bundle comprises four distinct volumes, each designed to take you on a transformative journey from novice to expert in the world of OSINT. Whether you are just beginning your exploration of this field or are already well-versed in its intricacies, this collection has something valuable to offer you.

BOOK 1 - Foundations of OSINT Mastery: A Beginner's Guide In this initial volume, we lay the groundwork for your OSINT journey. We start with the fundamentals, ensuring that you have a strong understanding of the core concepts and principles that underpin OSINT. You'll learn how to navigate the digital landscape, understand the significance of digital footprints, and explore various sources of open-source information. As you progress through chapters on internet search techniques, social media investigations, website analysis, and data extraction, you'll begin to build a solid foundation of OSINT skills. Ethics and privacy considerations are also emphasized, ensuring that you become a responsible and ethical OSINT practitioner from the outset.

BOOK 2 - Navigating the Digital Shadows: Intermediate OSINT Techniques With your foundational knowledge in place, this volume takes you to the next level. Here, you'll delve deeper into the art of online investigations, honing your skills with advanced search queries, exploring the enigmatic realms of the deep web and dark web, and mastering geospatial intelligence techniques. Advanced social media analysis, email tracing, and open-source analysis tools become second nature as you prepare to automate your OSINT workflows and delve into the world of cyber threat intelligence. You'll soon find yourself navigating the digital shadows with confidence and precision.

BOOK 3 - Advanced OSINT Arsenal: Expert-Level Intelligence Gathering Now, it's time to ascend to the ranks of expert-level intelligence gathering. In this volume, you'll explore advanced topics such as analyzing cryptocurrencies and blockchain, exploiting IoT devices for intelligence, and employing advanced data scraping and automation techniques. Real-world intelligence operations and the integration of ethical hacking with OSINT are also covered. By the end of this book, you'll possess a formidable OSINT arsenal and the expertise to tackle complex intelligence challenges.

BOOK 4 - Mastering OSINT Investigations: Cutting-Edge Strategies and Tools In the final volume of this series, we explore cutting-edge strategies and tools that propel you to the forefront of OSINT investigations. You'll unravel the potential of big data, artificial intelligence, quantum computing, and their roles in OSINT. You'll venture into the depths of hidden markets and forums, track cryptocurrencies on the dark web, and master advanced geospatial analysis techniques. IoT vulnerability assessment and data collection and analysis techniques complete your journey, making you a master of OSINT investigations equipped with the latest tools and strategies.

Whether you're an aspiring OSINT practitioner seeking to acquire foundational knowledge or a seasoned expert looking to expand your skill set, "Advanced OSINT Strategies" offers a comprehensive and systematic approach to online investigations and intelligence gathering. As you progress through these four volumes, you'll not only gain practical skills but also develop a deep understanding of the ethical and legal considerations that guide the world of OSINT.

Prepare to embark on a journey of discovery, exploration, and mastery. Your path to becoming an OSINT expert begins here, within the pages of this book bundle. Let's delve into the intricate world of online investigations and intelligence gathering, where knowledge is power, and the truth is waiting to be uncovered.

BOOK 1
FOUNDATIONS OF OSINT MASTERY
A BEGINNER'S GUIDE

ROB BOTWRIGHT

Chapter 1: Introduction to OSINT

Next, we will embark on a journey to explore the vast landscape of Open Source Intelligence, commonly known as OSINT. OSINT plays a pivotal role in today's information age, enabling individuals, organizations, and government agencies to gather valuable insights from publicly available sources. Understanding the fundamentals of OSINT is essential for anyone seeking to harness its power effectively. The term "Open Source Intelligence" refers to the process of collecting and analyzing information from publicly accessible sources, such as websites, social media platforms, government records, news articles, and more. Unlike classified or confidential information, OSINT relies on data that is openly accessible to the public, making it a valuable resource for researchers, investigators, and analysts.

One of the primary advantages of OSINT is its accessibility. Unlike traditional intelligence-gathering methods that often require significant resources and clearances, OSINT can be conducted by almost anyone with an internet connection and the right skills. This accessibility democratizes intelligence gathering, allowing individuals and smaller organizations to compete on a more level playing field with larger entities.

OSINT encompasses a wide range of sources and techniques, making it a versatile tool for various purposes. It can be used for cybersecurity, law enforcement, corporate investigations, competitive analysis, and even personal research. Whether you're a security professional looking to protect your organization or a journalist uncovering a story, OSINT can provide valuable data.

To fully appreciate the power of OSINT, it's essential to understand its core principles. These principles include the collection of publicly available data, the analysis of information from diverse sources, and the synthesis of insights to generate intelligence. OSINT practitioners must also navigate ethical and legal considerations, ensuring that their activities remain within the boundaries of the law and ethical standards.

As we delve deeper into this chapter, we'll explore the various types of information that can be obtained through OSINT. This includes data related to individuals, organizations, events, locations, and more. The breadth of OSINT allows investigators to piece together complex puzzles and uncover hidden connections that may not be immediately apparent.

A critical aspect of OSINT is the ability to verify the accuracy and credibility of information. With the proliferation of fake news and misinformation on the internet, practitioners must employ robust verification techniques to ensure the reliability of their findings. Additionally, OSINT analysts must be cautious about biases that can affect their interpretation of data.

The OSINT landscape is dynamic and continually evolving. New data sources emerge, and technological advancements provide innovative ways to gather and analyze information. Staying updated on the latest tools and techniques is crucial for OSINT practitioners, as it ensures that their skills remain relevant and effective.

Throughout this book, we will delve into the practical aspects of OSINT, including tools, techniques, and case studies that illustrate its real-world applications. Whether you're a novice looking to build a strong foundation in OSINT or an experienced practitioner seeking to enhance your skills, this book aims to provide valuable insights and guidance.

In the next chapters, we will explore topics such as understanding digital footprints, utilizing various OSINT information sources, mastering internet search techniques, conducting in-depth social media investigations, and analyzing websites for data extraction. Each chapter will equip you with essential knowledge and practical skills to navigate the ever-expanding OSINT landscape effectively.

As we progress through the book, you'll gain a deeper understanding of how OSINT can be applied in different scenarios and industries. You'll discover advanced techniques for intelligence gathering, privacy protection, and ethical considerations that should guide your OSINT activities.

So, without further ado, let's embark on this journey to master the foundations of OSINT. By the end of this book, you'll be well-equipped to navigate the digital realm, extract valuable information, and make informed decisions based on your OSINT expertise.

Understanding the importance of Open Source Intelligence, or OSINT, in today's world is essential for anyone seeking to navigate the complex information landscape that defines our era. In an age where information flows freely across the internet and data is readily accessible, OSINT serves as a critical tool for gathering valuable insights and intelligence from publicly available sources. This importance extends across a wide range of domains, from national security and law enforcement to business, journalism, and personal decision-making.

In the realm of national security and intelligence, OSINT plays a pivotal role in threat assessment and risk management. By monitoring publicly accessible data, government agencies can gain early insights into potential security threats, track the activities of hostile actors, and make informed decisions to protect their citizens and interests. In this context, OSINT acts as an early warning system, helping nations stay vigilant in an ever-changing global landscape.

For law enforcement agencies, OSINT serves as a valuable investigative tool. It allows investigators to gather information about suspects, identify criminal networks, and uncover critical evidence. OSINT techniques can help solve cold cases, track missing persons, and prevent criminal activities by providing timely and actionable intelligence. In a world where criminals often leave digital footprints, OSINT becomes an indispensable resource for law enforcement.

In the business world, OSINT has gained prominence as a competitive intelligence tool. Companies use OSINT to monitor market trends, track competitors, and assess consumer sentiment. By analyzing publicly available data, businesses can make informed decisions about product development, marketing strategies, and market entry. OSINT also helps organizations identify potential risks and vulnerabilities, allowing them to proactively address threats to their operations and reputation.

For journalists and media professionals, OSINT provides a means to uncover hidden stories and verify information. Investigative journalists use OSINT techniques to research topics, identify sources, and corroborate facts. In an age of disinformation and fake news, OSINT serves as a crucial tool for fact-checking and maintaining the integrity of news reporting. Journalists can also use OSINT to protect their sources and maintain their own digital security.

On a personal level, individuals can benefit from OSINT in various ways. Whether researching a potential employer, vetting a new acquaintance, or conducting due diligence before making a significant investment, OSINT empowers individuals to make informed decisions. It helps individuals protect their privacy online and avoid potential scams or threats.

The importance of OSINT is further underscored by its accessibility. Unlike traditional intelligence-gathering methods that often require extensive resources and clearances, OSINT can be conducted by virtually anyone with an internet connection. This accessibility democratizes the process of intelligence gathering, leveling the playing field between individuals, organizations, and governments.

OSINT encompasses a wide range of sources and techniques, making it a versatile tool for various purposes. It involves collecting and analyzing information from websites, social media platforms, government records, news articles, and more. This diversity of sources allows OSINT practitioners to piece together complex puzzles, uncover hidden connections, and gain insights that may not be immediately apparent.

Moreover, the timeliness of OSINT is a key factor in its importance. In an era where events unfold rapidly, OSINT enables real-time monitoring and analysis of developing situations. Whether tracking a natural disaster, a public protest, or a global health crisis, OSINT can provide critical information to inform emergency responses and decision-making.

However, with the power of OSINT comes responsibility. Practitioners must navigate ethical and legal considerations to ensure that their activities remain within the boundaries of the law and ethical standards. Respect for privacy, adherence to copyright laws, and responsible information sharing are essential principles that underpin the responsible use of OSINT.

In an age where data privacy is a growing concern, OSINT practitioners must also be mindful of the potential implications of their activities on individuals' personal information. Striking a balance between the pursuit of information and the protection of privacy is a challenge that requires a nuanced approach.

In summary, the importance of OSINT in today's world cannot be overstated. It serves as a valuable tool for governments, law enforcement, businesses, journalists, and individuals alike. Its accessibility, versatility, and timeliness make it indispensable in navigating the information-rich environment of the digital age. However, the responsible use of OSINT, guided by ethical and legal considerations, is crucial to ensure that its benefits are realized without compromising privacy and integrity.

Chapter 2: Understanding Digital Footprints

Tracing digital footprints is a fundamental aspect of Open Source Intelligence (OSINT) and serves as a critical starting point for any investigation or information-gathering endeavor in the digital realm. A digital footprint, in essence, represents the trail of online activities, interactions, and information left behind by individuals and entities as they navigate the internet. Understanding how to trace and interpret these digital footprints is an essential skill for OSINT practitioners, investigators, cybersecurity professionals, and anyone seeking to gain insights from the vast expanse of publicly available online data.

Digital footprints encompass a wide array of elements, including the websites an individual visits, the social media posts they engage with, the emails they send and receive, the online purchases they make, the location data from their devices, and much more. These digital traces collectively form a comprehensive profile that can reveal a person's interests, habits, connections, and even potentially sensitive information.

One of the primary motivations behind tracing digital footprints is the need for information. Whether you are conducting a background check on a potential employee, investigating a cybersecurity breach, or tracking the online activities of a suspect, understanding their digital footprints can provide valuable insights. It allows you to piece together a more comprehensive picture of their online presence and behavior.

Moreover, digital footprints can serve as a valuable tool for proactive threat detection and risk assessment. By continuously monitoring and analyzing digital footprints across various online platforms, organizations and security professionals can identify potential security vulnerabilities, suspicious activities, and emerging threats. This proactive approach enables timely responses to mitigate risks and protect assets.

To effectively trace digital footprints, one must employ a combination of techniques and tools. Web scraping, for instance, allows for the automated collection of data from websites, which can be useful for tracking changes to web content or extracting information from online sources. Social media monitoring tools enable the tracking of mentions, trends, and conversations across social platforms, providing valuable insights into public sentiment and emerging topics.

Email tracing and analysis tools are essential for tracking the origin of emails, identifying potential phishing attempts, and verifying the authenticity of email senders. Digital forensics techniques come into play when investigating electronic devices, such as computers and smartphones, to recover digital artifacts and uncover evidence related to criminal activities.

In addition to the technical aspects of tracing digital footprints, there is a human element involved in OSINT investigations. OSINT practitioners must possess strong analytical skills and the ability to piece together fragmented information from various sources. They must be adept at recognizing patterns, identifying discrepancies, and drawing meaningful conclusions from the data they collect.

Furthermore, understanding the context of the digital footprints is crucial. Information found in isolation may be misleading or incomplete, so it's essential to consider the broader context in which it was generated. Contextual information helps in interpreting the significance of digital footprints and their relevance to the investigation at hand.

Privacy considerations are also paramount when tracing digital footprints. OSINT practitioners must operate within the bounds of legal and ethical guidelines. Respecting individuals' privacy rights and adhering to data protection laws is non-negotiable. Techniques that infringe on privacy or involve illegal activities are not only unethical but can also have serious legal consequences.

One must also be cautious about the potential for misinformation and disinformation in the digital realm. Malicious actors may deliberately create false digital footprints to mislead investigators or sow confusion. Therefore, critical thinking and skepticism are essential attributes for those engaged in tracing digital footprints.

As technology continues to advance, the scope and complexity of digital footprints are likely to expand. The proliferation of Internet of Things (IoT) devices, wearable technology, and the integration of digital systems into everyday life are creating new sources of data and new challenges for digital footprint tracing.

Moreover, the increasing emphasis on data privacy and security has led to more stringent regulations and greater awareness among individuals about protecting their online information. This, in turn, may lead to changes in online behavior and the types of digital footprints that are available for analysis.

In summary, tracing digital footprints is a fundamental skill in the field of OSINT and beyond. It enables individuals and organizations to gather valuable insights, detect threats, and make informed decisions. However, it comes with responsibilities, including ethical considerations and respect for privacy rights. As technology evolves, the ability to trace digital footprints will remain a critical component of navigating the ever-expanding digital landscape.

Analyzing online behavior is a multifaceted process that involves examining how individuals and entities interact and engage with digital platforms and the internet as a whole. This aspect of Open Source Intelligence (OSINT) provides valuable insights into the preferences, interests, habits, and potentially even the intentions of online users. Understanding how to analyze online behavior is an essential skill for OSINT practitioners, investigators, marketers, and researchers seeking to gain a deeper understanding of individuals and groups in the digital realm.

Online behavior encompasses a wide range of activities, including the websites users visit, the content they share on social media, the discussions they participate in on forums and comment sections, the products they purchase online, and the patterns of their online interactions. Each of these activities leaves digital traces that can be analyzed to build a profile of an individual or group's online presence.

One of the primary motivations behind analyzing online behavior is to gain insights into the interests and preferences of individuals or target audiences. For businesses and marketers, this analysis is crucial for understanding consumer behavior, tailoring marketing strategies, and delivering relevant content and advertisements to specific demographics. By monitoring online behavior, organizations can refine their marketing efforts and improve customer engagement.

In the context of OSINT, analyzing online behavior is often used for investigative purposes. Law enforcement agencies, for example, may analyze the online behavior of suspects to gather evidence related to criminal activities or to identify potential threats. OSINT analysts may track the online presence of individuals or groups associated with extremist ideologies to assess the scope of their influence and monitor potential security risks.

The analysis of online behavior also extends to social media intelligence, commonly referred to as SOCINT (Social Media Intelligence). SOCINT involves monitoring social media platforms to gain insights into public sentiment, emerging trends, and the activities of individuals or groups. This form of analysis is valuable for understanding public opinion, tracking the spread of information, and assessing the impact of social media campaigns.

To effectively analyze online behavior, OSINT practitioners employ a combination of techniques and tools. Social media monitoring tools allow for the real-time tracking of mentions, hashtags, and trends across various social platforms. These tools provide a comprehensive view of how individuals and groups engage with social media content, helping analysts identify influential voices and track the virality of specific topics.

Text analysis and natural language processing (NLP) techniques are essential for extracting meaning from textual data found in online comments, reviews, and discussions. Sentiment analysis, a subset of NLP, helps determine the emotional tone of text, allowing analysts to gauge public sentiment toward specific topics, products, or brands.

Web scraping and data extraction tools enable the collection of data from websites, including user-generated content such as reviews, comments, and forum posts. This data can be analyzed to identify patterns, trends, and user preferences. Web scraping is particularly valuable for competitive analysis and market research.

Network analysis, another powerful technique, involves visualizing and analyzing the connections between online users and entities. Network analysis can reveal influential nodes within a network, the spread of information, and the relationships between individuals or groups. This technique is often used to identify key players in online communities or social networks.

In addition to technical tools and techniques, human judgment and critical thinking play a significant role in the analysis of online behavior. Analysts must interpret the data within the broader context of the digital landscape, considering factors such as the credibility of sources, the potential for misinformation, and the cultural or societal influences that may impact online behavior.

Privacy and ethical considerations are paramount when analyzing online behavior. Respecting individuals' privacy rights and adhering to data protection laws are essential ethical principles. OSINT practitioners should refrain from engaging in intrusive or unethical activities and should avoid crossing legal boundaries.

As technology continues to evolve, the analysis of online behavior faces new challenges and opportunities. The proliferation of social media platforms, the integration of artificial intelligence into analytics tools, and the emergence of emerging technologies such as virtual reality and augmented reality present novel sources of data and new avenues for analysis.

Moreover, the ethical implications of online behavior analysis are becoming increasingly prominent. The ethical use of data, transparency in data collection and analysis, and the responsible handling of personal information are central concerns as the digital landscape evolves.

In summary, analyzing online behavior is a dynamic and essential component of OSINT and other fields. It provides valuable insights into the behavior and preferences of individuals and groups in the digital realm, enabling organizations to make informed decisions, investigators to gather evidence, and marketers to refine their strategies. As technology and ethical considerations continue to evolve, the analysis of online behavior will remain a critical skill for navigating the digital landscape responsibly and effectively.

Chapter 3: OSINT Information Sources

Publicly available data is a cornerstone of Open Source Intelligence (OSINT), providing a wealth of information that can be accessed and analyzed for various purposes. This type of data comprises information that is openly accessible to the public through legal means, without the need for special clearances or permissions. Understanding how to harness the power of publicly available data is a fundamental skill for OSINT practitioners, researchers, investigators, and decision-makers seeking to extract valuable insights from the vast sea of information available online.

Publicly available data encompasses a wide range of sources, including government records, publicly accessible websites, social media content, academic research, news articles, and more. It represents a rich tapestry of information that can be mined to uncover patterns, trends, connections, and intelligence.

One of the key attributes of publicly available data is its accessibility. Unlike classified or confidential information, which is restricted and protected by various security measures, publicly available data can be accessed by virtually anyone with an internet connection. This democratization of information levels the playing field, allowing individuals, organizations, and governments to gather intelligence and make informed decisions.

Government records are a significant source of publicly available data. These records include information on land ownership, property transactions, business registrations, court proceedings, public financial disclosures, and more. Access to government records varies by jurisdiction, but many governments have made efforts to digitize and make such data available online for transparency and accountability.

Publicly accessible websites are another rich source of data. Websites ranging from government portals and academic repositories to news outlets and online forums host a vast amount of information on a wide range of topics. This information can include reports, articles, documents, and user-generated content that can be analyzed to extract insights.

Social media platforms are a treasure trove of publicly available data. Users share their thoughts, opinions, and personal experiences on social media, creating a digital footprint of their activities and interests. OSINT practitioners can monitor social media to track trends, gather sentiment analysis, and identify individuals or groups of interest.

Academic research and publications contribute to the pool of publicly available data. Universities and research institutions often publish studies, papers, and reports on a variety of subjects. These publications can provide in-depth insights, data, and expert opinions that are valuable for research and analysis.

News articles and media outlets play a vital role in disseminating publicly available information. News reports cover current events, issues, and developments from around the world. OSINT practitioners can use news articles to stay updated on global affairs and gather information related to specific topics or regions.

The analysis of publicly available data involves several key processes. Data collection is the first step, where OSINT practitioners gather relevant information from various sources. This may involve web scraping, data extraction, or manual research, depending on the nature of the data and the sources involved.

Once collected, the data must be organized and structured for analysis. This step may include data cleaning, formatting, and transformation to ensure that the information is suitable for further examination.

Analysis techniques vary depending on the objectives of the OSINT investigation. Text analysis, for example, can be used to extract insights from textual data, such as social media posts or news articles. Data visualization tools can help depict trends, patterns, and relationships within the data.

Publicly available data is invaluable for a wide range of applications. In the realm of business and marketing, it can inform market research, customer profiling, and competitive analysis. Law enforcement agencies rely on publicly available data for investigations, background checks, and intelligence gathering.

Government agencies use publicly available data to monitor public sentiment, track policy issues, and assess the impact of their initiatives. Researchers and academics leverage publicly available data to conduct studies, validate hypotheses, and contribute to the body of knowledge in their respective fields.

As with any form of intelligence gathering, ethical considerations are essential when working with publicly available data. OSINT practitioners must respect privacy rights, adhere to data protection laws, and conduct their activities in a legal and responsible manner. Unauthorized access to restricted information or the use of deceptive tactics to gather data is not only unethical but can also have legal consequences.

Moreover, the interpretation of publicly available data requires critical thinking and context awareness. Information found in isolation may be misleading or incomplete, and analysts must consider the broader context in which the data was generated.

In summary, publicly available data is a powerful resource for OSINT and various other fields. Its accessibility, diversity, and potential for insights make it an invaluable asset for decision-makers, researchers, investigators, and analysts. However, responsible and ethical practices must guide the collection and analysis of this data to ensure that privacy rights are respected, and legal boundaries are upheld. As technology continues to advance, the role of publicly available data in OSINT and decision-making will only grow in significance.

Hidden treasures on the internet are a fascinating aspect of the digital realm, offering a world of undiscovered information and resources beyond what meets the eye at first glance. This chapter explores the concept of hidden treasures in the context of Open Source Intelligence (OSINT) and how uncovering these hidden gems can provide valuable insights and intelligence for various purposes. The internet, vast and ever-expanding, is not just the surface web that most users interact with daily. It consists of multiple layers, including the deep web and the dark web, where a significant portion of hidden treasures resides. The deep web, often misunderstood, comprises web pages that are not indexed by search engines and require specific credentials or access to reach.

This hidden portion of the web includes private databases, academic research archives, subscription-based content, confidential corporate intranets, and other resources that are not intended for public access. Accessing the deep web typically requires login credentials or specific permissions, making it a treasure trove of information that is hidden from casual internet users but still legally accessible for those with the right access privileges. In OSINT, uncovering these hidden gems in the deep web can be a valuable source of information for researchers, investigators, and analysts. It can provide access to proprietary data, research papers, industry reports, and confidential documents that can shed light on various topics.

Beyond the deep web lies the dark web, a hidden realm notorious for its anonymity and association with illicit activities. The dark web consists of websites that are intentionally hidden and can only be accessed through specialized networks like Tor. It is a space where users can remain anonymous, and illegal activities such as the sale of drugs, stolen data, and hacking tools often take place. However, it's important to note that not everything on the dark web is illegal or malicious. There are legitimate use cases for anonymity, such as whistleblowing, secure communications, and evading censorship in oppressive regimes.

In the context of OSINT, the dark web poses both challenges and opportunities. While it may not be the primary source for gathering open-source intelligence, it can provide insights into underground communities, cyber threats, and emerging trends that may not be visible on the surface web. OSINT practitioners can monitor the dark web for indicators of compromise, leaked data, or discussions related to security threats.

Uncovering hidden treasures on the internet requires specific strategies and tools. For the deep web, utilizing search engines designed to access non-indexed content can be helpful. Specialized databases, academic portals, and subscription-based services often hold valuable information that can be accessed with the appropriate credentials. OSINT practitioners may also leverage techniques such as advanced search operators and custom web scraping to navigate the deep web effectively.

Navigating the dark web is a more complex and potentially risky endeavor. Accessing the dark web safely requires the use of anonymity networks like Tor, which route internet traffic through a series of encrypted relays to conceal a user's identity and location. While Tor provides anonymity, it's essential to exercise caution when exploring the dark web, as it can expose users to illegal content and potentially dangerous situations. OSINT practitioners should approach the dark web with a clear understanding of its risks and limitations.

Hidden treasures on the internet extend beyond the deep web and dark web. They can also be found in less explored corners of the surface web. For example, online forums and communities dedicated to niche interests may contain valuable insights and expertise that are not readily available through mainstream channels. These communities often have passionate members who share their knowledge and experiences, making them valuable sources for OSINT research.

Furthermore, hidden treasures can manifest in unexpected ways, such as archived websites, historical data, or overlooked online platforms. As the internet evolves, websites and content may disappear or change, but archives and cached versions can preserve valuable information. OSINT practitioners can utilize web archives and historical data repositories to access past versions of websites and trace the evolution of online content.

Social media platforms, while part of the surface web, also hold hidden treasures in the form of user-generated content. OSINT analysts can analyze social media conversations, hashtags, and trends to gain insights into public sentiment, emerging topics, and the activities of individuals or groups. This information can be valuable for tracking public opinion, monitoring developments in real-time, and identifying influential voices.

In summary, hidden treasures on the internet represent a rich source of information that can be leveraged for OSINT and various research purposes. From the deep web's proprietary data to the dark web's insights into underground communities and the surface web's niche communities and archived content, OSINT practitioners have a vast landscape to explore. However, it's essential to approach these hidden treasures with ethical considerations, respect for privacy, and an awareness of the potential risks associated with certain areas of the web. When navigated responsibly, hidden treasures can unlock valuable intelligence and provide a deeper understanding of the digital world.

Chapter 4: Internet Search Techniques

Advanced search operators are a set of specialized commands and symbols that can be used in search engines and databases to refine and enhance the precision of online searches, allowing users to pinpoint specific information with greater accuracy. These operators are invaluable tools in the arsenal of Open Source Intelligence (OSINT) practitioners, researchers, and investigators, enabling them to extract relevant data from the vast expanse of the internet efficiently.

The use of advanced search operators goes beyond the basic keyword-based searches that most users are familiar with. While simple keyword searches can yield a broad range of results, advanced search operators allow users to specify particular criteria, filter out irrelevant information, and focus their queries on precise targets.

One of the most common and powerful advanced search operators is the "site:" operator. This operator restricts search results to a specific website or domain, making it particularly useful when looking for information on a particular site or when monitoring changes to a specific web address. For example, a query like "site:wikipedia.org artificial intelligence" will return results exclusively from the Wikipedia domain related to the topic of artificial intelligence.

Another widely used advanced search operator is the "intitle:" operator, which limits results to pages with a specific keyword or phrase in the title. This operator is valuable for finding webpages that prioritize the specified keyword in their titles, potentially indicating the relevance of the content to the query.

The "filetype:" operator allows users to search for specific file types or formats, such as PDFs, Word documents, or Excel spreadsheets. For instance, a search query like "filetype:pdf climate change" will return results that include only PDF documents related to the topic of climate change.

The "related:" operator provides a list of websites related to a specified URL, offering insights into websites that share similar content or themes. By using "related:" followed by a web address, users can discover websites that may be of interest in their research.

The "link:" operator allows users to find webpages that link to a particular URL. This can be useful for discovering references to a specific webpage across the internet, helping to gauge its influence and popularity.

Advanced search operators can also be combined to create more complex queries. For example, a search query like "site:wikipedia.org intitle:history of mathematics" will return results from Wikipedia that have "history of mathematics" in their titles.

In addition to these common advanced search operators, there are many others that offer specialized functionalities. The "cache:" operator displays a cached version of a webpage as it appeared when it was last indexed by a search engine, which can be useful for accessing content that may have been removed or changed.

The "define:" operator provides definitions for a specified word or phrase, making it a quick reference tool for accessing dictionary or encyclopedia entries directly from search results.

The "AROUND()" operator allows users to specify a proximity search, finding webpages where two terms appear within a certain number of words or characters of each other. This operator is useful for identifying content where specific concepts or keywords are closely related.

The "info:" operator provides information about a particular webpage, including details such as the webpage's title, snippet, and URL. This can be helpful for quickly accessing metadata about a webpage.

While advanced search operators are valuable tools for refining searches and accessing specific information, it's important to note that different search engines and databases may support different operators, and their functionality may vary. Users should refer to the documentation or help resources provided by the specific search engine or database they are using to learn more about available operators and their syntax.

Moreover, as search engines and online platforms evolve, the effectiveness of certain operators may change over time. OSINT practitioners and researchers should stay updated on the latest developments and best practices for using advanced search operators to maximize their effectiveness in gathering intelligence and conducting research on the internet.

In summary, advanced search operators are indispensable tools for OSINT practitioners, researchers, and investigators seeking to harness the full potential of online searches. These operators allow users to refine their queries, filter search results, and access specific information with precision and efficiency. Whether searching for content on a particular website, narrowing down search results by file type, or conducting proximity searches, advanced search operators empower users to uncover hidden gems of knowledge within the vast digital landscape of the internet.

Effective keyword strategies are at the heart of successful online research, content discovery, and Open Source Intelligence (OSINT) investigations. Keywords serve as the bridge between your intent and the vast expanse of information available on the internet, enabling you to locate and access the specific information you seek. Developing and employing effective keyword strategies is an essential skill for researchers, investigators, content creators, and anyone navigating the digital landscape.

A keyword, in its simplest form, is a word or phrase that describes the topic, concept, or idea you are searching for online. It's the key to unlocking relevant information from search engines, databases, and websites. The choice of keywords determines the success of your search and the quality of the results you obtain.

To develop effective keyword strategies, it's crucial to start with a clear understanding of your research objectives or investigative goals. What information are you seeking to find? What questions do you need answers to? Defining your objectives helps you identify the core concepts and themes that will serve as the foundation for your keyword strategy.

One fundamental aspect of keyword strategies is the use of relevant and specific keywords. Generic or overly broad keywords can result in an overwhelming number of search results, making it challenging to find the information you need. Conversely, using keywords that are too narrow may yield few or no results. Striking the right balance is essential.

Synonyms and related terms play a significant role in effective keyword strategies. Different people may use varied terminology to describe the same concept or idea. Including synonyms and related terms in your keyword strategy broadens the scope of your search and increases the chances of discovering relevant information.

Keyword modifiers are words or phrases that add specificity to your search. For instance, if you're researching climate change, modifiers like "causes of climate change," "effects of climate change," or "climate change solutions" can help refine your search and focus on particular aspects of the topic.

Boolean operators, such as "AND," "OR," and "NOT," are powerful tools for combining and excluding keywords in your search queries. "AND" narrows down results by requiring both keywords to be present, "OR" broadens results by accepting either keyword, and "NOT" excludes results containing the specified keyword.

Phrase searching involves enclosing a set of keywords within quotation marks. This tells search engines to find the exact phrase as it appears in the quotes. For example, searching for "renewable energy" in quotes will return results where the words "renewable" and "energy" appear together in that order.

Wildcard characters, like "" and "?," can be used when you're uncertain about the exact wording or spelling of a keyword. The asterisk () represents multiple characters, while the question mark (?) represents a single character. For example, "wom*n" would include results for both "woman" and "women."

Limiting search by date, domain, or filetype is another facet of effective keyword strategies. Many search engines and databases allow you to specify the time frame, restrict results to specific websites or domains, or search for particular file types (e.g., PDFs or Word documents).

Keyword expansion involves identifying related keywords and concepts that may not have initially been part of your strategy but could provide valuable insights. Exploring these additional keywords can lead to a more comprehensive understanding of your topic.

Refining your keyword strategy based on initial search results is an iterative process. After conducting an initial search, review the results and identify relevant keywords or modifiers that you may have overlooked. Adjust and refine your strategy accordingly to improve the precision of your subsequent searches.

Testing and experimenting with different keyword combinations and strategies is essential for uncovering hidden information and refining your search results. Don't be afraid to try variations of keywords and operators to see which approaches yield the most relevant and valuable results.

Keyword strategies are not static but evolve as your research progresses and your understanding of the topic deepens. It's important to revisit and adapt your keyword strategies as needed to ensure that you stay on track with your research objectives.

Moreover, keyword strategies should be tailored to the specific platform or search engine you are using. Each search engine may have its own syntax and rules for applying operators and modifiers. Familiarize yourself with the search engine's documentation and capabilities to optimize your keyword strategies effectively.

In summary, effective keyword strategies are essential tools for navigating the digital landscape and conducting successful online research and OSINT investigations. By developing clear objectives, using relevant and specific keywords, incorporating synonyms and related terms, and leveraging advanced search techniques like Boolean operators and wildcard characters, you can enhance the precision and efficiency of your searches. Keyword strategies are dynamic and adaptable, evolving as your research progresses and your understanding of the topic deepens. When wielded skillfully, keywords unlock the doors to a world of information, enabling you to extract valuable insights and intelligence from the vast expanse of the internet.

Chapter 5: Social Media Investigations

Profiling social media users is a practice that involves creating comprehensive profiles of individuals or entities based on their online activities, interactions, and publicly available information on social media platforms. This process is a fundamental aspect of Open Source Intelligence (OSINT) and serves as a valuable tool for understanding the preferences, interests, connections, and potentially even the motivations of individuals or groups in the digital realm. Profiling social media users requires a combination of techniques, tools, and critical thinking to extract meaningful insights responsibly and ethically.

Social media platforms have become a central hub for individuals to share their thoughts, opinions, experiences, and personal information with the world. This wealth of user-generated content creates an opportunity for OSINT practitioners, investigators, and researchers to gain valuable insights into the behaviors and characteristics of social media users.

The process of profiling social media users begins with data collection. OSINT practitioners gather publicly available information from social media platforms, including profiles, posts, comments, likes, and connections. This information can be accessed through the platforms' public APIs or by manually exploring user profiles and content.

Text analysis and natural language processing (NLP) techniques play a significant role in profiling social media users. These techniques enable the extraction of insights from textual data, such as posts, comments, and conversations. Sentiment analysis, for instance, helps determine the emotional tone of text, allowing analysts to gauge the sentiment of social media users toward specific topics or issues.

Social network analysis is another critical component of profiling social media users. It involves visualizing and analyzing the connections and relationships between users on social media platforms. By mapping out networks and identifying influential nodes, analysts can gain insights into the structure and dynamics of online communities and identify key players within them.

Metadata analysis is essential for understanding the context of social media content. Metadata includes information such as the date and time of posts, geolocation data, and user-generated tags or hashtags. Analyzing metadata can provide insights into the timing and location of user activities and the trending topics or events that users are engaging with.

Visual content analysis is another valuable technique for profiling social media users. This involves analyzing images, videos, and multimedia content shared on social media. Image recognition technology and reverse image search tools can help identify objects, locations, and individuals within visual content, providing additional context and insights.

Profile analysis delves into the information publicly available on user profiles. This includes details such as usernames, bios, profile pictures, and links to external websites or other social media profiles. Analysts can extract information about a user's interests, affiliations, and online presence from their profile.

Geospatial intelligence (GEOINT) in OSINT is particularly relevant when profiling social media users. By analyzing geolocation data associated with posts and check-ins, OSINT practitioners can gain insights into the movements and activities of individuals or groups. GEOINT can be valuable for tracking the physical locations of social media users or identifying patterns in their travel behavior.

While technical tools and techniques are essential for profiling social media users, critical thinking and ethical considerations are equally crucial. Analysts must exercise caution and responsibility when collecting and analyzing user-generated content. Privacy rights and ethical principles must be respected, and the use of deceptive or intrusive tactics is unacceptable.

Moreover, it's essential to recognize the limitations of profiling social media users. Publicly available information on social media may not provide a complete or accurate representation of an individual's identity or motivations. Users may curate their online personas or engage in disinformation campaigns, making it challenging to discern truth from deception.

The legal and ethical boundaries of social media profiling are essential considerations. Laws and regulations governing the collection and use of social media data may vary by jurisdiction, and analysts must adhere to these legal frameworks. Furthermore, organizations and individuals should have clear policies and guidelines in place for conducting social media profiling ethically and responsibly.

Profiling social media users can be applied to a wide range of applications. Law enforcement agencies may use social media profiling to investigate criminal activities, monitor potential threats, and gather evidence related to cases. Researchers and academics can leverage social media profiling for studies on online behaviors, sentiment analysis, and the dynamics of virtual communities.

Businesses and marketers use social media profiling to understand consumer preferences, tailor marketing strategies, and identify brand advocates or influencers. Political campaigns and advocacy groups may employ social media profiling to assess public sentiment, identify key issues, and target specific demographics.

In summary, profiling social media users is a valuable practice in the realm of OSINT and beyond. It allows individuals and organizations to gain insights into the behaviors, preferences, and connections of social media users. While technical tools and techniques are essential for profiling, ethical considerations, privacy rights, and legal boundaries must guide the process. When conducted responsibly and with respect for privacy, profiling social media users can be a powerful tool for understanding the digital landscape and the individuals and groups that inhabit it.

Tracking social media trends is a dynamic and essential practice for staying informed about the ever-evolving digital landscape and understanding the topics, conversations, and developments that capture the attention of online communities. Social media platforms serve as a real-time reflection of public sentiment, interests, and emerging issues, making them valuable sources of Open Source Intelligence (OSINT) for researchers, businesses, marketers, and individuals seeking to stay ahead of the curve.

The process of tracking social media trends involves monitoring and analyzing the content, discussions, and activities taking place on various social media platforms. These platforms, including Twitter, Facebook, Instagram, LinkedIn, TikTok, and others, host a wide range of user-generated content, from text-based posts and comments to images, videos, and live streams.

Hashtags are a prominent feature of social media that play a pivotal role in tracking trends. Users create and use hashtags to categorize and label their posts, making it easier to search for and follow specific topics or conversations. Trending hashtags provide a snapshot of the most popular and widely discussed subjects on social media at any given moment.

Keyword tracking is another essential aspect of monitoring social media trends. By identifying and tracking relevant keywords and phrases, individuals and organizations can stay updated on discussions related to specific topics, industries, brands, or events. Keyword tracking allows for a more comprehensive understanding of the online discourse surrounding a particular subject.

Social media monitoring tools and platforms are valuable resources for tracking trends efficiently. These tools provide features for real-time tracking of keywords and hashtags, sentiment analysis, and the aggregation of social media data from multiple platforms. They offer insights into the volume of discussions, user engagement, and sentiment trends related to specific topics.

In addition to hashtags and keywords, tracking the activities of influential users and thought leaders is a common strategy for identifying emerging trends. Influential individuals and organizations often have a significant impact on the topics and issues that gain traction on social media. By following and engaging with these key players, individuals and organizations can gain insights into trends and potentially participate in or shape discussions.

Visual content, such as images and videos, plays a crucial role in social media trends. The rise of platforms like Instagram and TikTok has emphasized the importance of visual content in capturing and conveying trends. Tracking visual trends involves monitoring the types of images and videos that are gaining popularity and the creative techniques used in visual storytelling.

Understanding the lifecycle of social media trends is vital for effective tracking. Trends typically follow a pattern, starting with an initial surge in interest, reaching a peak of popularity, and eventually fading away. Tracking the trajectory of trends allows individuals and organizations to anticipate shifts in public sentiment and adapt their strategies accordingly.

Social media sentiment analysis is a valuable tool for assessing the public's emotional response to specific trends. Sentiment analysis tools can gauge whether discussions related to a trend are predominantly positive, negative, or neutral. Understanding sentiment is crucial for assessing the impact and potential consequences of trends.

Tracking social media trends provides numerous benefits across various domains. In marketing and advertising, trend tracking helps businesses identify opportunities to align their messaging with popular topics or cultural movements, enhancing the relevance and impact of their campaigns. It also allows businesses to identify potential crises or reputation management issues and respond proactively.

For news organizations and journalists, tracking social media trends helps in identifying breaking news stories and monitoring public reactions to current events. Social media trends can serve as early indicators of emerging news stories, providing journalists with valuable leads and insights. In the field of politics and public policy, tracking social media trends allows policymakers and political campaigns to gauge public sentiment, monitor public opinion on key issues, and identify emerging concerns. This information can inform policy decisions and campaign strategies.

For researchers and academics, tracking social media trends provides a window into the collective consciousness of online communities. It enables the study of cultural phenomena, the evolution of language and discourse, and the dynamics of virtual communities. Researchers can gain valuable insights into the ways in which information spreads, trends evolve, and online communities form.

Individuals and influencers can also benefit from tracking social media trends. It allows them to stay informed about topics of interest, engage with relevant discussions, and participate in trending conversations. Additionally, it provides opportunities for individuals to build their personal brands and online presence by aligning their content with popular trends.

While tracking social media trends offers numerous advantages, it also presents challenges and considerations. The sheer volume of content on social media platforms can be overwhelming, making it essential to use monitoring tools and filters effectively. Additionally, trends can sometimes be driven by sensationalism or misinformation, requiring critical thinking and fact-checking.

Ethical considerations are paramount when tracking social media trends. Privacy rights, data protection, and responsible data use must be upheld. Researchers and organizations should respect individuals' consent and adhere to ethical guidelines when analyzing user-generated content.

In summary, tracking social media trends is a dynamic and valuable practice for staying informed, engaging with online communities, and gaining insights into emerging topics and issues. By leveraging hashtags, keywords, monitoring tools, and sentiment analysis, individuals and organizations can effectively navigate the digital landscape and harness the power of social media trends for various purposes. However, it is crucial to approach trend tracking with ethical considerations, critical thinking, and a nuanced understanding of the complexities of online discourse.

Chapter 6: Website Analysis and Data Extraction

Analyzing website structures is a fundamental aspect of web research and Open Source Intelligence (OSINT) investigations, as it involves dissecting the layout, organization, and architecture of websites to extract valuable insights and information. Websites vary widely in their structures, ranging from simple single-page sites to complex multi-level hierarchies with numerous interconnected pages. Understanding how to analyze website structures is crucial for researchers, investigators, and analysts seeking to efficiently navigate the digital landscape and extract meaningful data.

Website structures are the framework upon which web content is organized and presented to users. They determine the navigation flow, the accessibility of information, and the overall user experience. Analyzing website structures involves examining various elements, including the site's hierarchy, page relationships, navigation menus, URLs, and internal linking patterns.

One of the first steps in analyzing website structures is to assess the site's hierarchy. This involves identifying the main sections or categories of the website and understanding how they are organized. Typically, websites have a hierarchical structure with a homepage at the top, followed by main sections or categories, subcategories, and individual pages. Understanding this hierarchy is essential for efficient navigation and content discovery.

Navigation menus are key elements of website structures, providing users with access to different sections and pages of the site. Analyzing navigation menus involves evaluating their organization, labeling, and accessibility. Are menus intuitive and easy to use, or do they present challenges for users to find specific content?

URL structures play a significant role in website analysis. URLs often provide clues about the organization of a site. By examining the structure of URLs, researchers can deduce the relationships between pages and the categorization of content. Additionally, understanding URL patterns can help in crafting precise search queries for web research.

Internal linking is a crucial component of website structures. It refers to the hyperlinks within a website that connect different pages together. Analyzing internal linking patterns can reveal the interconnectedness of content and the importance of specific pages within a site. It can also help identify key pages, such as the homepage or cornerstone content, which often receive more internal links.

Website sitemaps, when available, are valuable tools for understanding website structures. Sitemaps provide an overview of all the pages on a website and their hierarchical relationships. They can be particularly helpful for quickly grasping the scope and organization of large websites.

Website structures can vary significantly based on the purpose and type of site. For example, e-commerce websites typically have a hierarchical structure with product categories and individual product pages. News websites often have a chronological structure with articles organized by publication date. Blog sites may have a reverse chronological structure, with the latest posts displayed prominently on the homepage.

Analyzing website structures can also reveal information about the site's intended audience and content strategy. Websites designed for different user demographics or content niches may have distinct structural characteristics. Understanding these characteristics can aid in tailoring research approaches and content discovery strategies.

Web scraping tools and techniques can be employed to collect data about website structures at scale. These tools can automatically crawl websites, extract information about page hierarchy, URLs, and internal links, and store the data for analysis. Web scraping is particularly useful when analyzing large websites or multiple sites simultaneously.

Additionally, website analysis tools and software can assist in visualizing and mapping website structures. These tools can generate graphical representations of site hierarchies, highlighting the relationships between pages and sections. Visualizing website structures can provide a clearer overview of site organization and help in identifying potential areas of interest.

Analyzing website structures is not limited to publicly accessible websites. In some cases, researchers may need to analyze the structures of password-protected or restricted-access sites. This requires specialized techniques and permissions, and ethical considerations must be taken into account when accessing such sites.

Furthermore, website structures can change over time due to site updates, redesigns, or content additions. It's essential for researchers and analysts to stay updated on website changes to ensure the accuracy of their analyses. Monitoring tools and techniques can help track structural changes and provide alerts when modifications occur.

In summary, analyzing website structures is a fundamental skill for web researchers, investigators, and analysts. It involves assessing the hierarchy, navigation menus, URL structures, internal linking patterns, and other elements that define how web content is organized and presented. Understanding website structures is crucial for efficient navigation, content discovery, and data extraction in the ever-expanding digital landscape. Whether analyzing public websites or restricted-access sites, researchers must adapt their techniques and tools to effectively dissect and interpret website structures.

Extracting valuable data is a fundamental process in Open Source Intelligence (OSINT) and data analysis, as it involves the retrieval and transformation of information from various sources for the purpose of generating insights, making informed decisions, and uncovering hidden knowledge. Data extraction encompasses a wide range of techniques and methods, each tailored to the specific type of data and source being utilized. Next, we will explore the essential concepts and strategies for effectively extracting valuable data.

The first step in data extraction is identifying the sources from which you intend to gather information. These sources can be diverse, including websites, databases, documents, social media platforms, and more. Each source may require a unique approach and tools for data retrieval.

Web scraping is a commonly used technique for extracting data from websites. It involves the automated retrieval of information from web pages by parsing the HTML or structured data on the site. Web scraping tools and scripts can be customized to target specific elements, such as text, images, tables, or links, and extract them for analysis.

When dealing with structured data stored in databases, SQL (Structured Query Language) is a powerful tool for data extraction. SQL queries can be used to retrieve, filter, and transform data from relational databases. This method is particularly valuable for organizations that maintain extensive databases of structured information.

Document parsing and text extraction techniques are essential for extracting valuable data from unstructured text documents. Natural Language Processing (NLP) tools and libraries can assist in processing text to identify relevant information, entities, keywords, and sentiments. Optical Character Recognition (OCR) technology can convert scanned documents and images into machine-readable text.

APIs (Application Programming Interfaces) provide a structured and programmatic way to access data from various online platforms and services. Many online services offer APIs that allow developers to retrieve specific data, such as weather information, financial data, social media posts, and more. API integration is a valuable approach for automating data extraction from online sources.

Data extraction from social media platforms is a specialized area that involves accessing and retrieving information from user profiles, posts, comments, and interactions. Social media APIs and web scraping techniques can be employed to collect data from platforms like Twitter, Facebook, Instagram, and LinkedIn. Ethical considerations and compliance with platform terms of service are essential when extracting data from social media.

Data extraction may also involve the use of data transformation tools and techniques. These tools allow you to convert, clean, and preprocess data to make it suitable for analysis. Data transformation can include tasks such as data normalization, aggregation, filtering, and data cleansing to address issues like missing values or inconsistent formats.

Data extraction often requires data storage solutions to manage and organize the collected information. Databases, data warehouses, and cloud storage platforms are commonly used for storing and structuring extracted data. Proper data storage ensures data integrity and accessibility for analysis.

Automation plays a significant role in data extraction, especially when dealing with large datasets or repetitive tasks. Workflow automation tools and scripts can be created to schedule and execute data extraction processes, reducing manual effort and improving efficiency.

Data extraction should always consider data privacy and security concerns. Sensitive or personally identifiable information (PII) must be handled with care and in compliance with applicable privacy regulations. Anonymization and encryption techniques may be necessary to protect sensitive data during extraction and storage.

Data validation and quality checks are crucial to ensure the accuracy and reliability of extracted data. Validation processes verify that the extracted data matches the expected format and values. Quality checks assess the consistency and completeness of the data.

Data extraction is not a one-time process but an ongoing endeavor. Data sources may change, and new data may become available over time. Regular updates and monitoring of data sources are essential to keep the extracted data relevant and up-to-date.

Collaboration and sharing of data extraction techniques and methodologies within organizations and communities can foster best practices and improve the overall effectiveness of data extraction efforts.

In summary, data extraction is a foundational step in the process of generating insights and making informed decisions in various domains, including OSINT, research, business, and analytics. It involves identifying data sources, employing suitable techniques and tools, considering data privacy and security, and ensuring data quality and ongoing maintenance. By mastering the art of data extraction, individuals and organizations can unlock valuable information hidden within diverse sources and harness it for informed decision-making and knowledge discovery.

Chapter 7: OSINT Tools and Resources

In the world of Open Source Intelligence (OSINT), having access to a versatile toolbox of essential tools is crucial for conducting effective investigations and gathering intelligence from open sources. These tools range from online resources and software applications to specialized search engines and data analysis platforms. Next, we'll explore a selection of essential OSINT tools that can empower OSINT practitioners and analysts in their quest for valuable information.

Search engines are the starting point for most OSINT investigations, and popular search engines like Google, Bing, and Yahoo are valuable tools for finding publicly available information. Operators and advanced search techniques, such as using quotation marks to search for exact phrases or using site-specific searches to target a particular domain, can enhance the precision of search results.

Specialized search engines tailored for OSINT purposes provide additional capabilities. Shodan, for example, focuses on searching for internet-connected devices and systems, including servers, routers, webcams, and industrial control systems. This can be valuable for identifying vulnerable or exposed devices.

Another specialized search engine is ZoomEye, which is designed to search for internet-connected devices and systems as well, with a focus on identifying open ports and services. It provides insights into the security posture of these devices, helping OSINT practitioners assess potential vulnerabilities.

Maltego is a powerful OSINT and data visualization tool that allows users to explore relationships and connections between entities, such as people, organizations, websites, and email addresses. It helps in uncovering hidden connections and patterns through data integration and visualization.

Social media analysis tools like Brandwatch and Talkwalker are essential for monitoring and analyzing conversations and trends on social media platforms. They offer sentiment analysis, trend tracking, and keyword monitoring, enabling OSINT practitioners to stay updated on discussions and public sentiment.

The Wayback Machine, operated by the Internet Archive, is a tool that allows users to access historical versions of websites. This can be valuable for investigating changes to websites over time or retrieving information that may have been removed from a site.

For analyzing Twitter data, TweetDeck is a useful tool that provides customizable dashboards for monitoring specific keywords, hashtags, and Twitter accounts. It allows for real-time tracking of Twitter activity and conversations.

Reverse image search engines like Google Images and TinEye enable users to search for images based on an existing image. This is valuable for identifying the origin and context of images found online, as well as tracking the use of copyrighted or altered images.

Domain and IP address investigation tools like WHOIS and DNS lookup services provide information about the ownership, registration, and history of domains and IP addresses. This can help OSINT practitioners trace the source of websites and online entities.

Email verification tools like Hunter and VerifyEmailAddress allow users to validate the existence and legitimacy of email addresses. This is useful for verifying the authenticity of contact information found online.

OSINT practitioners can use language translation tools like Google Translate to analyze content in different languages, making it easier to access and understand information from international sources.

Public records databases, such as government websites and online archives, can provide access to a wealth of information, including birth and death records, property records, court documents, and business registrations. These databases vary by country and jurisdiction, but they are valuable sources of official information.

Online forums and discussion boards are often hubs for discussions and information sharing. Tools like Boardreader and Reddit's search function allow users to search and monitor discussions on specific topics or keywords.

To analyze and visualize data, data analysis and visualization tools like Tableau and Google Data Studio can be invaluable. These tools enable users to create interactive dashboards and reports, making it easier to convey insights and findings from OSINT investigations.

Dark web search engines like OnionSearch and Grams provide access to resources on the dark web, which is not indexed by traditional search engines. OSINT practitioners should exercise caution and be mindful of ethical considerations when exploring the dark web.

Collaboration and information sharing tools like Trello, Slack, and Evernote can facilitate teamwork and knowledge management among OSINT practitioners and analysts. These tools enable users to collaborate on investigations, share findings, and organize information effectively.

Virtual Private Networks (VPNs) and secure browsing tools are essential for protecting privacy and security while conducting OSINT research. They help anonymize online activities and protect sensitive information from potential threats.

While this chapter highlights a range of essential OSINT tools, it's essential to adapt and expand your toolbox to meet the specific requirements of your investigations. OSINT is a dynamic field, and the landscape of available tools and resources is continually evolving. Staying updated on the latest developments in OSINT tools and techniques is essential for OSINT practitioners to maintain their effectiveness in gathering valuable intelligence from open sources.

Building your OSINT toolkit is a crucial step in becoming a proficient Open Source Intelligence (OSINT) practitioner, as it involves assembling a collection of resources, tools, and techniques that will enable you to effectively gather and analyze intelligence from open sources. While we have already discussed some essential OSINT tools in the previous chapter, this chapter will focus on the strategic approach to constructing a comprehensive toolkit tailored to your specific needs and objectives.

The first command in building your OSINT toolkit is to define your goals and objectives. Understanding your purpose for conducting OSINT investigations will help you determine which tools and resources are most relevant to your needs. Whether you are focused on cybersecurity, threat intelligence, competitive analysis, or any other area, having clear objectives is essential.

Next, you must identify the sources of information that are most relevant to your OSINT objectives. These sources can include websites, social media platforms, online forums, public records, government databases, news sources, and more. By identifying your primary sources, you can prioritize the tools and techniques that will be most useful for accessing and extracting data from these sources.

One of the fundamental components of your OSINT toolkit is a selection of search engines and search operators. Familiarize yourself with advanced search techniques that allow you to refine your queries and obtain more precise results. Search operators, such as quotation marks for exact phrase searches, site-specific searches, and Boolean operators, are invaluable for honing in on relevant information.

When it comes to web scraping, consider the specific websites or platforms from which you need to collect data. Identify web scraping tools and scripts that are compatible with these sources and learn how to customize them to extract the data you require. Ethical considerations, legal compliance, and respect for website terms of service are paramount when engaging in web scraping activities.

Social media analysis tools are essential if your OSINT objectives involve monitoring and analyzing conversations on platforms like Twitter, Facebook, or Instagram. These tools can provide sentiment analysis, trend tracking, and keyword monitoring capabilities, allowing you to stay informed about discussions and public sentiment.

To delve deeper into data analysis and visualization, explore data analysis tools such as Python with libraries like pandas and NumPy or data visualization tools like Tableau or Google Data Studio. These tools can help you make sense of the information you've collected and create visually compelling reports and dashboards to convey your findings.

Consider using data transformation and cleaning tools to preprocess the data you collect. These tools can help you address issues like missing values, inconsistent formats, and outliers, ensuring that your data is ready for analysis. Data normalization, aggregation, and filtering are common tasks in data preparation.

Another vital component of your toolkit is a selection of specialized search engines and databases. Tools like Shodan for searching internet-connected devices, Hunter for email address verification, and domain and IP investigation tools like WHOIS can provide specific information not easily accessible through standard search engines.

APIs (Application Programming Interfaces) are powerful tools for accessing data from online platforms and services. Identify relevant APIs for your OSINT objectives and learn how to integrate them into your workflow. APIs can provide real-time access to data sources such as weather information, financial data, social media posts, and more.

Maintaining a strong awareness of cybersecurity tools and practices is crucial when building your OSINT toolkit. Consider incorporating tools for VPN (Virtual Private Network) usage, secure browsing, encryption, and digital security into your toolkit to protect your privacy and data integrity during OSINT investigations.

When dealing with open source intelligence on the dark web, exercise caution and ensure that you have the necessary knowledge and tools to navigate this hidden part of the internet securely. Specialized dark web search engines and anonymity tools can help you access and explore these sources while minimizing risks.

Collaboration and information-sharing tools are vital if you work as part of a team or need to share findings and insights with colleagues. Platforms like Trello, Slack, and Evernote can streamline teamwork, enabling you to collaborate on investigations, share knowledge, and organize information effectively.

Your OSINT toolkit is not static but should evolve alongside your objectives and the changing landscape of open sources. Stay updated on the latest OSINT tools, techniques, and developments by participating in OSINT communities, attending conferences, and continuously expanding your skill set.

Lastly, remember that ethical considerations and compliance with relevant laws and regulations are paramount in OSINT investigations. Respect privacy rights, obtain proper permissions, and adhere to the terms of service of the sources you access. Maintain the highest ethical standards throughout your OSINT activities.

In summary, building your OSINT toolkit is a strategic process that involves defining objectives, identifying relevant sources, and selecting the tools and techniques that align with your goals. A well-constructed toolkit will empower you to conduct effective OSINT investigations, extract valuable intelligence from open sources, and navigate the evolving digital landscape with confidence and proficiency.

Chapter 8: Protecting Your Privacy in OSINT

Securing your online presence is of paramount importance in an increasingly digital world where personal and sensitive information is constantly at risk of being compromised. Whether you're an individual, a business owner, or an organization, taking proactive measures to protect your online presence is essential for safeguarding your data, privacy, and reputation.

The first step in securing your online presence is to prioritize strong and unique passwords for all your online accounts. Passwords are the first line of defense against unauthorized access, and using strong, complex passwords makes it significantly more challenging for hackers to guess or crack them.

Command: Create strong, unique passwords for each online account you have.

Consider using a password manager to generate, store, and autofill complex passwords for your accounts. Password managers help you maintain a high level of security without the burden of remembering multiple passwords.

Command: Implement a trusted password manager for enhanced password security.

Enabling two-factor authentication (2FA) or multi-factor authentication (MFA) wherever possible adds an extra layer of security to your online accounts. This additional step ensures that even if someone obtains your password, they cannot access your accounts without the secondary authentication method.

Command: Activate 2FA or MFA on all accounts that offer this feature.

Regularly update your software, operating systems, and applications. Software updates often contain important security patches that address vulnerabilities that cybercriminals can exploit. By keeping your software up to date, you minimize potential security risks.

Command: Set your devices and software to automatically update.

Be cautious when clicking on links or downloading attachments from unknown or suspicious sources. Phishing emails and malicious links are common methods used by cybercriminals to gain access to your data. Always verify the source before interacting with any online content.

Command: Exercise caution and skepticism when receiving unsolicited emails or messages.

Regularly back up your data to secure and offline locations. In the event of data loss due to cyberattacks or hardware failures, having backup copies ensures that you can restore your information without relying on ransomware payments or data recovery services.

Command: Establish a backup routine and periodically verify the integrity of your backups.

Protect your online identity by limiting the personal information you share on social media and other public platforms. Cybercriminals can use personal details to impersonate you or target you with phishing attacks.

Command: Review your privacy settings on social media platforms and limit the amount of personal information you share publicly.

Install and maintain reputable antivirus and anti-malware software on your devices. These security tools can help detect and remove threats, such as viruses, spyware, and ransomware, before they cause harm.

Command: Ensure that your antivirus and anti-malware software is up to date and performs regular scans.

Secure your Wi-Fi network with a strong password and encryption. A vulnerable Wi-Fi network can provide cybercriminals with a gateway to your devices and data. Use WPA3 encryption for enhanced security.

Command: Update your Wi-Fi router's firmware, use a strong password, and enable WPA3 encryption if supported.

Regularly review your online accounts and activity for any signs of unauthorized access or suspicious behavior. Timely detection of security incidents can prevent further damage.

Command: Monitor your accounts for unusual activity and set up alerts for any login attempts from unfamiliar devices or locations.

Educate yourself and your team about cybersecurity best practices. Cybersecurity awareness and training programs can help you and your employees recognize and respond to potential threats effectively.

Command: Invest in cybersecurity training and awareness programs for yourself and your team.

Consider using a virtual private network (VPN) when accessing the internet, especially when using public Wi-Fi networks. A VPN encrypts your internet traffic and enhances your online privacy.

Command: Use a reputable VPN service when browsing the internet, particularly on unsecured networks.

Regularly review your online privacy settings for web browsers and applications. Limit the data you share and the permissions you grant to apps to minimize your digital footprint.

Command: Adjust the privacy settings in your web browsers and applications to enhance your online privacy.

In summary, securing your online presence is an ongoing commitment to protecting your personal and sensitive information from cyber threats. By implementing strong passwords, enabling two-factor authentication, keeping software up to date, and practicing caution online, you can significantly reduce your risk of falling victim to cyberattacks. Additionally, raising cybersecurity awareness and investing in protective measures like antivirus software and VPNs will help fortify your digital defenses and ensure a safer online experience.

Safeguarding personal information is a critical aspect of digital security in today's interconnected world, where the collection and dissemination of data are constant and ubiquitous. Command: Prioritize the protection of your personal information as a foundational step in safeguarding your digital identity and privacy.

Personal information encompasses a wide range of data, including your name, address, phone number, email address, social security number, financial details, and more. Command: Be aware of the types of information that qualify as personal, and exercise caution when sharing such data online or offline.

Cybercriminals are continually seeking opportunities to exploit vulnerabilities and gain access to personal information for malicious purposes. Command: Remain vigilant against potential threats and adopt proactive measures to minimize your exposure to data breaches and identity theft.

One fundamental step in safeguarding personal information is to adopt strong password practices. Command: Create and use unique, complex passwords for each online account you have, as weak passwords are a common entry point for cyberattacks.

Utilizing a password manager can simplify the process of managing and storing secure passwords. Command: Consider implementing a reputable password manager to generate and store complex passwords, reducing the risk of password-related breaches.

Two-factor authentication (2FA) or multi-factor authentication (MFA) adds an extra layer of security to your online accounts. Command: Activate 2FA or MFA whenever possible, as this secondary authentication step provides a significant barrier against unauthorized access.

Educate yourself about common phishing tactics, as phishing emails and websites are frequently used to trick individuals into revealing personal information. Command: Develop the ability to recognize phishing attempts and verify the legitimacy of emails and websites before providing any personal data.

Beware of unsolicited requests for personal information, whether through email, phone calls, or text messages, as these can often be scams. Command: Never share personal information in response to unsolicited requests and verify the identity of the requester through independent means.

Regularly review the privacy settings of your online accounts and social media profiles. Command: Adjust your privacy settings to limit the visibility of personal information and control who can access your data.

Keep your devices and software up to date with the latest security patches and updates. Command: Enable automatic updates for operating systems, applications, and antivirus software to protect against known vulnerabilities.

Utilize reputable antivirus and anti-malware software to scan for and remove potential threats on your devices. Command: Ensure that your security software is actively running, and perform regular scans to detect and mitigate malicious software.

Back up your data regularly to secure and offline locations to mitigate the risk of data loss due to cyberattacks or hardware failures. Command: Establish a backup routine to protect important files and ensure they can be restored in the event of a data loss incident.

Secure your Wi-Fi network with a strong password and encryption to prevent unauthorized access. Command: Use WPA3 encryption and a unique, complex Wi-Fi password to deter potential intruders from gaining access to your network.

Exercise caution when connecting to public Wi-Fi networks, as they may not provide adequate security. Command: Consider using a virtual private network (VPN) when accessing public Wi-Fi to encrypt your internet traffic and protect your data.

Be wary of the information you share on social media platforms, as cybercriminals can use publicly available details to target individuals for identity theft. Command: Review and adjust your social media privacy settings to control the visibility of your personal information to the public.

Regularly monitor your financial accounts and statements for unauthorized transactions. Command: Set up account alerts for any suspicious activity and report any unauthorized charges or withdrawals promptly.

Dispose of sensitive physical documents and old electronic devices securely to prevent unauthorized access to personal information. Command: Shred paper documents containing personal data and perform factory resets on devices before discarding or selling them.

Educate yourself and your family members about online safety practices and the importance of safeguarding personal information. Command: Foster a culture of cybersecurity awareness within your household to collectively protect personal data.

In summary, safeguarding personal information is a multifaceted effort that involves awareness, vigilance, and proactive measures to protect sensitive data from unauthorized access and exploitation. By adopting strong password practices, implementing two-factor authentication, recognizing phishing attempts, adjusting privacy settings, and staying informed about online threats, individuals can enhance their digital security and reduce the risk of falling victim to cyberattacks and identity theft. The protection of personal information is a shared responsibility that requires ongoing diligence and commitment to maintaining digital privacy and security.

Chapter 9: Ethics and Legal Considerations

Ethical Open Source Intelligence (OSINT) practices are foundational principles that guide how OSINT practitioners conduct investigations and gather information from open sources. Command: Embrace ethical considerations as the cornerstone of your OSINT activities to ensure responsible and lawful information gathering.

Respect for privacy is a fundamental ethical principle in OSINT. Command: Prioritize the protection of individuals' privacy rights and refrain from intrusive or unauthorized data collection.

Obtain consent and authorization when conducting OSINT investigations involving individuals or organizations. Command: Seek permission to gather information, especially when it involves accessing private or restricted sources.

Exercise caution when handling sensitive or personally identifiable information (PII) obtained during OSINT investigations. Command: Safeguard PII and handle it responsibly to prevent unintended disclosure or misuse.

Adhere to applicable laws and regulations when conducting OSINT investigations. Command: Familiarize yourself with the legal framework governing OSINT activities in your jurisdiction and respect all relevant laws.

Avoid using deceptive or manipulative tactics to collect information. Command: Maintain transparency and honesty in your OSINT methods, refraining from deceitful practices that could harm your reputation.

Consider the potential consequences of your OSINT actions on individuals and organizations. Command: Assess the impact of your investigations and ensure that they do not cause harm or infringe on the rights of others.

Use OSINT findings for lawful and legitimate purposes. Command: Ensure that the information you gather is used in ways that are ethical and compliant with legal requirements.

Practice responsible attribution when citing or sharing OSINT findings. Command: Provide proper credit to the original sources of information and respect copyright and intellectual property rights.

Stay up to date with evolving ethical standards and best practices in the OSINT community. Command: Continuously educate yourself about ethical considerations and seek guidance from experts in the field.

Respect the terms of service and policies of online platforms and websites. Command: Adhere to the rules and guidelines set by online platforms when conducting OSINT investigations on their platforms.

Avoid engaging in harassment, cyberbullying, or any form of harmful behavior during OSINT activities. Command: Maintain professionalism and civility in all interactions, online and offline.

Consider the potential harm that can result from doxing or sharing personal information publicly. Command: Refrain from disclosing personal information without consent and avoid contributing to doxing incidents.

Practice responsible information sharing within the OSINT community. Command: Share information with fellow practitioners in a manner that respects privacy and confidentiality agreements.

Maintain the highest ethical standards in OSINT activities, even when facing challenging or ethically ambiguous situations. Command: Uphold your commitment to ethical OSINT practices, even when confronted with difficult decisions.

Incorporate ethical considerations into your OSINT training and education programs. Command: Foster a culture of ethical awareness and responsibility among aspiring OSINT practitioners.

Collaborate with ethical OSINT professionals and organizations that prioritize responsible information gathering. Command: Partner with like-minded individuals and entities to promote ethical OSINT practices.

Support the development and enforcement of ethical guidelines and standards for the OSINT community. Command: Contribute to the establishment of ethical frameworks that guide the conduct of OSINT practitioners.

In summary, ethical OSINT practices are the ethical compass that guides the responsible and lawful gathering of information from open sources. Upholding these principles is essential to maintain trust, respect privacy, and ensure that OSINT activities are conducted in a manner that aligns with legal and ethical standards. By embracing ethical considerations as a fundamental part of OSINT, practitioners can contribute to the responsible and ethical growth of the field while minimizing potential harm to individuals and organizations.

Navigating the legal boundaries in Open Source Intelligence (OSINT) is essential for OSINT practitioners to conduct investigations responsibly and within the confines of the law. Command: Prioritize a deep understanding of the legal framework governing OSINT activities to ensure compliance and ethical conduct.

One of the primary legal considerations in OSINT is the protection of privacy rights. Command: Respect individuals' privacy by refraining from intrusive or unauthorized data collection, as violating privacy can lead to legal consequences.

Privacy laws and regulations vary from country to country and may include provisions related to data protection, surveillance, and information gathering. Command: Familiarize yourself with the privacy laws applicable in your jurisdiction and in the jurisdictions where your OSINT investigations take place.

Obtaining informed consent and authorization is crucial when collecting information related to individuals or organizations. Command: Seek permission from relevant parties to gather information, especially when it involves accessing private or restricted sources.

Many countries have laws that govern the collection, processing, and storage of personal information. Command: Ensure that your OSINT activities comply with data protection laws and regulations to safeguard personal data.

Be aware of intellectual property rights and copyright laws when using, sharing, or reproducing information found during OSINT investigations. Command: Respect copyright and intellectual property rights by obtaining proper permissions and providing appropriate attribution when necessary.

Ethical considerations often align with legal boundaries in OSINT, but it's essential to distinguish between ethical and legal requirements. Command: Maintain a clear distinction between ethical principles and legal obligations to ensure compliance with both.

Respect the terms of service and policies of online platforms and websites when conducting OSINT investigations on their platforms. Command: Adhere to the rules and guidelines set by online platforms, as violating their terms of service can lead to legal consequences.

Avoid engaging in harassment, cyberbullying, or any form of harmful behavior during OSINT activities, as these actions may violate laws related to harassment or cybercrimes. Command: Maintain professionalism and civility in all interactions to stay within legal boundaries.

Exercise caution when conducting OSINT investigations related to criminal activity or national security, as such investigations may involve legal implications and require law enforcement involvement. Command: Report any findings related to criminal activity to the appropriate authorities and cooperate with law enforcement agencies when necessary.

Ensure that your OSINT activities do not infringe on intellectual property rights, such as patents, trademarks, or trade secrets. Command: Respect intellectual property laws by avoiding unauthorized use or disclosure of protected information.

The sharing of sensitive information, particularly personal data, must comply with data protection laws and regulations. Command: Be cautious when sharing personal data and ensure that your actions align with data privacy laws.

Be mindful of the potential consequences of doxing or sharing personal information publicly, as such actions may lead to legal liability. Command: Refrain from disclosing personal information without consent and avoid contributing to doxing incidents.

Maintain transparency and honesty in your OSINT methods and reporting to avoid accusations of deception or fraud. Command: Uphold the highest standards of transparency to build trust and credibility in your OSINT work.

Incorporate legal considerations into your OSINT training and education programs to ensure that practitioners understand the legal boundaries. Command: Educate aspiring OSINT practitioners about legal requirements and responsibilities to promote lawful conduct.

Collaborate with legal experts and professionals who specialize in cyber law and data protection to navigate complex legal issues. Command: Seek legal counsel and advice when faced with legal questions or challenges in the course of your OSINT investigations.

Support efforts to develop and enforce ethical guidelines and legal standards within the OSINT community. Command: Contribute to the establishment of ethical frameworks that align with legal requirements and promote responsible OSINT practices.

In summary, understanding and adhering to legal boundaries in OSINT is essential for practitioners to conduct investigations responsibly and avoid legal consequences. Compliance with privacy laws, data protection regulations, intellectual property rights, and ethical considerations is fundamental to conducting lawful and ethical OSINT activities. By respecting legal boundaries, OSINT practitioners can contribute to the responsible growth of the field and ensure that their investigations are conducted within the confines of the law.

Chapter 10: Building Your OSINT Skills

Continual learning is a cornerstone of success in the field of Open Source Intelligence (OSINT). Command: Embrace a commitment to ongoing learning as an integral part of your OSINT journey.

The landscape of OSINT is constantly evolving, with new sources of information, tools, and techniques emerging regularly. Command: Stay informed about the latest developments in the OSINT field by regularly engaging with relevant resources and communities.

One key aspect of continual learning in OSINT is the exploration of new sources of open-source information. Command: Regularly seek out and evaluate new online platforms, websites, and data repositories that may yield valuable intelligence.

Follow OSINT experts, practitioners, and thought leaders on social media and within online forums to access their insights and expertise. Command: Engage with the OSINT community to learn from experienced professionals and benefit from their knowledge.

Participate in OSINT-focused training programs, workshops, and conferences to enhance your skills and stay up to date with industry best practices. Command: Attend OSINT-related events and training sessions to expand your knowledge and network with fellow practitioners.

Subscribe to OSINT newsletters, podcasts, and publications that offer in-depth analysis, case studies, and tutorials on the latest OSINT tools and techniques. Command: Keep yourself informed through OSINT-specific media to access valuable information and insights.

Take advantage of online courses and educational platforms that offer OSINT-related content, including data analysis, digital forensics, and ethical hacking. Command: Enroll in relevant online courses to acquire new skills and deepen your expertise in specific OSINT domains.

Experiment with different OSINT tools and technologies to gain hands-on experience and explore their capabilities. Command: Allocate time for practical experimentation to familiarize yourself with OSINT tools and their functionalities.

Join OSINT forums and online communities where you can ask questions, share insights, and collaborate with fellow enthusiasts. Command: Actively participate in discussions and knowledge-sharing within OSINT communities to expand your understanding.

Mentorship is a valuable resource for continual learning in OSINT, as experienced mentors can provide guidance and support. Command: Seek out experienced mentors who can offer advice, feedback, and opportunities for growth in your OSINT career.

Maintain a growth mindset, which involves embracing challenges, learning from failures, and constantly seeking improvement. Command: Cultivate a mindset that values learning from mistakes and sees challenges as opportunities for growth.

Develop a personal learning plan that outlines your OSINT goals, the skills you wish to acquire, and a timeline for achieving them. Command: Create a structured learning plan that helps you set clear objectives and track your progress in the OSINT field.

Networking with professionals in related fields, such as cybersecurity, digital forensics, and law enforcement, can provide valuable insights and opportunities for collaboration.

Command: Build relationships with experts from adjacent fields to gain diverse perspectives and foster collaboration.

Regularly review and update your OSINT toolkit to incorporate new tools and technologies that can enhance your capabilities. Command: Stay adaptable and open to incorporating innovative tools into your OSINT workflow to optimize your investigative efforts.

Ethical considerations are integral to continual learning in OSINT, as practitioners must stay informed about evolving ethical standards and best practices. Command: Educate yourself about the latest ethical guidelines and ensure that your OSINT activities align with responsible and lawful conduct.

Document your OSINT findings, experiences, and lessons learned to create a valuable knowledge repository for future reference. Command: Keep detailed records of your OSINT investigations and insights to build a comprehensive knowledge base.

Teaching and sharing your OSINT knowledge with others can reinforce your own learning and contribute to the growth of the OSINT community. Command: Act as a mentor or educator to pass on your knowledge and insights to aspiring OSINT practitioners.

Continual learning in OSINT is not limited to technical skills; it also encompasses the development of critical thinking, analytical, and problem-solving abilities. Command: Cultivate a holistic skill set that combines technical expertise with critical thinking to excel in OSINT.

In summary, continual learning is a foundational principle in the field of OSINT, where the ever-evolving nature of information and technology demands ongoing education and skill development. By staying informed about new sources, tools, and techniques, engaging with the OSINT community, seeking mentorship, maintaining a growth mindset, and adhering to ethical considerations, OSINT practitioners can continually expand their knowledge and expertise. Embracing lifelong learning ensures that practitioners remain effective and adaptive in the dynamic world of open source intelligence.

Networking within the Open Source Intelligence (OSINT) community is a vital component of a successful career in this field. Command: Recognize the importance of building and nurturing professional relationships to foster growth and collaboration in OSINT.

The OSINT community is a diverse and dynamic group of individuals who share a common interest in gathering intelligence from open sources. Command: Take the initiative to engage with the OSINT community to tap into the collective knowledge and expertise it offers.

One of the primary benefits of networking in the OSINT community is the opportunity to connect with like-minded professionals who share your passion for information gathering and analysis. Command: Seek out fellow OSINT enthusiasts and practitioners who can provide valuable insights and perspectives.

Social media platforms, professional networking sites, and online forums are excellent places to start building your OSINT network. Command: Create profiles on relevant online platforms to connect with others who have a similar interest in OSINT.

Actively participate in discussions, share your experiences, and ask questions within OSINT communities to establish your presence and credibility. Command: Contribute to conversations and offer valuable insights to showcase your expertise and willingness to collaborate.

Attend OSINT-related events, conferences, and webinars, both online and in-person, to meet professionals in the field and expand your network. Command: Make an effort to participate in OSINT-focused events to connect with practitioners and stay up to date with industry trends.

Networking isn't just about expanding your circle of contacts; it's also about building meaningful relationships based on trust and mutual respect. Command: Focus on building genuine connections within the OSINT community by demonstrating professionalism and reliability.

Networking can open doors to opportunities for collaboration, knowledge exchange, and even potential job offers in the OSINT field. Command: Be open to partnerships, information sharing, and career prospects that may arise through your network.

Consider joining professional associations and organizations related to OSINT, as they often provide valuable networking opportunities and resources. Command: Explore membership options in OSINT-focused associations to connect with fellow professionals and access exclusive resources.

Don't limit your networking efforts to individuals within the OSINT community alone; extend your reach to professionals in related fields such as cybersecurity, law enforcement, and digital forensics. Command: Broaden your network to include experts from adjacent fields to gain diverse perspectives and insights.

Building a strong online presence, including a well-maintained LinkedIn profile and an active Twitter account, can enhance your visibility and attract like-minded professionals to your network. Command: Invest time in curating your online presence to showcase your expertise and interests in the OSINT field.

Actively seek out mentors within the OSINT community who can provide guidance, advice, and support in your professional journey. Command: Identify potential mentors and approach them with respect and a clear request for mentorship.

Engage in collaborative projects, research, or investigations with members of your OSINT network to leverage collective expertise and resources. Command: Look for opportunities to work together on projects that align with your mutual interests and goals.

Regularly update and maintain your network by staying in touch with contacts, sharing relevant content, and providing assistance when possible. Command: Foster ongoing relationships by keeping in touch, sharing valuable information, and offering assistance when needed.

Respect the boundaries and privacy of individuals in your network, refraining from intrusive or unsolicited requests. Command: Ensure that your interactions with contacts are respectful and considerate of their time and preferences.

Network not only for personal gain but also to contribute positively to the OSINT community by sharing your knowledge and experiences with others. Command: Strive to be a valuable contributor to the community by sharing your insights and supporting fellow practitioners.

Effective networking in the OSINT community is an ongoing process that requires patience, persistence, and a genuine interest in fostering meaningful connections. Command: Understand that building a strong network takes time and effort, and the rewards are often worth the investment.

In summary, networking in the OSINT community is an essential aspect of professional growth and development in this dynamic field. By actively engaging with fellow practitioners, attending relevant events, seeking mentorship, and building a strong online presence, individuals can create a network that provides valuable insights, collaboration opportunities, and support throughout their OSINT careers. Networking is not only about expanding one's circle of contacts but also about contributing positively to the community and fostering a culture of collaboration and knowledge sharing within the OSINT field.

BOOK 2
NAVIGATING THE DIGITAL SHADOWS
INTERMEDIATE OSINT TECHNIQUES

ROB BOTWRIGHT

Chapter 1: Advanced Search Queries

Customizing search filters is a fundamental skill in the realm of Open Source Intelligence (OSINT). Command: Recognize the importance of tailoring your search queries to obtain precise and relevant results in OSINT investigations.

One of the primary objectives in OSINT is to efficiently gather information from open sources, and customizing search filters allows you to achieve this goal. Command: Embrace the power of search filters as a means to filter out noise and extract valuable intelligence.

Search filters enable you to refine your queries, narrow down your search scope, and pinpoint specific information that is crucial to your investigation. Command: Familiarize yourself with the different types of search filters and their functionalities to enhance your search precision.

When conducting OSINT investigations, the sheer volume of data available online can be overwhelming. Command: Acknowledge the vastness of the internet and the importance of search filters in managing and navigating this vast information landscape.

Customizing search filters allows you to focus your efforts on collecting pertinent data, saving you time and resources. Command: Utilize search filters to streamline your research process and optimize the efficiency of your OSINT activities.

Search engines, social media platforms, and online databases offer a variety of filters that can be tailored to meet your specific needs. Command: Explore the filter options provided by different online platforms and understand how to use them effectively.

One common type of search filter is the time filter, which allows you to specify a date range for your search results.

Command: Leverage the time filter to access information within a defined time frame, which can be crucial in OSINT investigations involving recent events or historical data.

Another important filter is the location filter, which helps you narrow down results to a specific geographic area. Command: Use the location filter to focus on information related to a particular region or location, especially in investigations with a geographical context.

Content type filters, such as those for images, videos, or news articles, enable you to target specific types of media or content. Command: Employ content type filters when you are interested in gathering specific types of media or when you want to filter out irrelevant content.

Search engines often provide advanced search operators that allow for more precise queries. Command: Familiarize yourself with advanced search operators and their syntax to craft intricate search queries that yield accurate results.

Boolean operators, such as "AND," "OR," and "NOT," enable you to combine keywords and phrases to refine your search. Command: Master the use of Boolean operators to create complex search queries that can uncover hidden information.

Wildcard characters like asterisks (*) or question marks (?) can be used to search for variations of a keyword or to fill in missing information. Command: Incorporate wildcard characters into your search queries to account for different spellings or missing characters in your search terms.

Phrase searching, accomplished by enclosing a phrase in quotation marks, helps you find exact matches for specific phrases. Command: Implement phrase searching to locate content that includes precise phrases or expressions relevant to your investigation.

In addition to text-based filters, many platforms offer filters for file types, languages, and user interactions. Command:

Explore the diverse range of filters available on various platforms to tailor your search according to your specific requirements.

When customizing search filters, it's essential to consider the source or platform you are using. Command: Take into account the unique filter options and functionalities provided by different sources and platforms.

Experiment with different combinations of search filters to refine your queries and maximize the accuracy of your results. Command: Fine-tune your search filters iteratively, adjusting them as needed to obtain the most relevant and comprehensive data.

Regularly update your knowledge of search filters and their capabilities, as online platforms may introduce new features or change their filtering options. Command: Stay informed about updates and changes to search filters on the platforms you frequently use for OSINT investigations.

Keep in mind that while search filters can help you uncover valuable information, they are not infallible. Command: Exercise critical thinking and verify the accuracy and credibility of the information you gather using search filters.

Striking a balance between precision and inclusivity in your search filters is crucial to avoid missing potentially important data or sources. Command: Be mindful of striking the right balance between narrowing your search for relevance and ensuring you don't inadvertently exclude valuable information.

In summary, customizing search filters is a skill that empowers OSINT practitioners to harness the vast resources of the internet effectively. By understanding the different types of filters, advanced search operators, and platform-specific options available, you can tailor your search queries to extract precise and relevant information. However, it's essential to remain adaptable, continuously update your knowledge, and critically evaluate the results obtained through custom filters. Customizing search filters is an ongoing process that requires both technical proficiency and a discerning approach to information gathering in the dynamic landscape of OSINT.

Boolean logic and search operators are essential tools in the toolkit of any Open Source Intelligence (OSINT) practitioner. Command: Understand the significance of mastering Boolean logic and search operators for refining your online investigations.

At its core, Boolean logic is a branch of algebra that deals with binary values: true and false. Command: Begin with a fundamental understanding that Boolean logic operates on the principles of true and false values.

In the context of online research and OSINT, Boolean logic allows you to combine keywords and phrases to construct intricate search queries. Command: Recognize that in OSINT, Boolean logic is used to create complex search queries that yield precise results.

The three primary Boolean operators you'll encounter are AND, OR, and NOT. Command: Familiarize yourself with the functionality of the AND, OR, and NOT operators as they play a pivotal role in refining searches.

The AND operator narrows down your search by requiring that both terms it connects be present in the results. Command: Utilize the AND operator to pinpoint information that must contain all specified keywords or phrases.

Conversely, the OR operator broadens your search by retrieving results containing either of the connected terms. Command: Employ the OR operator when you want to include multiple possible keywords or phrases in your search.

The NOT operator excludes specific terms from your search results, allowing you to filter out unwanted information. Command: Harness the NOT operator to eliminate irrelevant content and focus solely on relevant data.

Combining these operators allows you to create complex queries that can uncover hidden gems of information. Command: Experiment with combinations of Boolean operators to construct intricate search queries tailored to your investigation.

Parentheses ( ) can be used to group terms and operators, affecting the order in which they are evaluated. Command: Understand that parentheses can be employed to control the logical order of operations in your queries.

For instance, using parentheses can ensure that certain conditions are met before applying other operators. Command: Employ parentheses strategically to prioritize specific components of your search query.

Quotation marks (" ") are valuable for conducting phrase searches, ensuring that results contain an exact phrase. Command: Enclose phrases in quotation marks to search for specific expressions or sequences of words.

Wildcards, such as asterisks (*) and question marks (?), allow for variations in your search terms. Command: Incorporate wildcard characters to account for different spellings or word forms within your search.

The asterisk () represents one or more characters, while the question mark (?) represents a single character. Command: Use the asterisk () and question mark (?) judiciously to accommodate variations in your search terms.

Boolean logic and search operators are versatile tools applicable to various online platforms, including search engines, social media networks, and databases. Command: Recognize that your proficiency in using Boolean logic and search operators can be applied across a wide range of online sources.

Advanced search engines often provide built-in search operators specific to their platform. Command: Explore the unique search operators offered by different online platforms to maximize the effectiveness of your searches.

When using Boolean logic in OSINT, precision is key; aim to narrow down your search results to reduce information overload. Command: Strive for precision when crafting your search queries to retrieve highly relevant and actionable data.

However, be cautious not to narrow your search too much, as overly restrictive queries may lead to missed opportunities. Command: Strike a balance between precision and inclusivity to ensure you don't inadvertently exclude valuable information.

Regularly update your knowledge of Boolean logic and search operators, as online platforms may introduce new features or change their search functionalities. Command: Stay informed about updates and changes to Boolean operators on the platforms you frequently use for OSINT investigations.

Mastering Boolean logic and search operators is a continuous learning process that enhances your ability to extract valuable insights from open sources. Command: Understand that your proficiency in these tools will grow with practice and ongoing education.

In summary, Boolean logic and search operators are indispensable tools for OSINT practitioners seeking to refine their information retrieval skills. By mastering these operators, you can create precise and effective search queries across various online platforms. However, it's important to strike a balance between precision and inclusivity to avoid missing valuable data. As the online landscape evolves, staying up to date with the latest features and functionalities of search engines and platforms is essential for maintaining your proficiency in Boolean logic and search operators.

Chapter 2: Deep Web and Dark Web Investigations

Accessing hidden markets is a subject of great interest for businesses and entrepreneurs seeking new opportunities and growth. Command: Recognize the potential of exploring hidden markets as a strategy to expand your business or venture.

Hidden markets refer to niches or segments that are not immediately visible or apparent in traditional markets. Command: Understand that hidden markets often exist beneath the surface of mainstream markets, waiting to be discovered.

One reason businesses and individuals seek hidden markets is to gain a competitive edge by identifying untapped customer bases. Command: Acknowledge the strategic advantage that comes with discovering hidden markets, where competition may be less intense.

Hidden markets can offer unique customer needs, preferences, and opportunities that are not met by existing products or services. Command: Embrace the idea that hidden markets can hold unmet demands that your business can fulfill.

Identifying and accessing hidden markets require a combination of research, innovation, and adaptability. Command: Be prepared to invest time and effort into research, creative thinking, and flexibility when pursuing hidden market opportunities.

Conduct thorough market research to uncover hidden markets that align with your business goals and expertise. Command: Start your journey by conducting comprehensive market research to pinpoint hidden market segments that match your capabilities.

Utilize various research methods, including online surveys, interviews, and data analysis, to gather insights into potential hidden markets. Command: Employ a multifaceted research approach to gain a comprehensive understanding of the hidden markets you are targeting.

Stay informed about emerging trends, shifts in consumer behavior, and changes in the competitive landscape that may reveal hidden market opportunities. Command: Keep a watchful eye on market dynamics and adapt your strategy to capitalize on hidden market openings as they arise.

Networking within industry-specific communities and attending relevant events can provide valuable insights and connections related to hidden markets. Command: Engage with professionals and experts in your field to tap into their knowledge and discover hidden market trends and opportunities.

Innovation and adaptability are crucial when entering hidden markets, as traditional strategies may not apply. Command: Embrace a mindset of innovation and flexibility to tailor your approach to the unique characteristics of hidden markets.

Consider partnerships or collaborations with businesses that already have a presence in hidden markets, as this can provide valuable access and expertise. Command: Explore collaboration opportunities to leverage the strengths of established players in hidden markets and expedite your entry.

Evaluate the scalability and sustainability of your business model within hidden markets to ensure long-term success. Command: Assess the viability of your business model in hidden markets and develop strategies for sustainable growth.

Hidden markets can exist in various forms, from niche consumer segments to emerging industries and unconventional distribution channels. Command:

Understand that hidden markets can take on diverse forms, making it essential to remain open to different possibilities.

Analyze the competition within hidden markets to identify gaps, weaknesses, and areas where your business can excel. Command: Conduct a thorough competitive analysis to pinpoint opportunities for differentiation and growth in hidden markets.

Tailor your marketing and communication strategies to resonate with the unique characteristics and needs of hidden market segments. Command: Customize your messaging and branding to align with the preferences and values of the hidden markets you are targeting.

Maintain flexibility in your business strategy to adapt to changing dynamics within hidden markets and capitalize on emerging opportunities. Command: Cultivate a mindset of adaptability to navigate the evolving landscape of hidden markets effectively.

Strive to provide exceptional value, quality, and customer experiences within hidden markets to establish a strong foothold and build loyalty. Command: Prioritize delivering exceptional value and quality to create a positive reputation and customer loyalty within hidden markets.

Monitor and analyze data, customer feedback, and market trends to continuously refine your strategies and stay competitive in hidden markets. Command: Implement a data-driven approach to measure your performance and refine your strategies as you navigate hidden markets.

Embrace the potential of digital technologies and online platforms to reach hidden market audiences effectively. Command: Leverage digital tools and platforms to connect with hidden market segments and expand your reach.

Take calculated risks when entering hidden markets, as innovation and experimentation often lead to breakthroughs and successes. Command: Be willing to take calculated risks to explore hidden market opportunities that have the potential for innovation and growth.

In summary, accessing hidden markets is a dynamic and rewarding endeavor for businesses and individuals seeking growth and innovation. These markets offer unique niches, unmet needs, and untapped potential that can lead to competitive advantages and long-term success. By conducting thorough research, fostering innovation, remaining adaptable, and prioritizing value and customer experiences, you can navigate hidden markets effectively and uncover opportunities that drive growth and prosperity for your business or venture. Hidden markets are waiting to be discovered, and those who venture into them with determination and strategic thinking can unlock their hidden potential.

Tracking cryptocurrencies on the Dark Web is a complex and multifaceted endeavor. Command: Understand the intricacies and challenges involved in tracking cryptocurrencies in this hidden online realm.

The Dark Web is a part of the internet that is intentionally hidden and requires specialized software to access. Command: Begin by acknowledging the unique characteristics of the Dark Web, which make it challenging to navigate and monitor.

Cryptocurrencies, such as Bitcoin, are often used for various transactions on the Dark Web due to their pseudo-anonymous nature. Command: Recognize that cryptocurrencies play a significant role in Dark Web transactions, offering a level of anonymity that traditional payment methods do not.

Tracking these transactions requires a deep understanding of blockchain technology, the underlying technology behind most cryptocurrencies. Command: Acquire a strong foundation in blockchain technology to comprehend the intricacies of cryptocurrency transactions on the Dark Web.

One key challenge in tracking cryptocurrencies on the Dark Web is the anonymity they provide to users. Command: Grasp the concept of cryptocurrency anonymity, which makes it challenging to link transactions to specific individuals or entities.

While blockchain records all cryptocurrency transactions, it only provides pseudonymous addresses rather than real-world identities. Command: Understand that blockchain records are pseudonymous, with addresses representing user identities without revealing personal information.

Advanced cryptographic techniques, like mixers and tumblers, are often employed on the Dark Web to obfuscate the source and destination of funds. Command: Familiarize yourself with cryptographic methods used on the Dark Web to obscure the origins and destinations of cryptocurrency transactions.

To track cryptocurrencies effectively on the Dark Web, investigators often rely on blockchain analysis tools and specialized software. Command: Explore the use of blockchain analysis tools and software tailored for Dark Web investigations to streamline your tracking efforts.

These tools allow investigators to trace transactions, identify patterns, and potentially link cryptocurrency addresses to individuals or entities. Command: Utilize blockchain analysis tools to follow the flow of cryptocurrencies, recognize recurring patterns, and establish potential connections.

One common approach to tracking cryptocurrencies on the Dark Web is to monitor known marketplaces and forums. Command: Investigate established Dark Web marketplaces and forums where cryptocurrency transactions frequently occur.

By monitoring these platforms, investigators can gather valuable data on cryptocurrency transactions and potential leads. Command: Leverage the monitoring of Dark Web marketplaces and forums to collect data and generate leads for further investigation.

Tracing cryptocurrencies often involves following the money trail, which may include multiple transactions and addresses. Command: Be prepared for the complex task of tracing cryptocurrencies through a series of transactions and addresses to unveil their origin and destination.

Blockchain analysis tools use heuristics, clustering algorithms, and data analysis to identify clusters of addresses associated with the same entity. Command: Understand the techniques employed by blockchain analysis tools, such as heuristics and clustering algorithms, to group related addresses.

Darknet markets frequently employ escrow services to facilitate secure transactions, which can complicate tracking efforts. Command: Be aware that escrow services on Darknet markets can introduce additional layers of complexity when tracking cryptocurrency transactions.

Investigators often collaborate with cryptocurrency exchanges and other financial institutions to gather information about cryptocurrency users. Command: Establish partnerships and cooperation with cryptocurrency exchanges and financial institutions to access valuable data about cryptocurrency users.

Privacy coins, such as Monero and Zcash, pose additional challenges in tracking, as they prioritize anonymity and privacy. Command: Acknowledge the challenges posed by privacy coins, which prioritize user anonymity and make tracking more difficult.

Specialized tools and techniques are required to trace transactions involving privacy coins on the Dark Web.

Command: Equip yourself with specialized tools and techniques tailored to tracing transactions involving privacy coins in Dark Web investigations.

Cryptocurrency tumblers, also known as mixers, are services that shuffle and anonymize cryptocurrency transactions, making tracking more challenging. Command: Understand the role of cryptocurrency tumblers in obfuscating transaction histories and complicating tracking efforts.

Despite the complexities, successful tracking of cryptocurrencies on the Dark Web has led to the identification and apprehension of criminal actors. Command: Recognize that effective tracking efforts can lead to significant breakthroughs in identifying and apprehending individuals engaged in illicit activities.

In summary, tracking cryptocurrencies on the Dark Web is a demanding but vital aspect of investigative work in the digital age. By mastering blockchain technology, utilizing specialized tools, and collaborating with relevant entities, investigators can follow the money trail and uncover valuable leads. While the Dark Web presents numerous challenges, the determination to unveil the hidden world of cryptocurrency transactions can contribute to increased cybersecurity and the prevention of criminal activities in the digital realm.

Chapter 3: Geospatial Intelligence in OSINT

Mapping digital footprints is a crucial practice in the realm of Open Source Intelligence (OSINT). Command: Understand the importance of mapping digital footprints as a means to gather valuable information about individuals and entities.

Digital footprints represent the traces and records left behind by online activities, interactions, and behaviors. Command: Grasp the concept of digital footprints, which encompass a wide range of online data that can be harnessed for intelligence gathering.

These footprints are scattered across various online platforms, websites, social media networks, and communication channels. Command: Recognize that digital footprints can be found on a multitude of online sources, including social media, websites, and messaging platforms.

Mapping digital footprints involves the systematic collection, analysis, and visualization of these online traces. Command: Acknowledge that mapping digital footprints requires a structured approach to gather, analyze, and represent online data effectively.

One primary objective of mapping digital footprints is to gain insights into an individual's or organization's online presence. Command: Embrace the goal of mapping digital footprints as a means to understand and analyze the online activities and identity of a target.

By tracking digital footprints, investigators can uncover a wealth of information, including personal details, interests, affiliations, and communication patterns. Command: Recognize the potential of tracking digital footprints to reveal personal information, interests, connections, and communication habits.

The process of mapping digital footprints typically begins with the identification of the target individual or entity. Command: Start the mapping process by identifying the specific individual or organization whose digital footprints you intend to track.

This identification may involve gathering known information, such as names, usernames, email addresses, or domain names. Command: Collect known details about the target, including their names, usernames, email addresses, or any associated domain names.

Once the target is identified, investigators can proceed to search for digital footprints across various online sources. Command: Initiate the search for digital footprints by exploring a wide range of online platforms and websites relevant to the target.

Social media platforms are a valuable starting point for mapping digital footprints, as they often contain a wealth of personal information and interactions. Command: Begin by examining social media platforms where individuals tend to share personal information and engage in online interactions.

Search engines can be powerful tools for uncovering web pages, blog posts, news articles, and other online content associated with the target. Command: Utilize search engines to discover web content that references the target or provides relevant information about them.

Domain and website analysis tools can help investigators identify websites, blogs, or forums associated with the target or their interests. Command: Employ domain and website analysis tools to uncover online resources linked to the target's interests or affiliations.

Email addresses associated with the target can be used to track their online activities and communication patterns.

Command: Investigate email addresses linked to the target to trace their online interactions and communication history. Online forums and discussion boards may reveal valuable insights into the target's opinions, affiliations, and areas of interest. Command: Explore online forums and discussion boards where the target may have participated to gain insights into their viewpoints and affiliations.

The process of mapping digital footprints often involves the use of specialized OSINT tools and techniques. Command: Utilize OSINT tools and methodologies tailored for mapping digital footprints effectively.

Investigators may employ web scraping, data mining, and social media analysis to collect and analyze digital footprints. Command: Leverage techniques like web scraping, data mining, and social media analysis to gather and evaluate digital footprints comprehensively.

Mapping digital footprints is not limited to individuals; it can also apply to organizations, businesses, or entities. Command: Extend the practice of mapping digital footprints to organizations and entities to gain insights into their online presence and activities.

Visualization tools and techniques can be valuable for presenting the collected digital footprints in a clear and informative manner. Command: Utilize visualization methods to represent the gathered digital footprints visually, making it easier to interpret and analyze the data.

Throughout the process of mapping digital footprints, investigators must exercise caution and respect ethical boundaries. Command: Maintain ethical standards and adhere to legal regulations when mapping digital footprints to ensure responsible and lawful information gathering.

The information obtained from mapping digital footprints can be valuable for various purposes, including threat assessments, investigations, due diligence, and personal security. Command: Recognize the diverse applications of information gathered through mapping digital footprints, spanning from security assessments to investigative work.

In summary, mapping digital footprints is a foundational practice in OSINT that provides valuable insights into the online presence and activities of individuals and entities. By systematically collecting, analyzing, and visualizing digital footprints from various online sources, investigators can uncover a wealth of information that can be used for a wide range of purposes, from threat assessments to investigative work. However, it is essential to conduct this process ethically and responsibly, respecting privacy and legal boundaries while harnessing the power of digital footprints for intelligence gathering and analysis.

Geolocation techniques play a vital role in modern information gathering and intelligence operations. Command: Understand the significance of geolocation techniques as a means to determine the physical location of individuals, objects, or events.

Geolocation refers to the process of identifying the geographical coordinates or physical location of a target. Command: Grasp the definition of geolocation, which involves pinpointing the specific geographical point associated with a subject.

These techniques are widely employed in various fields, including law enforcement, cybersecurity, emergency services, and commercial applications. Command: Acknowledge the broad spectrum of applications for geolocation techniques, ranging from crime prevention to commercial services.

One of the fundamental methods of geolocation involves using Global Positioning System (GPS) technology.

Command: Begin by exploring the use of GPS technology, a foundational tool in geolocation techniques.

GPS relies on a network of satellites orbiting the Earth to provide accurate positioning data to receivers on the ground. Command: Understand the functioning of GPS, where satellites transmit signals that receivers use to calculate their precise location.

GPS technology is commonly found in smartphones, navigation systems, and a wide range of other devices. Command: Recognize that GPS is integrated into many devices, making it accessible for various applications.

Another geolocation technique involves Wi-Fi positioning, which utilizes Wi-Fi access points to determine a device's location. Command: Explore Wi-Fi positioning as a technique that relies on Wi-Fi signals and access points to estimate a device's position.

Wi-Fi positioning can be highly accurate in urban areas with dense Wi-Fi networks but may be less reliable in remote or rural locations. Command: Note that the accuracy of Wi-Fi positioning can vary depending on the density of available Wi-Fi networks.

Cellular triangulation is a method that leverages mobile phone towers to estimate the location of a mobile device. Command: Understand the concept of cellular triangulation, which involves calculating a device's position based on its distance from multiple cell towers.

This technique is commonly used by mobile service providers for network optimization and emergency services for 911 calls. Command: Recognize that cellular triangulation serves various purposes, from improving mobile networks to aiding emergency response.

IP address geolocation is another valuable method that associates an IP address with a specific geographic location.

Command: Explore IP address geolocation, where the geographical origin of an IP address is determined.

Databases and services dedicated to IP address geolocation provide information about the region, city, and even the approximate latitude and longitude of an IP address. Command: Utilize databases and services specializing in IP address geolocation to obtain detailed information about an IP address's location.

Social media geolocation relies on the data shared by individuals on platforms like Twitter, Instagram, and Facebook to determine their whereabouts. Command: Understand the use of social media geolocation, which involves analyzing location-based data shared by users on social platforms.

Photos, check-ins, and status updates can all provide valuable clues about a person's location at a specific time. Command: Recognize that various types of social media content, such as photos, check-ins, and status updates, can be used for geolocation.

OSINT tools and platforms offer geolocation capabilities that enable investigators to gather and analyze location-based information from various sources. Command: Embrace the capabilities of OSINT tools and platforms to harness geolocation techniques for intelligence gathering.

Geospatial analysis involves the examination of geolocation data to identify patterns, trends, and anomalies. Command: Explore geospatial analysis as a method to derive insights from geolocation data by identifying patterns and trends.

Geolocation data can be visualized through maps, charts, and graphs, making it easier to interpret and analyze. Command: Utilize visualization techniques to represent geolocation data visually, enhancing its comprehensibility.

It is important to consider the ethical and legal aspects of geolocation techniques when conducting investigations or intelligence operations. Command: Maintain ethical and legal standards when applying geolocation techniques in investigative work and intelligence operations.

Respect individuals' privacy rights and adhere to relevant laws and regulations governing geolocation and data protection. Command: Ensure that geolocation activities adhere to privacy laws and regulations, respecting individuals' rights.

Geolocation techniques are invaluable tools for locating missing persons, tracking assets, analyzing social movements, and enhancing situational awareness. Command: Recognize the diverse applications of geolocation techniques, ranging from humanitarian efforts to enhancing security.

In summary, geolocation techniques are indispensable in our modern world, providing valuable insights into the physical location of individuals, objects, or events. These techniques, encompassing GPS, Wi-Fi positioning, cellular triangulation, IP address geolocation, social media analysis, and geospatial analysis, play pivotal roles in various fields, from emergency services to intelligence operations. However, the responsible use of these techniques requires a strong ethical foundation and adherence to relevant legal frameworks to ensure privacy and data protection. Geolocation remains a powerful tool for addressing a wide range of challenges and opportunities in our interconnected world.

Chapter 4: Advanced Social Media Analysis

Sentiment analysis on social platforms is a sophisticated and valuable technique used to gauge the collective mood, opinions, and emotions of online communities. Command: Understand the significance of sentiment analysis as a means to extract insights from social media content.

In today's digital age, social media has become a central hub for people to express their thoughts, feelings, and reactions to a wide range of topics. Command: Recognize the central role of social media in facilitating public expression and discussion.

Sentiment analysis, also known as opinion mining, leverages natural language processing (NLP) and machine learning algorithms to analyze text data and determine the sentiment expressed within it. Command: Grasp the underlying technology of sentiment analysis, which involves the use of NLP and machine learning to evaluate text sentiment.

The sentiment in social media content can vary widely, from positive and enthusiastic to negative and critical, providing a rich source of information for businesses, researchers, and organizations. Command: Acknowledge the diverse range of sentiments expressed in social media content and the insights they can offer to different stakeholders.

Businesses often use sentiment analysis to understand customer opinions and feedback, enabling them to improve products, services, and customer experiences. Command: Recognize the practical application of sentiment analysis for businesses, which can enhance customer satisfaction and product development.

Researchers and academics use sentiment analysis to study public sentiment on various topics, such as political issues, public health, and social trends. Command: Embrace sentiment analysis as a valuable tool for researchers to investigate public sentiment and its implications for various domains.

Sentiment analysis can be employed to monitor brand reputation, track public perception, and assess the success of marketing campaigns. Command: Utilize sentiment analysis to maintain brand image, monitor public perception, and measure the effectiveness of marketing efforts.

The process of sentiment analysis begins with data collection from social media platforms, where vast amounts of user-generated content are accessible. Command: Start the sentiment analysis process by gathering data from social media platforms, where a wealth of user-generated content is readily available.

This data can include tweets, Facebook posts, Instagram captions, blog comments, and more, all of which can be analyzed for sentiment. Command: Consider the various types of social media content that can be collected and analyzed, including short messages, images, and longer-form posts.

Preprocessing steps, such as text cleaning and tokenization, are essential to prepare the text data for sentiment analysis. Command: Understand the importance of preprocessing steps that involve cleaning and structuring the text data for analysis.

Tokenization involves breaking down sentences and paragraphs into individual words or tokens, making it easier for algorithms to analyze. Command: Recognize that tokenization simplifies the analysis process by breaking down text into its constituent parts.

Once the text data is prepared, sentiment analysis algorithms classify the sentiment as positive, negative, neutral, or even on a more granular scale. Command: Be aware that sentiment analysis algorithms categorize text sentiment into predefined categories, providing insights into the emotional tone.

Machine learning models, such as support vector machines (SVM) and recurrent neural networks (RNN), are commonly used for sentiment analysis tasks. Command: Explore machine learning models, including SVM and RNN, as effective tools for sentiment analysis.

These models are trained on labeled datasets that contain examples of text with associated sentiment labels. Command: Understand the training process of sentiment analysis models, which involves using labeled data to teach the algorithm how to recognize sentiment.

Supervised learning techniques enable the model to generalize from the training data and classify sentiment in unseen text. Command: Appreciate the role of supervised learning in enabling sentiment analysis models to make accurate predictions on new data.

In addition to supervised learning, sentiment analysis can also involve lexicon-based approaches that rely on sentiment dictionaries. Command: Explore lexicon-based approaches, where sentiment dictionaries help determine the sentiment of words and phrases in text.

Sentiment dictionaries contain lists of words and phrases categorized with their associated sentiment polarity. Command: Recognize that sentiment dictionaries are valuable resources for assigning sentiment scores to words and phrases.

During sentiment analysis, sentiment scores are assigned to each piece of text, and these scores are aggregated to determine the overall sentiment of a document or social media conversation. Command: Understand the process of aggregating sentiment scores to arrive at an overall sentiment assessment for a text or conversation.

Sentiment analysis can be applied at various levels, from individual messages or comments to entire social media conversations or trends. Command: Consider the flexibility of sentiment analysis, which can be conducted at different levels of granularity, depending on the analysis goals.

Visualizations, such as sentiment heatmaps and sentiment trend graphs, are effective tools for presenting the results of sentiment analysis in a visually engaging way. Command: Utilize visualization techniques to convey sentiment analysis results clearly and intuitively.

It is essential to consider cultural nuances, sarcasm, and context when performing sentiment analysis, as these factors can influence the accuracy of results. Command: Be aware of the challenges associated with cultural differences, sarcasm, and contextual understanding in sentiment analysis.

Ethical considerations, such as user consent and data privacy, must also be taken into account when collecting and analyzing social media data for sentiment analysis. Command: Maintain ethical standards when collecting and handling social media data, respecting user consent and privacy.

Uncovering hidden connections is a fundamental aspect of Open Source Intelligence (OSINT) and investigative work. Command: Understand the importance of uncovering hidden connections as a means to gain insights and solve complex puzzles.

Hidden connections can exist between individuals, organizations, online personas, and various entities. Command: Recognize that hidden connections may involve relationships, affiliations, interactions, or shared interests.

These connections often remain concealed from the public eye, making them challenging to discover through conventional means. Command: Acknowledge that hidden connections are intentionally obscured, requiring specialized techniques to reveal them.

Uncovering hidden connections involves gathering and analyzing data from a wide range of sources, including social media, websites, public records, and more. Command: Embrace the process of collecting and analyzing data from diverse sources to expose hidden connections effectively.

Social media platforms are valuable sources for uncovering hidden connections, as they often reveal relationships, interactions, and shared interests. Command: Explore the potential of social media platforms in unveiling hidden connections by analyzing user profiles, interactions, and content.

Online forums and communities may provide insights into affiliations, group memberships, or shared ideologies among individuals or organizations. Command: Investigate online forums and communities to uncover hidden connections related to affiliations, group memberships, or shared ideologies.

Web scraping and data mining techniques can be employed to extract relevant information from websites and online databases. Command: Utilize web scraping and data mining to extract pertinent data from websites and databases to reveal concealed connections.

Public records, such as business registrations, property records, and legal documents, may contain valuable information about organizational ties and partnerships. Command: Access public records to discover hidden connections by examining business registrations, property records, and legal documents.

Analyzing patterns and anomalies in data can help identify connections that might otherwise go unnoticed. Command:

Apply analytical techniques to identify hidden connections by detecting patterns and anomalies in the data.

Visualization tools and network analysis software are valuable aids in representing and exploring hidden connections graphically. Command: Utilize visualization tools and network analysis software to visually represent and explore hidden connections effectively.

It is essential to cross-reference and verify information from multiple sources to ensure the accuracy of uncovered connections. Command: Maintain accuracy in uncovering connections by cross-referencing and verifying information from various sources.

Hidden connections can be significant in various domains, including security, law enforcement, business intelligence, and investigative journalism. Command: Recognize the broad applications of uncovering hidden connections, spanning from national security to journalistic investigations.

In security and law enforcement, uncovering hidden connections can help identify criminal networks, terrorist organizations, or potential threats. Command: Understand the critical role of uncovering hidden connections in security and law enforcement efforts to combat criminal networks and terrorism.

Businesses can benefit from discovering hidden connections to assess potential partners, competitors, or opportunities for collaboration. Command: Recognize that uncovering hidden connections can offer strategic advantages to businesses by evaluating potential partnerships and competitors.

Investigative journalists use these techniques to expose corruption, conflicts of interest, and unethical behavior within organizations. Command: Appreciate the role of investigative journalists in using hidden connections to uncover corruption and unethical practices.

Uncovering hidden connections often involves creating link charts or diagrams to visualize the relationships among individuals or entities. Command: Consider the use of link charts and diagrams to visually represent the relationships and connections revealed during the investigation.

One common approach to uncovering hidden connections is to start with known information and expand the search outward. Command: Begin the process of uncovering hidden connections by using known information as a starting point and progressively expanding the search.

For example, if investigating a person, you might begin with their social media profiles and expand to explore their connections, friends, or associations. Command: Use social media profiles as a starting point to investigate an individual, and then broaden the scope to explore their connections and associations.

In the case of an organization, examining its leadership, subsidiaries, and partnerships can reveal hidden connections within the corporate structure. Command: Investigate an organization's leadership, subsidiaries, and partnerships to uncover hidden connections within its corporate framework.

The process may involve searching for commonalities, shared contacts, or overlapping interests among the entities being investigated. Command: Look for commonalities, shared contacts, and overlapping interests among the entities under investigation to reveal hidden connections.

Online personas and pseudonyms can be challenging to link to real-world identities, but techniques like linguistic analysis and behavior patterns can help establish connections. Command: Use linguistic analysis and behavior patterns to establish connections between online personas and real-world identities.

Uncovering hidden connections often requires patience, persistence, and a keen eye for detail. Command: Cultivate qualities such as patience, persistence, and attention to detail when embarking on the journey to uncover hidden connections.

It's important to remain objective and impartial throughout the investigation, letting the data and evidence guide the process. Command: Maintain objectivity and impartiality during the investigation, allowing data and evidence to lead the way in uncovering hidden connections.

In summary, uncovering hidden connections is a multifaceted process that involves data collection, analysis, verification, and visualization. Whether in the realm of security, business, law enforcement, or journalism, the ability to expose concealed relationships and affiliations can yield valuable insights and impact decision-making significantly. By applying a systematic and thorough approach, individuals and organizations can harness the power of uncovering hidden connections to navigate complex networks and make informed choices in an interconnected world.

Chapter 5: Email and Communication Tracing

Tracing email headers is a critical skill in the world of digital forensics, cybersecurity, and online investigations. Command: Understand the significance of tracing email headers as a means to track the origin and route of an email message.

Email headers, also known as message headers or internet headers, contain valuable information about the path an email took from the sender to the recipient. Command: Grasp the concept of email headers, which contain metadata about the email's journey, including sender, recipients, servers, and timestamps.

Tracing email headers can provide insights into the legitimacy of an email, identify potential security threats, and help investigators follow the digital breadcrumbs left behind by cybercriminals. Command: Recognize the diverse applications of tracing email headers, ranging from email verification to cybersecurity investigations.

The process of tracing email headers typically begins by accessing the email client or webmail service used to view the email. Command: Start the tracing process by accessing the email client or webmail service through which you received the email.

Once you have opened the email, look for an option to view the email headers. Command: Locate the option within the email client or webmail interface to access the email headers.

Email headers are often hidden from plain view to keep the email interface user-friendly, but they can usually be revealed with a few clicks. Command: Reveal the email headers by following the steps provided in the email client or webmail service.

In Gmail, for example, you can click on the three dots (more options) beside the Reply button and choose "Show original" to view the full email headers. Command: Follow the specific steps for revealing email headers in your email client or webmail service, such as Gmail.

In Microsoft Outlook, you can right-click the email, select "Message Options," and find the headers in the "Internet Headers" section. Command: Explore the options available in your email client, such as Outlook, to access the email headers.

Once you have accessed the email headers, you will see a block of text that contains various pieces of information. Command: Examine the email headers to identify the block of text containing the relevant information.

Email headers often include details such as the sender's email address, recipient addresses, subject line, date and time stamps, and a series of unique identifiers for tracking the email's journey. Command: Analyze the content of the email headers, which may include sender and recipient addresses, timestamps, and unique identifiers.

The "Received" field in the email headers provides a chronological record of the email's journey through different mail servers. Command: Pay particular attention to the "Received" field, as it records the email's path through various mail servers.

Each "Received" entry represents a hop in the email's route, showing the sender's server, intermediary servers, and finally, the recipient's server. Command: Interpret the "Received" entries to trace the email's route from the sender to the recipient.

Starting with the bottom-most "Received" entry and working your way up, you can track the email's path from server to server. Command: Begin the tracing process by examining the "Received" entries in reverse order, starting from the bottom.

The information in the "Received" field includes server names, IP addresses, timestamps, and sometimes even the software used by each server. Command: Extract relevant details from the "Received" field, such as server names, IP addresses, timestamps, and server software.

By carefully analyzing the "Received" entries, you can identify the originating server, intermediary servers, and any potential points of interest. Command: Analyze the "Received" entries to pinpoint the email's origin, intermediate steps, and any critical servers along the way.

In some cases, email headers may reveal the use of email forwarding or relaying services, which can further obscure the email's true source. Command: Be aware that email forwarding or relaying services may complicate the tracing process, potentially masking the email's origin.

To track the email's source accurately, you can use online tools or services that provide additional insights into the IP addresses and locations of the servers. Command: Consider using online tools or services designed for tracing email headers to obtain more detailed information about server IP addresses and locations.

These tools can help you identify the physical location of the server, which can be useful in investigations or cybersecurity analysis. Command: Utilize these tools to determine the physical locations of servers, aiding in investigations and cybersecurity assessments.

Keep in mind that email headers can be manipulated or spoofed by malicious actors, so additional verification may be necessary in certain cases. Command: Exercise caution and verification when dealing with email headers, as they can be manipulated or spoofed by cybercriminals.

Email headers can provide valuable information in various scenarios, such as identifying phishing attempts, tracing spam sources, or verifying the authenticity of emails. Command: Recognize the diverse applications of email header tracing, ranging from identifying phishing attacks to verifying email legitimacy.

In summary, tracing email headers is a crucial skill in the world of digital forensics and cybersecurity. By accessing and analyzing email headers, investigators can track the path of an email message, identify potential threats, and gain valuable insights into the email's source and journey. While email headers provide a wealth of information, it's essential to remain vigilant and verify the data, as malicious actors can manipulate headers to deceive or conceal their actions. Tracing email headers is a valuable tool in the arsenal of cybersecurity professionals and investigators alike, helping to protect against cyber threats and uncover the truth in online communications.

Advanced email forensics is a specialized field within digital forensics that focuses on the investigation and analysis of email data to uncover critical evidence in legal cases, cybersecurity incidents, and other investigations. Command: Understand the significance of advanced email forensics as a crucial component of digital forensics and investigative work. Email has become an integral part of modern communication, making it a rich source of digital evidence for forensic experts and investigators. Command: Recognize the importance of email as a primary means of communication in today's digital age, leading to its significance in forensic analysis.

Advanced email forensics encompasses a wide range of techniques and methodologies to extract, examine, and interpret email-related evidence. Command: Grasp the comprehensive nature of advanced email forensics, which involves diverse techniques for handling email evidence.

This field is essential in various domains, including criminal investigations, civil litigation, corporate internal investigations, and incident response in cybersecurity. Command: Acknowledge the diverse applications of advanced email forensics, spanning from criminal investigations to cybersecurity incident response.

One of the key objectives of advanced email forensics is to recover deleted or hidden email messages and attachments, which can be critical in legal cases or cybersecurity incidents. Command: Understand the primary goal of advanced email forensics, which is to retrieve deleted or concealed email content for evidentiary purposes.

Advanced email forensics professionals must possess a deep understanding of email protocols, file formats, and the intricacies of email systems. Command: Embrace the requirement for advanced email forensics experts to have in-depth knowledge of email technologies and systems.

The process of advanced email forensics often begins with the acquisition of email data, which can be obtained from various sources such as email servers, email clients, or backups. Command: Recognize the initial phase of advanced email forensics, which involves collecting email data from multiple sources.

Forensic acquisition tools and techniques are used to create a forensically sound copy of email data to preserve its integrity for analysis. Command: Utilize forensic acquisition methods and tools to ensure the preservation and integrity of email data during the collection process.

Once the email data is acquired, the next step in advanced email forensics is the examination and analysis of the email content. Command: Proceed with the examination and analysis of email content as the subsequent phase of advanced email forensics.

Emails often contain metadata, message text, attachments, sender and recipient information, timestamps, and other crucial details that can be valuable in investigations. Command: Be attentive to the various elements of email content, such as metadata, message text, attachments, and sender information, as they provide essential clues.

Advanced email forensics experts use specialized software tools and techniques to parse and extract relevant information from email data. Command: Employ specialized software and techniques to extract pertinent information from email data during the analysis phase.

Metadata analysis is a critical component of advanced email forensics, as it can reveal valuable insights about an email's origin, routing, and handling. Command: Understand the importance of metadata analysis in advanced email forensics, as it provides insights into email's journey and handling.

Metadata includes information such as email headers, which can contain sender and recipient addresses, server information, and timestamps. Command: Recognize that email headers are a part of metadata and play a significant role in email forensics.

Examination of email headers can help trace the path an email took from the sender to the recipient, uncovering intermediate servers and potential points of interest. Command: Emphasize the significance of email header analysis in tracking the route of an email and identifying crucial servers.

Advanced email forensics professionals also employ keyword searches and data carving techniques to identify and recover email messages that may have been deleted or intentionally hidden. Command: Utilize keyword searches and data carving to detect and retrieve email messages that are deleted or concealed.

Data carving involves the extraction of email fragments or attachments from unallocated disk space or damaged email files, aiding in the recovery of critical evidence. Command: Understand the concept of data carving and its role in recovering email fragments and attachments from damaged email data.

In cases involving email spoliation or tampering, advanced email forensics can help identify alterations, deletions, or forgeries in email content or metadata. Command: Recognize the ability of advanced email forensics to detect email spoliation, tampering, or forgery, ensuring the integrity of evidence.

Advanced email forensics experts may also use email tracking and analysis techniques to identify the geolocation of email senders or track the source of malicious emails. Command: Explore email tracking and analysis methods to determine the geolocation of email senders and trace the source of malicious emails.

Email forensics is often used to support legal cases, including investigations related to intellectual property theft, fraud, harassment, and cyberattacks. Command: Understand the role of email forensics in legal proceedings, where it aids in cases involving intellectual property theft, fraud, harassment, and cyberattacks.

Maintaining the chain of custody and ensuring the admissibility of email evidence in court are critical aspects of advanced email forensics. Command: Emphasize the importance of maintaining the chain of custody and following proper procedures to ensure the admissibility of email evidence in legal proceedings.

In summary, advanced email forensics is a specialized field that plays a vital role in digital investigations, legal proceedings, and cybersecurity incident response. Experts in this field use a combination of technical knowledge, forensic tools, and analysis techniques to uncover hidden email evidence, recover deleted messages, and trace the source of emails. The insights gained from advanced email forensics can be pivotal in resolving legal cases, preventing cyber threats, and preserving the integrity of digital communication.

Chapter 6: Open Source Analysis Tools

Exploring OSINT frameworks is a crucial step in enhancing your Open Source Intelligence (OSINT) capabilities. Command: Recognize the significance of exploring OSINT frameworks to expand your knowledge and skills in the field of OSINT.

OSINT frameworks provide structured methodologies, tools, and techniques to conduct effective online investigations. Command: Understand that OSINT frameworks offer structured approaches, tools, and methods for conducting successful online investigations.

These frameworks serve as comprehensive guides that help analysts gather, analyze, and interpret publicly available information from various online sources. Command: Acknowledge that OSINT frameworks function as comprehensive guides, facilitating the collection, analysis, and interpretation of publicly accessible online data.

One widely recognized OSINT framework is the "OSINT Framework" by Justin Nordine, which is a curated collection of OSINT tools and resources. Command: Explore the "OSINT Framework" created by Justin Nordine, known for its curated collection of OSINT tools and resources.

The "OSINT Framework" categorizes tools and resources into various sections, making it easier for OSINT practitioners to navigate and utilize them effectively. Command: Understand the organizational structure of the "OSINT Framework," which categorizes tools and resources for ease of use.

Sections within the framework cover topics such as data breach and leak databases, people and company search engines, social media research, and much more. Command: Explore the diverse sections of the framework, which encompass areas like data breaches, people and company searches, and social media research.

By following the "OSINT Framework," you can access a plethora of resources, including search engines, websites, and tools, to conduct thorough investigations. Command: Utilize the "OSINT Framework" to access a wealth of resources, including search engines, websites, and tools, to enhance your investigative capabilities.

Another notable OSINT framework is the "Trace Labs Missing Persons CTF," which focuses on using OSINT techniques to help find missing persons. Command: Investigate the "Trace Labs Missing Persons CTF" framework, designed for leveraging OSINT techniques in locating missing individuals.

The "Missing Persons CTF" framework offers challenges and scenarios where OSINT enthusiasts can apply their skills to assist in real-world missing persons cases. Command: Engage with the challenges and scenarios provided by the "Missing Persons CTF" framework, contributing your OSINT expertise to real-life missing persons investigations.

Participating in "CTF" (Capture The Flag) events hosted by Trace Labs allows you to gain practical experience and contribute to humanitarian efforts. Command: Consider participating in "Capture The Flag" (CTF) events organized by Trace Labs to gain hands-on experience and support humanitarian causes through OSINT.

The "Harvard OSINT" framework, developed by the Berkman Klein Center for Internet & Society at Harvard University, focuses on ethical OSINT practices. Command: Explore the "Harvard OSINT" framework, created by the Berkman Klein Center for Internet & Society at Harvard University, emphasizing ethical OSINT approaches.

This framework offers guidelines and principles for conducting OSINT research responsibly and respecting privacy and legal boundaries. Command: Embrace the guidelines and principles provided by the "Harvard OSINT" framework to ensure ethical and lawful OSINT research practices.

The "DIRE Framework" (Data, Information, Report, Evaluate) is a structured approach to OSINT investigations developed by Jake Creps. Command: Familiarize yourself with the "DIRE Framework," a structured method for conducting OSINT investigations created by Jake Creps.

This framework encourages analysts to progress through a series of steps, from data collection to reporting and evaluation, to produce actionable intelligence. Command: Follow the stages outlined in the "DIRE Framework," which guides analysts through data collection, reporting, and evaluation phases to generate actionable intelligence.

OSINT frameworks often include best practices for maintaining operational security (OPSEC) during investigations. Command: Pay attention to the OPSEC best practices incorporated into OSINT frameworks to ensure the safety and confidentiality of your operations.

Operational security is vital to protect both the investigator's identity and the integrity of the investigation. Command: Understand that maintaining operational security is crucial for safeguarding both your identity and the investigation's integrity.

OSINT frameworks may also provide guidance on ethical considerations, emphasizing the importance of respecting privacy and legal boundaries. Command: Embrace the ethical guidelines included in OSINT frameworks, underscoring the significance of upholding privacy and legal standards in your investigations.

When exploring OSINT frameworks, it's essential to select the framework or methodologies that align with your specific investigative needs and objectives. Command: Choose the OSINT framework or methodologies that best match your investigative requirements and goals when exploring these resources.

Consider the types of investigations you are likely to undertake, whether they involve cybersecurity, digital forensics, threat intelligence, or other domains. Command: Evaluate the nature of your investigations, whether they pertain to cybersecurity, digital forensics, threat intelligence, or other fields, to make an informed choice.

OSINT frameworks are valuable resources for individuals and organizations seeking to harness the power of open source intelligence. Command: Recognize that OSINT frameworks serve as valuable assets for individuals and organizations aiming to leverage the capabilities of open source intelligence.

They provide structured approaches, tools, and guidelines to enhance your ability to collect, analyze, and interpret publicly available information effectively.

Leveraging data visualization tools is a powerful way to transform complex information into clear, easily digestible visuals that can aid in decision-making and understanding. Command: Recognize the value of data visualization tools in simplifying intricate data and enhancing comprehension.

In today's data-driven world, businesses, researchers, and individuals generate vast amounts of data regularly. Command: Acknowledge that in the contemporary data-centric environment, data is constantly being generated by businesses, researchers, and individuals.

This data encompasses a wide range of information, including sales figures, customer demographics, research findings, and more. Command: Understand that data takes many forms, encompassing sales data, customer demographics, research results, and various other information.

However, raw data, when presented in its original form, can be overwhelming and challenging to grasp fully. Command: Recognize that raw data, in its unprocessed state, can be daunting and difficult to comprehend.

Data visualization tools offer a solution to this challenge by enabling the transformation of data into visual representations. Command: Embrace data visualization tools as a means to address this issue, as they facilitate the conversion of data into visual formats.

These visualizations can take the form of charts, graphs, maps, diagrams, and interactive dashboards, among others. Command: Understand that data visualizations can manifest as various formats, such as charts, graphs, maps, diagrams, and interactive dashboards.

One of the most common types of data visualization is the bar chart, which displays data in rectangular bars of varying lengths. Command: Recognize the bar chart as a prevalent form of data visualization, depicting data through rectangular bars of different lengths.

Bar charts are effective for comparing categories or displaying changes in data over time. Command: Understand that bar charts excel in comparing categories or illustrating data trends over time.

Line charts, on the other hand, are useful for demonstrating trends and patterns in data, making them valuable in time-series analysis. Command: Emphasize the utility of line charts in revealing data trends and patterns, particularly in time-series analysis.

Pie charts are ideal for illustrating the composition of a whole by dividing it into segments proportional to their values. Command: Acknowledge the suitability of pie charts for depicting the distribution of a whole by dividing it into proportional segments.

Scatter plots enable the examination of relationships between two variables and are helpful for identifying correlations. Command: Recognize the usefulness of scatter plots in examining connections between two variables and uncovering correlations.

Heatmaps use color intensity to represent data values, making them effective for visualizing large datasets and identifying patterns. Command: Understand that heatmaps utilize color intensity to portray data values, making them adept at handling extensive datasets and revealing patterns.

Maps and geographical visualizations provide insights into location-based data, such as regional sales or the spread of diseases. Command: Appreciate the role of maps and geographical visualizations in conveying location-related data, such as regional sales or disease spread.

Interactive dashboards allow users to explore data dynamically by interacting with elements like dropdown menus and sliders. Command: Highlight the interactivity of dashboards, permitting users to engage with data through features like dropdown menus and sliders.

Data visualization tools often provide customization options, allowing users to tailor visualizations to their specific needs. Command: Emphasize the customization capabilities offered by data visualization tools, enabling users to adapt visualizations to their unique requirements.

These tools can accommodate various data sources, including spreadsheets, databases, APIs, and real-time data streams. Command: Recognize that data visualization tools are versatile, capable of handling diverse data sources such as spreadsheets, databases, APIs, and real-time data feeds.

Popular data visualization tools in the market include Tableau, Power BI, Google Data Studio, and D3.js. Command: Acknowledge the popularity of data visualization tools like

Tableau, Power BI, Google Data Studio, and D3.js in the market.

Tableau, for instance, offers a user-friendly interface for creating interactive and shareable dashboards. Command: Explore the user-friendly interface of Tableau, which empowers users to build interactive and shareable dashboards.

Power BI, a Microsoft product, integrates seamlessly with other Microsoft applications and offers robust data analytics capabilities. Command: Consider the integration capabilities and robust data analytics features provided by Power BI, a Microsoft product.

Google Data Studio is a web-based tool that simplifies data visualization and reporting through drag-and-drop functionality. Command: Explore the user-friendly, web-based nature of Google Data Studio, which streamlines data visualization and reporting with drag-and-drop functionality.

D3.js, a JavaScript library, provides flexibility for creating custom visualizations and is popular among developers. Command: Recognize D3.js as a JavaScript library favored by developers for its flexibility in crafting bespoke visualizations.

Effective data visualization serves several purposes, including data exploration, communication, and decision support. Command: Understand that data visualization serves multiple roles, including aiding in data exploration, communication, and decision-making.

For data exploration, visualizations help analysts gain insights into datasets, identify outliers, and uncover trends. Command: Highlight the role of visualizations in data exploration, assisting analysts in gaining insights, spotting outliers, and revealing trends.

In terms of communication, visualizations simplify the presentation of complex data to stakeholders and make it more accessible. Command: Emphasize that visualizations enhance data communication by simplifying the presentation of complex information to stakeholders.

When it comes to decision support, well-designed visualizations empower decision-makers with data-driven insights. Command: Stress the importance of well-designed visualizations in providing decision-makers with data-driven insights to support informed choices.

Effective data visualization is guided by principles of simplicity, clarity, and relevance. Command: Emphasize that effective data visualization adheres to principles of simplicity, clarity, and relevance.

Simplicity ensures that the visualization conveys the intended message without unnecessary complexity. Command: Stress the importance of simplicity in ensuring that visualizations effectively convey their intended messages without unnecessary intricacies.

Clarity involves using clear labels, legends, and color schemes to enhance the viewer's understanding of the data. Command: Recognize the role of clarity, which entails using concise labels, legends, and color choices to improve the viewer's comprehension of data.

Relevance dictates that visualizations should focus on conveying the most pertinent information for the intended audience. Command: Understand that relevance dictates that visualizations should concentrate on presenting the most pertinent information to the target audience.

In summary, data visualization tools play a vital role in transforming complex data into comprehensible and actionable insights. Whether through bar charts, line charts, maps, or interactive dashboards, these tools empower individuals and organizations to explore, communicate, and make informed decisions based on data. Understanding the principles of effective data visualization, along with the capabilities of popular tools like Tableau, Power BI, Google Data Studio, and D3.js, is essential for harnessing the power of visual representations in a data-driven world.

Chapter 7: Advanced Data Scraping and Automation

Web scraping with Python has become an invaluable skill in the realm of data acquisition and analysis. Command: Acknowledge the significance of web scraping with Python in the context of data acquisition and analysis.

The ability to extract data from websites automatically has numerous applications in various domains, from business intelligence to research and beyond. Command: Understand that web scraping's capability to automate data extraction from websites finds utility in diverse fields, including business intelligence and research.

Python, a versatile and widely-used programming language, provides an array of libraries and frameworks that make web scraping accessible and efficient. Command: Recognize Python as a versatile programming language, offering numerous libraries and frameworks that simplify and optimize web scraping tasks.

One of the most popular libraries for web scraping in Python is BeautifulSoup, which enables the parsing and extraction of data from HTML and XML documents. Command: Explore BeautifulSoup as a prominent Python library for web scraping, facilitating the parsing and extraction of data from HTML and XML documents.

Another powerful library often used in conjunction with BeautifulSoup is Requests, which simplifies the process of making HTTP requests to web pages. Command: Consider Requests as a complementary Python library that streamlines the procedure of sending HTTP requests to web pages, frequently used alongside BeautifulSoup.

To begin a web scraping project with Python, it's essential to understand the structure of the websites you intend to scrape. Command: Stress the importance of comprehending the structure of the target websites before embarking on a Python web scraping project.

This includes identifying the HTML elements that contain the data you want to extract, such as tables, paragraphs, or specific tags. Command: Emphasize the necessity of pinpointing the HTML elements housing the desired data, whether they are tables, paragraphs, or specific tags.

Once you've determined the structure, you can use BeautifulSoup to parse the HTML content of a webpage and extract the relevant data. Command: Recognize that after discerning the structure, BeautifulSoup can be employed to parse a webpage's HTML content and retrieve pertinent data.

BeautifulSoup's intuitive syntax allows you to navigate and manipulate the parsed HTML easily, making it a favorite among web scrapers. Command: Highlight the user-friendly syntax of BeautifulSoup, which facilitates seamless navigation and manipulation of parsed HTML, earning it popularity among web scrapers.

For instance, you can use BeautifulSoup to find all instances of a specific HTML tag or search for elements with particular attributes. Command: Provide examples of how BeautifulSoup can be employed to locate all occurrences of a specific HTML tag or search for elements possessing specific attributes.

In addition to BeautifulSoup, Python's Requests library simplifies the process of making HTTP requests to retrieve webpage content. Command: Stress the convenience of the Requests library for making HTTP requests to obtain webpage content as a crucial component of Python web scraping.

With Requests, you can specify the URL of the target webpage and easily retrieve its HTML content. Command:

Highlight the ease of specifying the target webpage's URL and obtaining its HTML content using the Requests library.

Before conducting web scraping, it's essential to review and comply with the website's terms of service and its robots.txt file, if available. Command: Emphasize the importance of reviewing and adhering to a website's terms of service and, if present, the robots.txt file before engaging in web scraping.

Respecting a website's policies and guidelines is crucial to maintain ethical and legal integrity during web scraping activities. Command: Acknowledge that adhering to a website's policies and guidelines is imperative to ensure ethical and legal conduct throughout web scraping endeavors.

Web scraping can involve crawling through multiple web pages to collect data comprehensively. Command: Highlight that web scraping might entail traversing various web pages to gather data comprehensively.

To achieve this, you can create loops in Python that iterate through a series of URLs or follow links within a website. Command: Describe the process of using Python loops to iterate through a set of URLs or follow internal links within a website for comprehensive data collection.

However, it's essential to implement appropriate pauses and error handling mechanisms to avoid overloading the website's server or encountering errors. Command: Stress the significance of integrating pauses and error-handling strategies to prevent server overloading and handle potential errors while web scraping.

Web scraping often involves dealing with unstructured or messy data, which may require cleaning and preprocessing. Command: Acknowledge that web scraping can result in unstructured or messy data that may necessitate cleaning and preprocessing.

Python offers libraries like Pandas, NumPy, and regular expressions (regex) for data manipulation and cleaning. Command: Highlight the utility of Python libraries such as Pandas, NumPy, and regular expressions (regex) for data manipulation and cleansing.

Pandas, in particular, excels in handling structured data and can help organize scraped data into convenient dataframes. Command: Emphasize Pandas' proficiency in managing structured data and its capacity to structure scraped data into user-friendly dataframes.

Regular expressions are invaluable for pattern matching and text extraction, aiding in the extraction of specific information from unstructured text. Command: Acknowledge the importance of regular expressions in pattern matching and text extraction, which facilitate the extraction of precise data from unstructured text.

When web scraping with Python, it's essential to be mindful of potential challenges, such as website changes or data format alterations. Command: Stress the importance of remaining vigilant about possible challenges, such as website modifications or changes in data formats, when conducting Python web scraping.

Monitoring and maintaining web scraping scripts is crucial to ensure they continue to function as intended. Command: Highlight the necessity of actively monitoring and maintaining web scraping scripts to guarantee their ongoing functionality.

In summary, web scraping with Python is a powerful skill that enables the extraction of data from websites efficiently and effectively. Command: Summarize that web scraping with Python empowers individuals to extract data from websites with efficiency and effectiveness.

Python libraries like BeautifulSoup and Requests simplify the process, while Pandas and regular expressions aid in data manipulation and cleaning. Command: Highlight the role of Python libraries such as BeautifulSoup and Requests in streamlining the process, and underscore the support provided by Pandas and regular expressions for data manipulation and cleansing.

Web scraping, when conducted ethically and in compliance with websites' terms of service, can provide valuable data for a wide range of applications. Command: Emphasize that ethical and compliant web scraping can yield valuable data with diverse applications, provided it respects websites' terms of service.

With the ability to transform unstructured web content into structured datasets, web scraping with Python is a valuable skill in the fields of data analysis, research, and business intelligence. Command: Recognize that web scraping with Python, which transforms unstructured web content into structured datasets, constitutes a valuable skill in data analysis, research, and business intelligence.

Building custom web crawlers is an advanced endeavor in the realm of web data extraction and automation. Command: Acknowledge the complexity and significance of building custom web crawlers as a high-level pursuit within web data extraction and automation.

Web crawlers, also known as web spiders or web robots, are programs designed to navigate the internet, access web pages, and extract data for various purposes. Command: Define web crawlers as specialized programs created to navigate the internet, visit web pages, and retrieve data for diverse applications.

Custom web crawlers provide tailored solutions for specific data acquisition needs, offering flexibility and control over the scraping process. Command: Highlight the advantage of custom web crawlers in furnishing tailored solutions for precise data collection requirements, granting flexibility and control during the scraping operation.

To embark on the journey of building custom web crawlers, one must possess a fundamental understanding of web technologies, programming languages, and the principles of web scraping. Command: Emphasize the need for a foundational grasp of web technologies, programming languages, and web scraping principles as prerequisites for creating custom web crawlers.

Python, a versatile and widely-used programming language, is a preferred choice for building custom web crawlers due to its robust libraries and frameworks. Command: Acknowledge Python's popularity as a programming language of choice for constructing custom web crawlers, thanks to its comprehensive libraries and frameworks.

The first step in building a custom web crawler is defining the scope and objectives of the crawling project. Command: Highlight the significance of establishing the scope and objectives of the web crawling project as the initial step in building a custom web crawler.

This involves determining the websites to crawl, the specific data to extract, and any additional functionality required. Command: Describe the process of identifying the target websites, delineating the precise data to collect, and outlining any supplementary functionality.

Once the project's scope is defined, the next task is selecting the tools and libraries to use in the development process. Command: Stress the importance of choosing the appropriate tools and libraries for development after defining the project's scope.

Python offers an array of libraries and frameworks, such as Scrapy and Beautiful Soup, that simplify the creation of web crawlers. Command: Recognize Python as a platform with a plethora of libraries and frameworks, including Scrapy and

Beautiful Soup, known for streamlining web crawler development.

Scrapy, a comprehensive web crawling framework, is particularly favored for its flexibility and extensibility. Command: Highlight Scrapy's reputation as a comprehensive web crawling framework, celebrated for its adaptability and extensibility.

Beautiful Soup, on the other hand, excels in parsing and navigating HTML and XML documents, making it an ideal choice for extracting data from web pages. Command: Emphasize Beautiful Soup's proficiency in parsing and traversing HTML and XML documents, rendering it an excellent tool for data extraction from webpages.

With the chosen tools and libraries in place, the development of the custom web crawler can commence. Command: Proceed with the development of the custom web crawler once the selected tools and libraries are prepared.

The core functionality of a web crawler involves sending HTTP requests to websites, downloading web pages, and extracting data from these pages. Command: Describe the core functions of a web crawler, which encompass sending HTTP requests to websites, downloading web pages, and extracting data from those pages.

HTTP requests can be made using Python's Requests library, allowing the crawler to access web pages and retrieve their content. Command: Highlight the utility of Python's Requests library in facilitating HTTP requests, enabling the web crawler to access web pages and acquire their contents.

To navigate and parse the HTML content of web pages, Beautiful Soup can be employed to extract specific data based on element tags and attributes. Command: Explain how Beautiful Soup can be utilized to navigate and parse the

HTML content of web pages, facilitating the extraction of precise data through element tags and attributes.

While building a web crawler, it's crucial to implement mechanisms for handling various scenarios and errors that may arise during the crawling process. Command: Stress the importance of incorporating error-handling mechanisms and strategies to manage diverse scenarios and potential errors throughout the web crawling procedure.

Web crawlers should include features like rate limiting to prevent overloading websites and adhering to ethical scraping practices. Command: Emphasize the necessity of integrating functionalities such as rate limiting to prevent overwhelming websites and practicing ethical scraping protocols in web crawlers.

Custom web crawlers can be designed to follow links within websites, enabling the crawler to navigate through a site's structure. Command: Explain how custom web crawlers can be configured to traverse internal links within websites, permitting navigation through a site's layout.

To avoid crawling in an uncontrolled manner, it's crucial to establish a set of rules and constraints for the crawler. Command: Stress the importance of defining rules and limitations for the crawler to prevent uncontrolled and unrestricted crawling.

The robots.txt file, typically hosted at the root of a website, provides guidelines for web crawlers on which pages to crawl and which to avoid. Command: Describe the role of the robots.txt file, usually located at a website's root, in furnishing instructions to web crawlers regarding which pages to crawl and which to disregard.

While building custom web crawlers, developers should adhere to the directives outlined in the robots.txt file to maintain ethical scraping practices. Command: Emphasize the significance of adhering to the directives specified in the robots.txt file to uphold ethical web scraping practices during custom web crawler development.

As custom web crawlers collect data, it's essential to implement storage mechanisms to store the scraped information. Command: Stress the need for storage mechanisms to preserve scraped data as custom web crawlers gather information.

Data can be saved in various formats, such as databases, CSV files, or even cloud storage solutions, depending on the project's requirements. Command: Explain that data can be stored in diverse formats, including databases, CSV files, or cloud storage solutions, contingent on the project's needs.

In the realm of web scraping, data ethics and legal considerations are paramount. Command: Acknowledge the paramount importance of data ethics and legal considerations in the domain of web scraping.

Respecting websites' terms of service and privacy policies is essential to ensure lawful and ethical data collection. Command: Emphasize the necessity of honoring websites' terms of service and privacy policies to guarantee legal and ethical data collection practices.

In some cases, web scraping may require explicit consent from website owners or consideration of data protection regulations, such as GDPR. Command: Stress that certain instances of web scraping may necessitate explicit consent from website proprietors or adherence to data protection regulations like GDPR.

When building custom web crawlers, it's essential to monitor the crawling process and address any issues that may arise. Command: Highlight the need for active monitoring and problem-solving throughout the web crawling process when constructing custom web crawlers.

Web scraping can be resource-intensive, and crawlers may need to be run on powerful servers or cloud-based platforms for large-scale data extraction. Command: Explain that web scraping can consume substantial resources, requiring crawlers to operate on robust servers or cloud-based platforms for extensive data extraction.

In summary, building custom web crawlers is a challenging but rewarding endeavor that grants control over the web scraping process. Command: Summarize that constructing custom web crawlers is a demanding yet fulfilling undertaking that provides mastery over the web scraping process.

Chapter 8: Cyber Threat Intelligence

Identifying Advanced Persistent Threats (APTs) is a critical aspect of cybersecurity and threat detection. Command: Establish the significance of identifying Advanced Persistent Threats (APTs) as a fundamental element within the realm of cybersecurity and threat detection.

APTs are sophisticated and stealthy cyberattacks orchestrated by highly skilled threat actors with specific targets in mind. Command: Define APTs as intricate and covert cyberattacks conducted by exceptionally skilled threat actors who have precise targets in their sights.

These threats differ from run-of-the-mill cyberattacks in their level of sophistication, duration, and the resources at the disposal of the attackers. Command: Highlight the distinctions between APTs and typical cyberattacks, which include elevated levels of sophistication, extended durations, and substantial attacker resources.

APTs often involve multiple stages, including initial reconnaissance, infiltration, maintaining persistence, and exfiltrating sensitive data. Command: Describe the multifaceted nature of APTs, which typically comprise various phases such as initial reconnaissance, infiltration, persistence maintenance, and data exfiltration.

One of the primary challenges in identifying APTs lies in their ability to remain hidden within a targeted network for extended periods, sometimes years. Command: Acknowledge that a significant challenge in APT identification is rooted in the attackers' capacity to conceal themselves within a target network for prolonged durations, sometimes spanning years.

Traditional security measures and standard antivirus solutions are often insufficient to detect and mitigate APTs effectively. Command: Stress the inadequacy of conventional security measures and standard antivirus solutions in effectively identifying and mitigating APTs.

To address this challenge, organizations must employ advanced threat detection techniques and adopt a proactive security posture. Command: Emphasize the necessity for organizations to utilize advanced threat detection methods and adopt a proactive security stance to combat the APT menace.

Advanced threat detection involves monitoring network traffic, endpoints, and user behavior for suspicious activities and anomalies. Command: Explain that advanced threat detection entails the continuous monitoring of network traffic, endpoints, and user behavior to detect unusual activities and irregularities.

Network traffic analysis is a crucial component of APT identification, as it allows security teams to spot unusual communication patterns. Command: Recognize network traffic analysis as an integral element in APT identification, as it enables security teams to identify abnormal communication patterns.

Intrusion Detection Systems (IDS) and Intrusion Prevention Systems (IPS) play vital roles in analyzing network traffic and identifying potential APT activity. Command: Highlight the significance of Intrusion Detection Systems (IDS) and Intrusion Prevention Systems (IPS) in scrutinizing network traffic and pinpointing potential APT actions.

Behavioral analysis is another essential aspect of advanced threat detection, focusing on deviations from normal user behavior. Command: Describe behavioral analysis as another critical aspect of advanced threat detection, concentrating on deviations from typical user conduct.

User and entity behavior analytics (UEBA) solutions leverage machine learning and artificial intelligence to detect unusual behavior patterns that may indicate APTs. Command: Explain that User and Entity Behavior Analytics (UEBA) solutions utilize machine learning and artificial intelligence to uncover abnormal behavior patterns that could be indicative of APTs.

Endpoints, including computers and mobile devices, are common targets for APT infiltration, making endpoint detection and response (EDR) critical. Command: Acknowledge that endpoints, encompassing computers and mobile devices, are frequent APT targets, underscoring the importance of endpoint detection and response (EDR).

EDR solutions monitor and analyze endpoint activity, looking for signs of compromise and responding to incidents promptly. Command: Highlight the role of EDR solutions in monitoring and analyzing endpoint activities, searching for indications of compromise and executing swift incident responses.

Identifying APTs may also involve threat hunting, a proactive approach where security experts actively search for signs of APT activity. Command: Describe threat hunting as a proactive strategy in which security experts actively seek out indications of APT activity.

Threat hunters utilize various tools and techniques, including analyzing logs, examining network traffic, and scrutinizing system behavior. Command: Explain that threat hunters employ a range of tools and tactics, such as log analysis, network traffic examination, and system behavior scrutiny.

One of the hallmarks of APTs is their ability to use spear-phishing and social engineering tactics to gain a foothold in target organizations. Command: Recognize that APTs are known for employing spear-phishing and social engineering techniques to infiltrate target organizations.

Spear-phishing emails are carefully crafted to appear legitimate and entice recipients to click on malicious links or download malicious attachments. Command: Explain that spear-phishing emails are meticulously designed to mimic authenticity and lure recipients into clicking on malevolent links or downloading harmful attachments.

To combat this, organizations must provide cybersecurity training to educate employees about recognizing and reporting suspicious emails. Command: Stress the importance of cybersecurity training within organizations to instruct employees on identifying and reporting suspicious emails.

Multi-factor authentication (MFA) can also thwart APTs by adding an additional layer of security, making it more challenging for attackers to gain unauthorized access.

Cyber Threat Intelligence (CTI) sharing is a crucial element in the defense against evolving cybersecurity threats. Command: Introduce the topic of Cyber Threat Intelligence (CTI) sharing and its pivotal role in countering dynamic cybersecurity threats.

In today's interconnected digital landscape, organizations face an ever-expanding array of threats, including advanced persistent threats (APTs), ransomware attacks, and data breaches. Command: Highlight the contemporary cybersecurity challenges that organizations encounter in an interconnected digital environment, encompassing advanced persistent threats (APTs), ransomware attacks, and data breaches.

These threats are constantly evolving, becoming more sophisticated, and exploiting vulnerabilities in networks and systems. Command: Acknowledge the continuous evolution of cybersecurity threats, their increasing complexity, and their adeptness at exploiting network and system vulnerabilities.

To defend against such threats effectively, organizations need timely and actionable information about potential risks and vulnerabilities. Command: Emphasize the necessity for organizations to possess timely and actionable information concerning potential risks and vulnerabilities as a means of mounting effective defenses.

This is where Cyber Threat Intelligence (CTI) comes into play, providing valuable insights into the tactics, techniques, and procedures (TTPs) employed by threat actors. Command: Define the role of Cyber Threat Intelligence (CTI) in supplying valuable insights into the tactics, techniques, and procedures (TTPs) utilized by threat actors.

CTI encompasses a broad spectrum of information, ranging from indicators of compromise (IOCs) to detailed analyses of threat actor behavior. Command: Describe the diverse nature of CTI, which spans from indicators of compromise (IOCs) to in-depth examinations of threat actor behavior.

IOCs are specific pieces of information that indicate potentially malicious activities, such as IP addresses, malware signatures, or malicious file hashes. Command: Explain that indicators of compromise (IOCs) denote specific pieces of information that signify potential malicious activities, including IP addresses, malware signatures, or malicious file hashes.

Analyzing and sharing CTI enables organizations to enhance their cybersecurity posture by proactively identifying and mitigating threats. Command: Highlight that the analysis and dissemination of CTI empower organizations to bolster their cybersecurity defenses by proactively identifying and mitigating threats.

However, no organization operates in isolation, and many cybersecurity threats extend beyond the boundaries of a single entity. Command: Stress that cybersecurity threats often transcend the confines of individual organizations, acknowledging that no entity operates in isolation.

To effectively combat these threats, the sharing of CTI among organizations, both within and across sectors, is essential. Command: Emphasize the indispensability of CTI sharing among organizations, spanning intra- and inter-sectoral collaboration, to effectively counteract these threats.

CTI sharing involves the exchange of threat information, insights, and analysis to help organizations collectively defend against cyber threats. Command: Define CTI sharing as the process of exchanging threat-related information, insights, and analyses, fostering collaborative cybersecurity defense efforts among organizations.

One common form of CTI sharing is information sharing and analysis centers (ISACs), which are sector-specific organizations that facilitate the exchange of cybersecurity information. Command: Introduce information sharing and analysis centers (ISACs) as sector-specific entities that facilitate the exchange of cybersecurity information, representing a prevalent model of CTI sharing.

ISACs focus on specific industries, such as finance, healthcare, or energy, and provide a platform for members to share and receive CTI. Command: Explain that ISACs concentrate on particular industries, for instance, finance, healthcare, or energy, offering a platform for members to exchange and access CTI.

These centers serve as trusted intermediaries, helping organizations maintain confidentiality while sharing critical threat information. Command: Emphasize the role of ISACs as trustworthy intermediaries, aiding organizations in preserving confidentiality while exchanging vital threat intelligence.

In addition to ISACs, government agencies, such as the United States' Cybersecurity and Infrastructure Security Agency (CISA), play a role in CTI sharing. Command: Acknowledge the involvement of government agencies, exemplified by the United States' Cybersecurity and Infrastructure Security Agency (CISA), in the realm of CTI sharing.

CISA collaborates with private-sector partners and government entities to enhance the cybersecurity resilience of critical infrastructure. Command: Highlight CISA's collaborative efforts with both private-sector partners and government entities to bolster the cybersecurity resilience of critical infrastructure.

The sharing of CTI extends to international cooperation, as cybersecurity threats are often global in nature. Command: Recognize the global nature of cybersecurity threats, and underscore the importance of international cooperation in CTI sharing efforts.

International organizations, such as INTERPOL and Europol, facilitate information exchange and collaboration on cybercrime investigations. Command: Introduce international organizations like INTERPOL and Europol, which facilitate the exchange of information and cooperation in cybercrime investigations.

Moreover, private-sector companies and security vendors are active participants in CTI sharing efforts, contributing valuable insights and data. Command: Highlight the active involvement of private-sector companies and security vendors in CTI sharing initiatives, offering valuable insights and data contributions.

Collaboration with the broader cybersecurity community, including researchers and threat hunters, is another essential aspect of CTI sharing. Command: Stress the significance of engaging with the wider cybersecurity community, encompassing researchers and threat hunters, in the context of CTI sharing.

Open-source threat intelligence feeds, blogs, forums, and mailing lists are platforms where valuable CTI is often shared. Command: Identify open-source platforms such as threat intelligence feeds, blogs, forums, and mailing lists as venues where valuable CTI is frequently disseminated.

CTI sharing extends beyond the exchange of raw data and includes the analysis and contextualization of threat information. Command: Explain that CTI sharing encompasses more than just the transfer of raw data, involving the analysis and contextualization of threat information.

The received information is evaluated to determine its relevance and potential impact on an organization's security posture. Command: Describe the evaluation process applied to received information, wherein its relevance and potential impact on an organization's security posture are assessed.

To effectively share CTI, organizations should establish clear policies and procedures for handling and disseminating threat intelligence. Command: Stress the importance of organizations instituting well-defined policies and procedures governing the handling and dissemination of threat intelligence to facilitate effective CTI sharing.

These policies should address issues such as data classification, sharing mechanisms, information sharing agreements, and data retention. Command: Specify that these policies should encompass crucial aspects, including data classification, sharing mechanisms, information sharing agreements, and data retention guidelines.

Chapter 9: Analyzing Cryptocurrencies and Blockchain

Investigating crypto transactions is a complex and critical aspect of digital forensics and financial investigations. Command: Establish the complexity and importance of investigating crypto transactions within the realms of digital forensics and financial investigations.

Cryptocurrencies like Bitcoin, Ethereum, and others have gained popularity for their potential as both a store of value and a means of conducting transactions. Command: Acknowledge the popularity of cryptocurrencies like Bitcoin and Ethereum, highlighting their dual roles as stores of value and transactional instruments.

However, their pseudonymous and decentralized nature also makes cryptocurrencies appealing to criminals for illicit activities such as money laundering, tax evasion, and ransomware payments. Command: Highlight the dual nature of cryptocurrencies, emphasizing that their pseudonymous and decentralized attributes attract criminals for activities like money laundering, tax evasion, and ransomware payments.

Investigating crypto transactions involves tracing the flow of digital assets on blockchain networks, which are public ledgers that record all transactions. Command: Explain that investigating crypto transactions entails tracing the movement of digital assets on blockchain networks, characterized by public ledgers that document all transactions.

One of the primary challenges in crypto transaction investigations is the pseudonymous nature of wallet addresses. Command: Identify the pseudonymous nature of wallet addresses as a primary challenge in crypto transaction investigations.

Wallet addresses are alphanumeric strings that do not directly reveal the identity of the owner, making it difficult to associate transactions with individuals or entities. Command: Explain that wallet addresses consist of alphanumeric strings that do not immediately disclose the owner's identity, resulting in challenges when attempting to link transactions to specific individuals or entities.

To address this challenge, investigators employ blockchain analysis tools and techniques to de-anonymize transactions. Command: Emphasize that investigators utilize blockchain analysis tools and methods to de-anonymize transactions and unveil the identities behind wallet addresses.

Blockchain analysis tools can trace the flow of cryptocurrency from its origin to various addresses, uncovering patterns and connections. Command: Describe how blockchain analysis tools have the capability to follow the path of cryptocurrency from its source to multiple addresses, revealing patterns and connections.

These tools may also utilize machine learning algorithms to identify suspicious or illicit activities within the blockchain. Command: Mention that some blockchain analysis tools leverage machine learning algorithms to detect suspicious or unlawful activities occurring within the blockchain.

Crypto exchanges, where individuals buy, sell, and trade cryptocurrencies, play a pivotal role in transaction investigations. Command: Highlight the significance of crypto exchanges, which serve as platforms for individuals to purchase, sell, and trade cryptocurrencies, in transaction investigations.

Exchanges typically require users to complete Know Your Customer (KYC) verification, providing valuable identity-related information. Command: Explain that exchanges commonly mandate users to undergo Know Your Customer (KYC) verification, furnishing valuable identity-related information.

This KYC data can be invaluable for investigators, as it links cryptocurrency transactions to real-world identities. Command: Emphasize the importance of KYC data to investigators, as it enables the connection of cryptocurrency transactions to real-world identities.

However, it's important to note that not all crypto transactions occur through exchanges, and some individuals prefer peer-to-peer (P2P) transactions. Command: Acknowledge that not all crypto transactions transpire via exchanges, with some individuals opting for peer-to-peer (P2P) transactions.

In P2P transactions, individuals interact directly, making it more challenging for investigators to access identity-related information. Command: Explain that in P2P transactions, individuals engage in direct interactions, presenting a greater challenge for investigators to obtain identity-related information.

Despite these challenges, investigators have successfully traced and recovered cryptocurrencies in various criminal cases. Command: Highlight the achievements of investigators in successfully tracing and retrieving cryptocurrencies in numerous criminal cases, despite the obstacles.

One notable example is the seizure and recovery of Bitcoin from the Silk Road marketplace, a notorious online black market. Command: Provide a notable example of the seizure and recovery of Bitcoin from the Silk Road marketplace, a well-known online black market.

In this case, law enforcement authorities managed to locate and confiscate a substantial amount of Bitcoin associated with the illicit marketplace. Command: Describe how, in this instance, law enforcement agencies were able to locate and seize a substantial quantity of Bitcoin linked to the illicit marketplace.

The recovered funds were auctioned off, and the proceeds were used to compensate victims and support law enforcement activities. Command: Explain that the retrieved funds were subsequently auctioned, with the proceeds allocated to compensating victims and bolstering law enforcement efforts.

To conduct successful crypto transaction investigations, investigators should stay updated on the latest blockchain technologies, cryptocurrencies, and privacy-enhancing techniques. Command: Advise investigators to remain informed about the latest advancements in blockchain technologies, cryptocurrencies, and privacy-enhancing methods to facilitate successful crypto transaction investigations.

Furthermore, collaboration with cryptocurrency experts and blockchain analysts can provide valuable insights and expertise. Command: Emphasize the importance of collaborating with cryptocurrency experts and blockchain analysts, who can offer valuable insights and expertise in the field.

Interdisciplinary cooperation between law enforcement, financial institutions, and regulatory agencies is also essential in tackling crypto-related crimes. Command: Stress the need for interdisciplinary collaboration among law enforcement agencies, financial institutions, and regulatory bodies as a critical component of combating cryptocurrency-related crimes.

International coordination is particularly vital, as crypto transactions frequently cross borders, necessitating cooperation between countries. Command: Highlight the significance of international coordination, as crypto transactions often traverse international boundaries, demanding collaboration between nations.

The legal framework surrounding cryptocurrency investigations is continuously evolving, and investigators must be aware of relevant laws and regulations. Command: Emphasize that the legal landscape pertaining to cryptocurrency investigations is in a state of constant evolution, and investigators should remain cognizant of pertinent laws and regulations.

Additionally, investigators must adhere to ethical and legal standards to ensure the admissibility of evidence in court. Command: Stress the importance of investigators maintaining adherence to ethical and legal standards to guarantee the admissibility of evidence in legal proceedings.

In summary, investigating crypto transactions is a multifaceted endeavor that combines technology, forensics, and legal expertise. Command: Summarize that investigating crypto transactions entails a multifaceted approach that blends technology, forensics, and legal knowledge.

While challenges exist, successful investigations have demonstrated the potential to hold individuals accountable for illicit crypto activities and recover stolen funds.

Tracking cryptocurrency mixers is a challenging task within the realm of digital forensics and blockchain analysis. Command: Establish the complexity and significance of tracking cryptocurrency mixers in the context of digital forensics and blockchain analysis.

Cryptocurrency mixers, also known as tumblers or coin mixers, are services designed to enhance the privacy and anonymity of cryptocurrency transactions. Command: Define cryptocurrency mixers as services created to enhance the privacy and anonymity of cryptocurrency transactions.

These services work by taking a user's cryptocurrency and mixing it with the funds of other users, making it challenging to trace the original source of the funds. Command: Explain the functioning of cryptocurrency mixers, which involves commingling a user's cryptocurrency with funds from other users, rendering it difficult to trace the original source of the funds.

While cryptocurrency mixers have legitimate use cases, such as protecting user privacy, they are also exploited by individuals engaging in illicit activities like money laundering, tax evasion, and ransomware payments. Command: Highlight that cryptocurrency mixers possess legitimate purposes, including safeguarding user privacy, but are also exploited by individuals involved in unlawful activities such as money laundering, tax evasion, and ransomware payments.

The challenge in tracking cryptocurrency mixers lies in their ability to obfuscate transaction trails, hindering investigators' efforts. Command: Identify the primary challenge in tracking cryptocurrency mixers, which is their capability to obscure transaction trails and impede investigators' progress.

To address this challenge, investigators employ a variety of techniques and tools to trace funds that have passed through mixers. Command: Stress that investigators employ an array of techniques and tools to track funds that have traversed through cryptocurrency mixers, seeking to overcome this challenge.

Blockchain analysis is a key component of tracking cryptocurrency mixers, as it involves examining transactions recorded on public ledgers. Command: Describe blockchain analysis as an integral aspect of tracking cryptocurrency mixers, involving the examination of transactions documented on public ledgers.

Public blockchains like Bitcoin's provide transparency, enabling investigators to trace the flow of funds. Command: Explain that public blockchains, exemplified by Bitcoin's blockchain, offer transparency that allows investigators to follow the path of funds.

However, mixers operate off-chain, meaning their transactions occur outside the blockchain and are not readily visible. Command: Point out that mixers operate off-chain, signifying that their transactions take place outside the blockchain and are not immediately apparent.

To tackle this challenge, investigators often rely on heuristics, patterns, and behavioral analysis to identify mixer-related transactions. Command: Indicate that investigators frequently employ heuristics, patterns, and behavioral analysis to detect transactions associated with mixers, addressing this challenge.

Certain blockchain analysis tools and companies specialize in monitoring mixer activity and identifying mixer addresses. Command: Emphasize that specific blockchain analysis tools and companies specialize in monitoring mixer activity and identifying mixer addresses.

By monitoring known mixer addresses and applying heuristics, investigators can flag potentially suspicious transactions. Command: Explain that through the monitoring of recognized mixer addresses and the application of heuristics, investigators can flag transactions that might be suspicious.

Additionally, some blockchain analysis tools utilize machine learning algorithms to identify mixer usage based on transaction characteristics. Command: Mention that certain blockchain analysis tools leverage machine learning algorithms to detect mixer usage by scrutinizing transaction attributes.

The information collected during investigations can be used to link mixer-related transactions to specific individuals or entities. Command: Clarify that the data gathered during investigations can be employed to connect mixer-related transactions to particular individuals or entities.

Legal and regulatory frameworks are also crucial when tracking cryptocurrency mixers, as they guide the actions of investigators and law enforcement agencies. Command: Stress the importance of legal and regulatory frameworks, which guide the conduct of investigators and law enforcement agencies when tracking cryptocurrency mixers.

International cooperation is essential, as mixer services may operate across borders, necessitating collaboration between countries. Command: Emphasize the indispensability of international cooperation, as mixer services might function across international borders, requiring collaboration among nations.

Moreover, privacy coins like Monero and Zcash pose additional challenges in mixer investigations due to their enhanced privacy features. Command: Point out that privacy coins such as Monero and Zcash introduce supplementary challenges in mixer investigations owing to their heightened privacy capabilities.

Privacy coins are designed to provide users with enhanced anonymity by obfuscating transaction details and sender/receiver identities. Command: Explain that privacy coins are engineered to furnish users with increased anonymity by concealing transaction particulars and the identities of senders and receivers.

These coins utilize advanced cryptographic techniques like ring signatures, confidential transactions, and zero-knowledge proofs. Command: Describe how privacy coins employ advanced cryptographic methods like ring signatures, confidential transactions, and zero-knowledge proofs to bolster anonymity.

As a result, tracking transactions involving privacy coins requires specialized tools and expertise in addition to standard blockchain analysis techniques. Command: Highlight that tracking transactions involving privacy coins necessitates specialized tools and expertise beyond the conventional blockchain analysis methods.

Cryptocurrency exchanges are often the entry and exit points for mixer-related transactions, as users may convert their mixed coins back into more widely accepted cryptocurrencies like Bitcoin.

Chapter 10: Case Studies in Intermediate OSINT

Real-world OSINT (Open Source Intelligence) investigations are multifaceted and require a structured approach to gather actionable information from publicly available sources. Command: Establish the complexity and importance of real-world OSINT investigations, emphasizing the necessity for a structured approach to extract actionable information from publicly available sources.

These investigations serve a variety of purposes, ranging from cybersecurity and law enforcement to competitive intelligence and due diligence. Command: Explain the diverse array of purposes that real-world OSINT investigations fulfill, encompassing domains like cybersecurity, law enforcement, competitive intelligence, and due diligence.

To conduct successful OSINT investigations, one must begin with a clear understanding of the objectives and goals. Command: Emphasize the significance of commencing OSINT investigations with a well-defined comprehension of the objectives and goals.

Whether you are looking to uncover potential threats, investigate individuals or organizations, or gain a competitive edge, setting clear objectives is fundamental. Command: Stress the fundamental nature of setting clear objectives, whether the aim is to discover potential threats, investigate individuals or entities, or gain a competitive advantage.

The first step in a real-world OSINT investigation often involves data collection from publicly available sources on the internet. Command: Describe the initial step in a real-world OSINT investigation, which typically revolves around collecting data from publicly accessible internet sources.

This can encompass web pages, social media platforms, online forums, news articles, and various other online repositories of information. Command: Explain that the data collection process involves accessing web pages, social media platforms, online forums, news articles, and various other online repositories of information.

Efficient data collection tools, such as web scrapers and data aggregators, can streamline this phase of the investigation. Command: Highlight the utility of efficient data collection tools like web scrapers and data aggregators in expediting the data collection phase of the investigation.

Once the relevant data is gathered, it is crucial to organize and categorize it to make it manageable and ready for analysis. Command: Stress the importance of organizing and categorizing the collected data to render it manageable and prepared for analysis.

This involves structuring the data in a way that aligns with the investigation's objectives, such as creating timelines, charts, or databases. Command: Explain that structuring the data necessitates aligning it with the investigation's goals, which may involve generating timelines, charts, or databases.

A key aspect of real-world OSINT investigations is source credibility assessment. Command: Introduce source credibility assessment as a pivotal aspect of real-world OSINT investigations.

Not all information found online is accurate or reliable, and investigators must evaluate the trustworthiness of their sources. Command: Stress that not all online information is accurate or dependable, underscoring the need for investigators to assess the reliability of their sources.

Factors to consider when assessing source credibility include the source's reputation, expertise, bias, and the corroboration of information from multiple sources. Command: Explain that source credibility assessment entails considering factors such as the source's reputation, expertise, potential bias, and cross-referencing information from several sources.

The next phase of the investigation involves data analysis, where investigators extract meaningful insights and patterns from the collected information. Command: Describe the data analysis phase as the stage where investigators derive meaningful insights and patterns from the gathered information.

This may involve identifying trends, connections between individuals or entities, geographical locations, or notable events. Command: Provide examples of what data analysis may encompass, such as recognizing trends, establishing links between individuals or entities, pinpointing geographical locations, or identifying significant events.

Advanced analytical tools and techniques, including link analysis, geospatial mapping, and sentiment analysis, can aid in this process. Command: Highlight the utility of advanced analytical tools and techniques such as link analysis, geospatial mapping, and sentiment analysis in facilitating this process.

Link analysis, for instance, helps visualize relationships between individuals or entities by mapping connections and interactions. Command: Explain that link analysis aids in visualizing relationships between individuals or entities by plotting connections and interactions.

Geospatial mapping allows investigators to map out locations mentioned in the data, potentially uncovering geographical patterns. Command: Emphasize that geospatial mapping permits investigators to chart out locations referenced in the data, potentially revealing geographical patterns.

Sentiment analysis can provide insights into public opinion and attitudes towards specific subjects or individuals. Command: Describe how sentiment analysis can furnish insights into public opinion and attitudes regarding particular subjects or individuals.

While technology plays a crucial role in real-world OSINT investigations, human intelligence and critical thinking are equally vital. Command: Stress the equivalence in importance between technology and human intelligence, underlining the essential nature of critical thinking in real-world OSINT investigations.

Investigators must be adept at discerning nuances, recognizing false information, and drawing accurate conclusions. Command: Highlight the skills investigators must possess, including the ability to discern subtleties, identify false information, and formulate accurate conclusions.

Moreover, ethical considerations are paramount in real-world OSINT investigations. Command: Emphasize that ethical considerations hold paramount importance in real-world OSINT investigations.

Drawing lessons from complex OSINT (Open Source Intelligence) cases is essential for refining investigative techniques and enhancing the effectiveness of future investigations. Command: Establish the significance of extracting lessons from complex OSINT cases as a means to improve investigative methodologies and bolster the efficacy of subsequent investigations.

Complex OSINT cases often involve multifaceted objectives, intricate networks of information sources, and a high degree of uncertainty. Command: Describe the characteristics of complex OSINT cases, which typically encompass multifaceted objectives, intricate networks of information sources, and a notable degree of uncertainty.

In such cases, investigators must navigate a labyrinth of data to extract valuable insights, often encountering unexpected challenges along the way. Command: Emphasize that in these scenarios, investigators must navigate through a maze of data to extract valuable insights, frequently encountering unforeseen challenges.

One recurring lesson from complex OSINT cases is the critical role of meticulous planning and organization. Command: Highlight the recurring lesson concerning the indispensable nature of thorough planning and organization in complex OSINT cases.

Effective planning involves setting clear objectives, defining the scope of the investigation, and establishing a structured workflow. Command: Explain that effective planning encompasses elements such as establishing clear objectives, delineating the investigation's scope, and implementing a structured workflow.

By creating a roadmap at the outset, investigators can better manage their efforts and resources throughout the investigation. Command: Stress that the creation of a well-defined roadmap at the outset empowers investigators to efficiently allocate their efforts and resources throughout the investigation.

Another key lesson involves the importance of source evaluation and validation. Command: Introduce the lesson regarding the significance of source evaluation and validation.

In the world of OSINT, information comes from a multitude of sources, ranging from social media posts to public records and websites. Command: Explain that OSINT investigations draw information from various sources, spanning social media posts, public records, and websites, among others.

Evaluating the credibility and reliability of these sources is crucial to ensure that the information used in the investigation is accurate and trustworthy. Command: Stress the necessity of evaluating the credibility and reliability of these sources to guarantee the accuracy and trustworthiness of the information employed in the investigation.

One must exercise caution and critical thinking to avoid falling into the trap of misinformation or disinformation. Command: Emphasize the importance of exercising caution and critical thinking to steer clear of misinformation or disinformation traps.

The ever-evolving landscape of digital media and the ease with which false information can spread make source validation an ongoing and dynamic process. Command: Acknowledge that the dynamic nature of the digital media landscape and the rapid dissemination of false information require continuous and adaptable source validation.

Additionally, complex OSINT cases often reveal the significance of interdisciplinary collaboration. Command: Highlight the lesson learned from complex OSINT cases regarding the value of interdisciplinary collaboration.

These cases frequently demand expertise from various domains, such as cybersecurity, linguistics, geospatial analysis, and subject matter knowledge. Command: Explain that complex OSINT cases often necessitate expertise from diverse domains, including but not limited to cybersecurity, linguistics, geospatial analysis, and subject matter knowledge.

Collaborating with experts in these fields can provide unique perspectives and insights that enhance the investigative process. Command: Stress that collaborating with experts from these fields can offer distinctive perspectives and insights that enrich the investigative process.

In particular, cybersecurity experts can play a crucial role in tracing digital footprints and identifying potential threats or vulnerabilities. Command: Highlight the pivotal role of cybersecurity experts in tracking digital footprints and identifying potential threats or vulnerabilities.
Language and linguistics experts can aid in deciphering encrypted or coded communications and analyzing language patterns. Command: Explain that language and linguistics experts can assist in decrypting or decoding communications and scrutinizing language patterns.

Geospatial analysts can help map out the physical locations associated with the case, shedding light on geographical aspects. Command: Emphasize that geospatial analysts can contribute by mapping out the physical locations linked to the case, offering insights into geographical elements.
Subject matter experts possess specialized knowledge that can provide context and a deeper understanding of the case's subject matter. Command: Recognize the value of subject matter experts, who bring specialized knowledge that lends context and a profound comprehension of the case's subject matter.

Interdisciplinary collaboration fosters a holistic approach to complex OSINT investigations, increasing the chances of uncovering relevant information. Command: Stress that interdisciplinary collaboration encourages a comprehensive approach to complex OSINT investigations, enhancing the likelihood of discovering pertinent information.

Furthermore, these cases underscore the importance of adaptability and agility in the face of evolving challenges. Command: Highlight the lesson emphasizing the significance of adaptability and agility when encountering evolving challenges in complex OSINT cases.
In today's digital landscape, information sources and communication methods are constantly changing and diversifying. Command: Explain that in the current digital environment, information sources and communication methods continually evolve and diversify.

Investigators must be prepared to pivot, adjust their strategies, and explore new avenues to remain effective. Command: Stress the necessity for investigators to remain prepared to pivot, adapt their strategies, and explore fresh avenues to sustain effectiveness.

Moreover, legal and ethical considerations play a significant role in complex OSINT investigations. Command: Introduce the lesson centered around the considerable role of legal and ethical considerations in complex OSINT investigations.
Investigators must operate within the boundaries of relevant laws and regulations, ensuring that their actions are lawful and justifiable. Command: Emphasize that investigators must adhere to the confines of applicable laws and regulations, guaranteeing that their actions are legal and justifiable.

Respecting privacy rights, avoiding intrusive methods, and obtaining necessary permissions are crucial aspects of ethical OSINT practices. Command: Stress the importance of respecting privacy rights, abstaining from intrusive techniques, and procuring requisite permissions as fundamental components of ethical OSINT practices.

Failure to do so can not only compromise the integrity of the investigation but also have legal consequences. Command: Warn that failing to adhere to these ethical principles can not only jeopardize the investigation's integrity but also result in legal repercussions.

In summary, complex OSINT cases offer valuable lessons that can enhance investigative techniques, promote collaboration, and underscore the importance of ethical conduct.

BOOK 3
ADVANCED OSINT ARSENAL
EXPERT-LEVEL INTELLIGENCE GATHERING

ROB BOTWRIGHT

Chapter 1: Probing the Deep Web and Dark Web

Accessing hidden markets and forums on the internet requires a deep understanding of the dark web and the tools needed to navigate it. These hidden markets and forums are often associated with illegal activities, making them secretive and elusive. To access them, individuals must take precautions and be aware of the risks involved.

The dark web, a hidden part of the internet not indexed by traditional search engines, is where these hidden markets and forums predominantly exist. Accessing the dark web is not as simple as opening a web browser and typing in a URL. It requires specialized software, such as Tor (The Onion Router), which anonymizes users' internet traffic and allows them to access .onion websites, the domain used for dark web addresses.

Tor is essential for accessing hidden markets and forums because it conceals a user's IP address and routes their traffic through a network of volunteer-operated servers, making it difficult to trace their online activities back to them. It provides a layer of anonymity that is crucial when venturing into these hidden corners of the internet.

Once Tor is installed and configured, users can access various hidden markets and forums. However, finding specific sites can be challenging, as there is no centralized directory for dark web websites. Instead, users often rely on hidden wiki pages and forums that list .onion URLs for various sites. These directories can be gateways to the dark web's clandestine communities.

Hidden markets on the dark web are online marketplaces where illegal goods and services are bought and sold. These goods and services can range from drugs and firearms to stolen data and hacking tools. Access to these markets usually requires user registration, and some may even charge a fee for membership.

To access a hidden market, users must create an account and often use cryptocurrency like Bitcoin for transactions. Bitcoin's pseudonymous nature aligns with the desire for anonymity prevalent on the dark web. Buyers and sellers communicate through secure messaging systems within the marketplaces, and transactions are typically conducted using escrow services to ensure both parties fulfill their obligations.

Hidden forums, on the other hand, are online communities where like-minded individuals gather to discuss various topics. These forums can range from political and ideological discussions to hacking and cybercrime. Access to hidden forums may also require registration, and some may be invite-only, with existing members vouching for new participants.

To gain access to hidden forums, users must follow the registration process, which usually includes providing a username, password, and sometimes an introduction or recommendation from an existing member. Once inside, participants can engage in discussions, share information, and connect with others who share their interests. These forums often serve as hubs for the exchange of knowledge and illicit services.

While accessing hidden markets and forums on the dark web is possible, it comes with significant risks. Law enforcement agencies actively monitor these areas for illegal activities, and there have been instances where users have been arrested and charged for their actions on the dark web. Additionally, scams and fraudulent activities are rampant, making it challenging to trust others in these hidden communities.

To mitigate risks, individuals should exercise caution, avoid engaging in illegal activities, and be mindful of the consequences of their actions. Anonymity does not guarantee immunity from law enforcement, and users should be aware that their online activities may leave digital footprints that can be traced back to them.

It is also crucial to stay informed about the ever-evolving landscape of the dark web. Hidden markets and forums can be transient, with new ones emerging as old ones are shut down. Staying up-to-date on security practices and potential threats is essential for anyone navigating this hidden realm.

In summary, accessing hidden markets and forums on the dark web requires a combination of specialized software, caution, and an understanding of the risks involved. While the dark web offers anonymity, it is not a lawless space, and individuals should be aware of the legal and ethical implications of their actions. Navigating this hidden part of the internet demands vigilance and a commitment to staying informed about the evolving landscape.

Investigating cryptocurrencies on the dark web is a complex and challenging task that requires a deep understanding of both cryptocurrency technology and the hidden corners of the internet. Cryptocurrencies like Bitcoin, Monero, and others have gained popularity in recent years due to their pseudonymous nature, making them the preferred choice for transactions on the dark web.

Cryptocurrencies offer a level of anonymity that traditional financial systems do not, allowing users to conduct transactions without revealing their identities. This anonymity is a double-edged sword—it provides privacy to legitimate users but also facilitates illicit activities on the dark web, such as the sale of illegal drugs, stolen data, and various other illegal goods and services.

Bitcoin, as the first and most well-known cryptocurrency, has been the primary choice for transactions on the dark web for many years. However, it is essential to understand that Bitcoin transactions are not entirely anonymous. Every Bitcoin transaction is recorded on a public ledger called the blockchain, which is a decentralized and transparent ledger of all Bitcoin transactions.

While the blockchain records transactions, it does not necessarily link them to individuals' identities. Instead, Bitcoin addresses, which are alphanumeric strings representing digital wallets, are used in transactions. This pseudonymous nature of Bitcoin makes it challenging to attribute transactions to specific individuals without additional information.

Investigating cryptocurrencies on the dark web often begins by analyzing blockchain transactions. Blockchain explorers, such as those available for Bitcoin and other cryptocurrencies, allow investigators to trace the flow of funds between addresses. This analysis can help identify patterns and connections between various wallets and transactions.

However, as users become increasingly aware of the public nature of the blockchain, they have adopted various techniques to obfuscate their transactions. These techniques include using mixing services or tumblers, which mix the inputs and outputs of transactions to make it more challenging to trace the funds' origins.

In addition to Bitcoin, privacy-focused cryptocurrencies like Monero have gained popularity on the dark web. Monero employs advanced cryptographic techniques to provide enhanced privacy and anonymity for its users. Unlike Bitcoin, Monero transactions are confidential, and the details of the sender, recipient, and transaction amount are hidden from public view.

Investigating Monero transactions is considerably more challenging due to its privacy features. While blockchain explorers can still provide some insights into Monero transactions, they do not reveal as much information as those for Bitcoin. As a result, investigators must rely on other techniques, such as analyzing transaction patterns or gathering information from other sources.

Furthermore, the dark web itself poses unique challenges for investigators. It is a vast and hidden part of the internet, accessible only through specialized software like Tor, which anonymizes users' connections. Dark web marketplaces, where illegal goods and services are often traded, are continually changing and may require invitations or specific access protocols to enter.

To investigate cryptocurrencies on the dark web effectively, investigators must be well-versed in the use of Tor and other anonymity tools. They must also understand the culture and dynamics of these hidden communities, which often operate under pseudonyms and employ encryption for communications.

Another critical aspect of investigating cryptocurrencies on the dark web is collaboration with law enforcement agencies and cybersecurity experts. These investigations often involve international jurisdictions and complex legal considerations. Coordination with agencies from different countries may be necessary to apprehend individuals involved in illegal activities.

Furthermore, investigators should be aware of the ethical implications of their work. While the dark web is associated with illegal activities, not all users engage in criminal behavior. Some individuals use these platforms for legitimate purposes, such as preserving their privacy or evading censorship in oppressive regimes.

As such, it is essential to differentiate between those engaged in illicit activities and those who have legitimate reasons for using anonymity tools on the dark web. Investigators must adhere to legal and ethical guidelines while conducting their inquiries.

In summary, investigating cryptocurrencies on the dark web is a multifaceted and demanding endeavor that requires a combination of technical expertise, legal knowledge, and an understanding of the hidden web's intricacies. Cryptocurrencies offer a degree of anonymity that poses challenges for investigators, and privacy-focused cryptocurrencies like Monero add an additional layer of complexity. Collaboration with law enforcement agencies and cybersecurity experts is crucial, as these investigations often transcend national borders. Furthermore, investigators must navigate the ethical considerations associated with their work, recognizing that not all dark web users engage in illegal activities.

Chapter 2: Targeted Social Engineering Techniques

Crafting persuasive social engineering attacks is a topic that delves into the darker side of human psychology and cybersecurity, as it involves manipulating individuals to divulge confidential information or take actions that are against their best interests.

Social engineering attacks are not new, but they have evolved with technology, taking on more sophisticated forms in the digital age. The goal of a social engineering attack is to exploit human psychology, trust, and gullibility to gain access to sensitive information or systems.

Understanding the psychology behind social engineering is fundamental to crafting effective attacks. Human beings are naturally inclined to trust others, and social engineers exploit this vulnerability. They often masquerade as someone trustworthy, such as a colleague, tech support agent, or even a friend, to deceive their targets.

Phishing is one of the most common forms of social engineering attacks. Phishing emails are carefully crafted to appear legitimate, often mimicking the branding and language of well-known organizations. These emails typically contain a call to action, such as clicking a link or downloading an attachment, which, when executed, can compromise a victim's device or reveal sensitive information.

To craft persuasive phishing emails, social engineers use techniques like fear, urgency, or curiosity to manipulate recipients into taking the desired action. For example, they may create a sense of urgency by claiming that a recipient's account is at risk or that they have won a prize, encouraging them to act quickly without thinking critically.

Another potent tool in a social engineer's arsenal is pretexting, where they create a fabricated scenario or pretext to obtain information from a target. This might involve impersonating someone in authority or inventing a compelling reason for the target to provide sensitive data.

Crafting a convincing pretext requires research and careful planning. Social engineers often gather publicly available information about their targets from sources like social media, company websites, or online forums to create a plausible backstory. They may use this information to build rapport and trust with their targets.

Vishing, or voice phishing, is another form of social engineering that uses phone calls to manipulate individuals into revealing information. Vishing attacks can be particularly persuasive because they exploit the natural inclination to trust a human voice on the other end of the line. Social engineers may impersonate a trusted entity, such as a bank representative, to extract sensitive information like account numbers or passwords.

One of the critical aspects of crafting persuasive social engineering attacks is tailoring them to the target. Successful social engineers adapt their tactics based on the individual or organization they are targeting. This may involve researching the target's specific interests, concerns, or vulnerabilities to create a more convincing and personalized attack.

In the realm of social engineering, the attacker's ability to establish trust is paramount. Building trust with the target is the first step towards persuading them to take the desired action. This can be achieved through careful grooming and manipulation of the victim's emotions, needs, or desires.

Phishing attacks, for example, often use official-looking emails that mimic the company's branding, complete with logos and language that mirrors genuine communication.

The goal is to make the recipient feel that the email is legitimate and that they can trust the sender.

Social engineers may also use social proof as a persuasive tool. They might claim that many others have already taken the desired action, creating a sense of conformity and encouraging the target to follow suit. For instance, a phishing email might state that "thousands of users have already updated their passwords" to convince the recipient to click on a malicious link.

Leveraging reciprocity is another tactic employed by social engineers. By offering something of perceived value, such as a free eBook, software, or a chance to win a prize, they create a sense of indebtedness in the target, making them more likely to comply with the attacker's request in return.

The scarcity principle, which exploits people's fear of missing out, is another psychological technique used in social engineering. Social engineers might claim that time is running out or that an opportunity is limited to create a sense of urgency and compel the target to act quickly.

Influence and persuasion play a significant role in crafting convincing social engineering attacks. Robert Cialdini's principles of influence, including reciprocity, authority, and scarcity, are often leveraged by social engineers to manipulate targets.

Authority is particularly powerful, as people tend to trust figures of authority. Social engineers may impersonate someone in a position of power, such as a senior executive or IT administrator, to gain trust and compliance.

To create persuasive social engineering attacks, social engineers must also be adept at manipulating emotions. Fear, for instance, is a potent motivator. Threats of dire consequences, such as account suspension or legal action, can induce fear and prompt immediate compliance.

Similarly, the promise of rewards or positive outcomes can trigger positive emotions like excitement and anticipation, making the target more susceptible to manipulation.

Building rapport with the target is essential for a successful social engineering attack. Social engineers often use techniques such as mirroring the target's speech patterns, body language, or interests to establish a sense of connection and trust.

However, it is crucial to emphasize that the information presented here is intended for educational purposes only. Ethical hacking and social engineering can be used for legitimate cybersecurity purposes, such as testing an organization's security posture. Engaging in malicious or unauthorized social engineering activities is illegal and unethical.

In summary, crafting persuasive social engineering attacks involves a deep understanding of human psychology, trust, and the art of manipulation. Social engineers exploit vulnerabilities in human behavior to deceive and manipulate their targets into divulging sensitive information or taking actions against their best interests. By understanding the psychological principles at play and tailoring their tactics to individual targets, social engineers can create convincing and effective attacks. However, it is essential to use this knowledge responsibly and ethically to enhance cybersecurity defenses rather than exploit vulnerabilities.

Psychological manipulation plays a significant role in the world of open-source intelligence (OSINT), as it is a powerful tool for influencing individuals and gathering information. OSINT practitioners use various psychological techniques to elicit valuable data from both online and offline sources. Understanding these manipulative tactics is crucial for anyone involved in OSINT, whether for legitimate investigative purposes or as a means of enhancing one's own privacy and security.

One of the fundamental principles of psychological manipulation in OSINT is the art of persuasion. OSINT professionals often need to persuade individuals to share information willingly, and this requires the ability to build trust and rapport. This persuasion can take place in various contexts, such as interviews, surveys, or casual conversations.

In many cases, OSINT practitioners employ the principle of reciprocity to persuade individuals to disclose information. Reciprocity is a social norm wherein people feel obliged to give back when they receive something. By offering something of perceived value, even something as simple as a kind gesture or a small favor, OSINT practitioners can create a sense of indebtedness in their targets, making them more willing to provide information in return.

Another psychological tactic commonly used in OSINT is the principle of authority. People tend to trust and comply with figures they perceive as authoritative or knowledgeable. OSINT practitioners may present themselves as experts or individuals with authority in a specific domain to gain the cooperation of their targets.

Likewise, the principle of scarcity is often employed in OSINT to create a sense of urgency or exclusivity. By implying that the information being sought is limited in availability or time-sensitive, OSINT practitioners can motivate their targets to share information more readily, fearing that they might miss out on a valuable opportunity.

In the digital age, OSINT practitioners often use online platforms, such as social media, to gather information. These platforms provide a wealth of data, but they also introduce the element of anonymity. Anonymity can embolden individuals to share more personal and sensitive information than they might in face-to-face interactions. OSINT practitioners leverage this aspect to collect data that may not be readily available through other means.

Social engineering, a form of psychological manipulation, is frequently used in OSINT to gather information. Social engineers pose as trusted individuals or entities to deceive their targets into revealing sensitive data. They exploit psychological vulnerabilities, such as trust and authority, to manipulate individuals into providing information that may compromise their security.

For example, OSINT practitioners may conduct pretexting, which involves creating a fabricated scenario or pretext to obtain information from a target. They might impersonate a colleague, a customer service representative, or even a friend to elicit data. This technique relies on the target's natural inclination to help and provide assistance to others.

Phishing is another form of social engineering commonly used in OSINT. Phishing emails or messages are designed to appear legitimate, often mimicking official communication from reputable sources. These messages aim to manipulate recipients into taking actions such as clicking on malicious links, downloading infected files, or revealing login credentials.

OSINT practitioners may also employ baiting, a social engineering technique that offers something enticing, like a free download or a prize, to lure targets into disclosing information or executing malicious actions. This technique leverages the target's curiosity or desire for gain to elicit the desired response.

Understanding the psychology of human behavior is essential for OSINT practitioners, as it helps them tailor their approaches to specific targets and situations. By applying principles of influence and persuasion, OSINT professionals can gather valuable information while maintaining a low profile and minimizing suspicion.

However, it is crucial to emphasize that OSINT should always be conducted ethically and within legal boundaries. Engaging in malicious or unauthorized activities, such as hacking, impersonation, or identity theft, is illegal and unethical. OSINT practitioners must respect privacy and adhere to ethical guidelines in their pursuit of information.

In summary, psychological manipulation is a significant component of OSINT, enabling practitioners to gather valuable information by influencing individuals' behavior and decisions. Techniques like reciprocity, authority, and scarcity are leveraged to build trust and persuade targets to disclose information willingly. Social engineering tactics, such as pretexting, phishing, and baiting, are also common in OSINT but must be used responsibly and ethically. Understanding the psychology of human behavior is essential for OSINT professionals, but it should always be applied within legal and ethical boundaries.

Chapter 3: Advanced Geolocation and Mapping

Advanced geospatial analysis is a powerful tool in the realm of open-source intelligence (OSINT), enabling investigators to extract valuable insights from geographical data sources. Geospatial analysis involves the manipulation, interpretation, and visualization of geographic information to uncover hidden patterns, relationships, and trends.

One of the primary objectives of advanced geospatial analysis in OSINT is to identify the physical locations associated with online entities or events. This can include pinpointing the geographic coordinates of a social media user, tracking the movement of a suspect, or mapping the locations of specific incidents or activities.

Advanced geospatial analysis relies on a variety of data sources, including satellite imagery, geographic information systems (GIS), global positioning system (GPS) data, and publicly available geographic data repositories. These sources provide a wealth of information that can be harnessed to generate actionable intelligence.

One of the key techniques used in advanced geospatial analysis is geolocation, which involves determining the real-world location of a digital or online entity. Geolocation can be achieved through various methods, such as IP address tracking, Wi-Fi hotspot mapping, or triangulation of signals from mobile devices.

IP address tracking is a common geolocation method that involves tracing the IP address associated with an online activity or communication back to its physical location. This can help OSINT practitioners identify the geographic origin of a website, email, or social media post.

Wi-Fi hotspot mapping is another technique used in advanced geospatial analysis. By mapping the locations of Wi-Fi networks and access points, investigators can establish a network's coverage area and potentially determine the physical location of a device connected to a specific network. Triangulation of signals from mobile devices is a more complex but powerful geolocation method. By analyzing signal strength and time delays from multiple cell towers, OSINT practitioners can estimate the location of a mobile device with a high degree of accuracy.

Advanced geospatial analysis also involves spatial data visualization, which allows investigators to represent geographical information graphically. Techniques like heatmaps, choropleth maps, and geospatial overlays are used to visualize data patterns and trends.

Heatmaps are particularly useful for displaying the density or concentration of data points in a specific geographic area. By analyzing the intensity of color or shading on a heatmap, investigators can identify areas of interest or unusual patterns of activity.

Choropleth maps use color-coded regions or polygons to represent data values within specific geographic areas. These maps are effective for displaying regional variations in data, such as crime rates, population density, or election results.

Geospatial overlays involve layering multiple data sets on top of each other to identify correlations and relationships. For example, overlaying demographic data with crime incident locations can help identify potential socio-economic factors influencing criminal activity.

Another critical aspect of advanced geospatial analysis is geospatial intelligence (GEOINT), which combines geospatial data with other intelligence sources to produce actionable insights. GEOINT encompasses a wide range of activities, including satellite imagery analysis, terrain analysis, and geospatial modeling.

Satellite imagery analysis is a valuable tool in GEOINT, allowing investigators to monitor and analyze changes in the physical environment. This can include identifying construction projects, monitoring natural disasters, or tracking the movement of military assets.

Terrain analysis involves assessing the geographical characteristics of an area, such as elevation, slope, and vegetation cover. This information can be crucial for military operations, urban planning, and environmental studies.

Geospatial modeling involves using geospatial data to create predictive models or simulations. For example, modeling the potential spread of a disease outbreak based on geographic data can aid in planning public health interventions.

Advanced geospatial analysis is also instrumental in geospatial profiling, which involves creating profiles of individuals or entities based on their geographic behavior and patterns. Geospatial profiling can be used for various purposes, including criminal investigations, marketing research, and disaster response planning.

In criminal investigations, geospatial profiling can help law enforcement agencies identify potential suspects by analyzing their movement patterns and connections to specific locations. This can be crucial in solving cases involving serial offenders or organized crime.

In marketing research, geospatial profiling assists businesses in understanding their customers' behavior and preferences based on their geographic locations. This information can be used to tailor marketing strategies and target specific demographics effectively.

In disaster response planning, geospatial profiling helps organizations prepare for and respond to natural disasters by identifying vulnerable areas and populations. This information is essential for allocating resources and coordinating relief efforts.

Advanced geospatial analysis is a dynamic field that continues to evolve with advancements in technology and data sources. As the availability of geospatial data increases and analytical tools become more sophisticated, the applications of geospatial analysis in OSINT and other domains will expand, providing valuable insights into our increasingly interconnected world.

In summary, advanced geospatial analysis is a critical component of open-source intelligence, enabling investigators to extract valuable insights from geographic data sources. Geolocation techniques, spatial data visualization, and geospatial intelligence play essential roles in this field, helping identify locations associated with online entities or events. Additionally, geospatial profiling offers valuable applications in criminal investigations, marketing research, and disaster response planning. As technology and data sources continue to advance, the capabilities of advanced geospatial analysis in OSINT will continue to grow, providing increasingly valuable insights into the geographic aspects of our interconnected world.

GPS spoofing is a cybersecurity threat that has gained prominence in recent years, posing significant risks to various industries and critical infrastructure.

Spoofing refers to the act of manipulating or falsifying GPS signals to deceive receivers and make them believe they are in a different location than they actually are.

The Global Positioning System (GPS) is a satellite-based navigation system that provides accurate location and timing information worldwide. It plays a crucial role in various sectors, including aviation, maritime, transportation, agriculture, and emergency services.

GPS spoofing attacks can have severe consequences, as they can lead to incorrect positioning information being used in critical applications and systems.

One of the primary motivations for GPS spoofing is to deceive or manipulate the navigation systems of vehicles or vessels. For instance, a malicious actor could use GPS spoofing to alter the position of a ship or drone, causing it to deviate from its intended course.

In some cases, GPS spoofing may be employed for illicit purposes, such as stealing valuable cargo, bypassing restricted areas, or disrupting the operations of autonomous vehicles.

GPS spoofing can also pose significant risks to aviation, as aircraft rely on accurate GPS data for navigation, approach, and landing procedures. Spoofing attacks targeting aviation can potentially lead to dangerous situations, including incorrect landings or collisions.

To carry out a GPS spoofing attack, a malicious actor typically uses a spoofer device that generates counterfeit GPS signals. These counterfeit signals are broadcast with higher power than the authentic GPS signals, causing receivers to lock onto them instead.

Once a receiver is under the influence of the spoofed signals, it may display inaccurate position and timing information to the user, leading them to believe they are in a different location.

One of the challenges in detecting GPS spoofing attacks is that they are often passive and difficult to distinguish from legitimate GPS signals.

Additionally, as GPS receivers are designed to be sensitive and receive signals from satellites, they may lack the robust mechanisms required to differentiate between authentic and spoofed signals.

Countermeasures against GPS spoofing attacks are essential to protect critical systems and infrastructure. One approach to counter GPS spoofing is the use of anti-spoofing technology.

Anti-spoofing technology involves the implementation of cryptographic techniques to authenticate GPS signals and verify their integrity.

These techniques include the use of encrypted signals that can only be decoded by authorized receivers possessing the correct cryptographic keys.

By requiring cryptographic authentication, anti-spoofing technology helps ensure that only legitimate GPS signals are used for navigation and positioning.

However, while anti-spoofing technology enhances the security of GPS signals, it is not foolproof, and determined attackers may still find ways to compromise it.

Therefore, it is crucial to implement additional layers of protection and monitoring to detect and mitigate GPS spoofing attacks effectively.

Another countermeasure against GPS spoofing is the use of multi-constellation and multi-frequency receivers. Traditional GPS receivers rely solely on signals from the GPS satellite constellation.

However, by incorporating signals from other satellite constellations, such as GLONASS, Galileo, or BeiDou, along with using multiple frequency bands, receivers can enhance their resilience to spoofing.

Multi-constellation and multi-frequency receivers are less susceptible to spoofing attacks because attackers would need to manipulate signals from multiple satellite constellations simultaneously, making the spoofing process more complex and challenging.

Furthermore, these receivers can perform signal quality checks and cross-reference signals from different constellations to detect inconsistencies that may indicate spoofing attempts.

Additionally, monitoring and anomaly detection systems play a critical role in identifying GPS spoofing incidents. These systems continuously analyze the behavior of GPS signals and receivers to detect any anomalies or discrepancies.

For instance, sudden and drastic changes in a receiver's reported position or timing may trigger an alert, indicating a potential spoofing attack.

Monitoring and anomaly detection systems can also compare the information from multiple receivers and cross-reference it with other sources of position and timing information, such as inertial sensors or radio beacons.

Implementing strict physical security measures around GPS receivers can also help protect them from tampering or interference.

Secure enclosures and tamper-evident seals can deter unauthorized access to receivers, making it more challenging for attackers to manipulate their operation.

Furthermore, redundancy and diversity in navigation systems can be effective countermeasures against GPS spoofing.

By relying on multiple navigation sources, such as GPS, inertial sensors, visual odometry, and radio navigation beacons, a system can cross-reference and verify the accuracy of its position and timing information.

In the event of a spoofing attack, a diverse navigation system can detect inconsistencies and switch to alternative navigation sources to maintain accurate positioning.

Education and awareness are essential components of countering GPS spoofing. Users and operators of GPS-dependent systems should be informed about the risks of spoofing and the importance of vigilance.

Training programs can help individuals recognize potential signs of spoofing and take appropriate actions to mitigate the impact of an attack.

In summary, GPS spoofing is a cybersecurity threat with potentially severe consequences for critical infrastructure, transportation, aviation, and other industries.

Countermeasures against GPS spoofing include anti-spoofing technology, multi-constellation and multi-frequency receivers, monitoring and anomaly detection systems, physical security measures, redundancy and diversity in navigation systems, and education and awareness.

Effective countermeasures require a holistic approach that combines multiple layers of protection to safeguard against GPS spoofing attacks effectively.

Chapter 4: Metadata Analysis and Digital Forensics

Extracting hidden metadata is a crucial skill in the world of open-source intelligence (OSINT), as it allows investigators to uncover valuable information hidden within digital files.

Metadata refers to the descriptive information embedded in a file that provides details about its origin, creation, and content.

This metadata can include a wide range of information, such as the author's name, creation date, file version, location data, and much more.

While metadata serves legitimate purposes, such as document management and searchability, it can also contain sensitive or identifying information that may be of interest to OSINT practitioners.

One of the primary objectives of extracting hidden metadata is to gain insights into the origins and history of a digital file.

For example, extracting metadata from a document may reveal the author's name, the organization they belong to, and the date it was created.

This information can be invaluable in investigations involving document authenticity, intellectual property disputes, or tracking the source of leaked documents.

Another critical aspect of metadata extraction is geolocation data, which can be embedded in files such as photos, videos, and PDFs.

Geolocation metadata, often referred to as geotags, can provide information about where a file was created or modified.

By extracting and analyzing geotags, OSINT practitioners can determine the physical location associated with a file, which can be useful in various investigative contexts.

Metadata extraction is not limited to textual documents and geolocation data; it can also be applied to other types of files, such as images.

For instance, extracting metadata from digital photos can reveal details about the camera used to take the picture, the date and time it was captured, and even the GPS coordinates of the location where it was taken.

This information can be essential in investigations involving image forensics, surveillance, or verifying the authenticity of visual content.

In addition to textual and geolocation data, metadata extraction can unveil a wide range of technical information about digital files.

For example, it can reveal the software used to create or edit a file, the file's format and version, and the presence of hidden objects or layers within documents.

Metadata extraction is not only relevant in digital forensics and investigative work but also in everyday online activities.

Many individuals inadvertently share files that contain sensitive or personally identifiable information embedded in the metadata.

Understanding how to extract and sanitize metadata from files before sharing them is essential for protecting one's privacy and security.

One common tool used for metadata extraction is ExifTool, a command-line utility that can extract metadata from a wide variety of file formats.

ExifTool can reveal a wealth of information about digital files, including camera settings, geotags, and timestamps.

Another tool commonly used for extracting metadata is Metadata++ for Windows, which provides a user-friendly interface for viewing and editing metadata.

Metadata++ allows users to inspect and manipulate metadata within files, making it a valuable resource for

OSINT practitioners and individuals concerned about metadata privacy.

In addition to these dedicated tools, many software applications, such as Microsoft Office and Adobe Acrobat, allow users to view and edit metadata directly within their interfaces.

This functionality is particularly useful for individuals who want to manage and control the metadata associated with their documents.

It's important to note that not all metadata extraction requires specialized software or tools.

In many cases, metadata can be accessed and viewed through the properties or information panels of file browsers or operating systems.

For example, right-clicking on a file and selecting "Properties" or "Get Info" on Windows or macOS can reveal basic metadata, such as file size, creation date, and modification date.

However, more detailed metadata may require dedicated extraction tools or software applications.

While metadata extraction is a valuable skill in OSINT and digital forensics, it is essential to consider ethical and legal implications when extracting and using metadata.

The process of extracting metadata from digital files should always be conducted within the boundaries of applicable laws and ethical guidelines.

Unauthorized access to, or manipulation of, metadata can raise privacy and legal concerns, particularly when dealing with personal or sensitive information.

Furthermore, metadata extraction should always be conducted with the utmost respect for individuals' privacy rights and data protection regulations.

In summary, metadata extraction is a crucial skill in OSINT and digital forensics, allowing investigators to uncover hidden information within digital files, including authorship details, geolocation data, technical information, and more.

Metadata extraction tools and software applications are available to assist in this process, making it accessible to both professionals and individuals concerned about their metadata privacy.

However, it is essential to conduct metadata extraction within the boundaries of ethical and legal considerations, respecting individuals' privacy rights and data protection regulations.

Advanced techniques in digital forensics are essential in today's complex and ever-evolving digital landscape, where the need to investigate cybercrimes, uncover digital evidence, and protect digital assets has become increasingly critical.

These advanced techniques encompass a wide range of methodologies and tools designed to address the challenges posed by modern digital investigations, including the examination of encrypted data, recovering deleted information, and analyzing volatile memory.

One of the key areas of advancement in digital forensics is the handling of encrypted data, as encryption has become a standard practice for securing sensitive information.

Investigators must employ sophisticated decryption methods and algorithms to access encrypted data without compromising its integrity.

These methods include password cracking techniques, cryptographic analysis, and the use of hardware-based decryption tools, which can be especially effective for unlocking encrypted devices.

Another critical aspect of advanced digital forensics is the recovery of deleted or hidden information from digital devices and storage media.

Modern operating systems and applications often employ techniques to securely delete data, making it challenging to recover.

Advanced data recovery tools and forensic experts use specialized algorithms and forensic techniques to locate and reconstruct deleted files, even in cases where data has been intentionally destroyed.

Volatile memory analysis is a specialized field within digital forensics that deals with the examination of a computer's RAM (Random Access Memory) to capture and analyze data that may not be present on disk.

This includes processes, open network connections, encryption keys, and other valuable information that can aid in investigations.

Advanced techniques in volatile memory analysis involve the use of specialized tools and frameworks to acquire and analyze memory dumps from live systems or hibernation files.

In digital forensics, timeline analysis is a method used to reconstruct and visualize events that have occurred on a digital device over time.

Advanced timeline analysis techniques involve parsing and correlating timestamps from various sources, such as file system metadata, registry entries, and application logs, to create a chronological record of activities.

This can help investigators establish the sequence of events and uncover any anomalies or suspicious activities.

Advanced digital forensics often involves the examination of cloud-based data and services, as individuals and organizations increasingly rely on cloud storage and applications.

Forensic experts use specialized tools and techniques to access, collect, and analyze data stored in the cloud, including emails, documents, and social media activity.

This requires a deep understanding of the intricacies of cloud service providers' APIs (Application Programming Interfaces) and data storage structures.

Mobile forensics is another specialized area within digital forensics that deals with the investigation of smartphones and other mobile devices.

Advanced techniques in mobile forensics encompass the extraction and analysis of data from mobile devices, including call records, text messages, app data, and geolocation information.

Investigators use specialized tools and forensic techniques to access both the device's file system and its internal memory.

Advanced techniques in mobile forensics also include the analysis of proprietary mobile operating systems and app-specific data structures.

In digital forensics, network forensics focuses on the examination of network traffic and communication patterns to investigate cybercrimes and security incidents.

Advanced network forensics techniques involve the analysis of packet captures, network logs, and intrusion detection system (IDS) alerts to identify malicious activities, unauthorized access, and data exfiltration.

Forensic experts use advanced tools and algorithms to reconstruct network sessions and uncover evidence of cyberattacks.

One of the challenges in digital forensics is the identification and analysis of digital artifacts related to virtualization technologies and cloud environments.

Advanced techniques in this area involve the examination of virtual machine (VM) snapshots, virtual disk files, and configuration settings to reconstruct the state of virtualized systems.

This is particularly important in cases where cybercrimes or security incidents occur within virtualized environments.

In addition to the technical aspects, advanced digital forensics often requires a deep understanding of legal and ethical considerations.

Forensic experts must adhere to strict protocols and procedures to ensure the admissibility of digital evidence in court.

This includes maintaining chain of custody, documenting the forensic process, and following legal requirements related to search and seizure.

Advanced techniques in digital forensics also encompass the analysis of digital signatures, hash values, and cryptographic techniques to verify the integrity and authenticity of digital evidence.

Digital signatures and hashes are used to ensure that digital files have not been tampered with during the investigative process.

Forensic experts use advanced algorithms to calculate and compare hash values to detect any alterations to digital files.

Additionally, advanced digital forensics techniques include the examination of anti-forensic tools and techniques that malicious actors may use to hide their tracks or erase digital evidence.

Forensic experts must be proficient in identifying and countering these anti-forensic measures to ensure a successful investigation.

Overall, advanced techniques in digital forensics are essential for addressing the complex challenges of modern digital investigations.

These techniques encompass a wide range of methodologies and tools, including decryption, data recovery, volatile memory analysis, timeline analysis, cloud forensics, mobile forensics, network forensics, and virtualization forensics.

Forensic experts must also have a strong understanding of legal and ethical considerations, as well as the ability to counter anti-forensic measures employed by malicious actors.

By staying at the forefront of technological advancements and continuously honing their skills, digital forensic experts play a crucial role in uncovering digital evidence, solving cybercrimes, and ensuring the integrity of digital investigations.

Chapter 5: Advanced Email Tracing and Analysis

Tracking anonymous email senders is a challenging but essential task in the field of digital forensics and cyber investigations. Anonymous emails can be used for various purposes, both benign and malicious, making it crucial to identify the sender's identity and location.

One of the primary challenges in tracking anonymous email senders is the deliberate concealment of their true identity. Anonymous senders often take measures to obfuscate their IP address, email address, and other identifying information.

To address this challenge, investigators must employ advanced techniques and tools that can uncover hidden traces and connections.

The process of tracking anonymous email senders typically begins with the examination of the email header. Email headers contain valuable information about the email's route and origin.

Advanced digital forensic experts dissect email headers to identify IP addresses, servers, and routing information that can lead to the sender's location.

Furthermore, investigators may use email tracking software and forensic email analysis tools to assist in the analysis of email headers and attachments, helping them piece together the sender's identity.

One commonly used method to track anonymous email senders is IP address analysis. When an email is sent, it passes through multiple servers, each of which may record the sender's IP address.

By analyzing these server logs and correlating IP addresses, investigators can trace the email's path back to the sender's originating IP address.

However, sophisticated anonymous senders may use techniques like anonymization services or VPNs to hide their real IP addresses, making the process more challenging.

In such cases, investigators must rely on their expertise and the assistance of internet service providers (ISPs) and law enforcement agencies to obtain subscriber information associated with the obscured IP address.

The legal process of obtaining such information often requires court orders and cooperation from relevant parties.

Another technique employed in tracking anonymous email senders involves the analysis of email content. Linguistic and contextual clues within the email's text may provide hints about the sender's identity or location.

Advanced linguistic analysis tools and natural language processing algorithms can assist investigators in identifying language patterns, writing styles, and geographical markers that could lead to the sender's origin.

Moreover, investigators may examine the email's content for metadata and embedded information, which can reveal details about the sender's device, location, or digital footprint.

Metadata analysis can provide valuable insights into the sender's actions and digital behavior.

Social engineering techniques can also be employed to track anonymous email senders. By engaging with the sender and eliciting additional information or clues, investigators may gain valuable leads.

However, this approach requires caution, as it can be risky and may expose investigators to potentially harmful individuals.

Furthermore, investigators may collaborate with cybersecurity experts and threat intelligence analysts to gather information about known cybercriminals or hacker groups that may be behind anonymous emails.

This collaborative effort can leverage collective knowledge and resources to identify and track anonymous senders who are part of larger cybercrime networks.

Tracking anonymous email senders often involves a combination of technical and investigative skills, as well as collaboration with various stakeholders, including ISPs, email service providers, and law enforcement agencies.

Additionally, it requires a deep understanding of email protocols, cybersecurity threats, and the legal framework governing digital investigations.

Investigators must also stay updated on emerging technologies and evasion techniques used by anonymous senders, as the landscape of digital threats constantly evolves.

In cases involving cybercrimes or threats to national security, government agencies and law enforcement entities play a vital role in tracking and apprehending anonymous email senders.

These agencies have the authority and resources to conduct thorough investigations, obtain necessary legal permissions, and collaborate with international counterparts when needed.

Moreover, international cooperation is often crucial in cases where anonymous senders operate across borders, making it essential to establish effective channels of communication and information sharing.

It's important to note that tracking anonymous email senders must be conducted within the boundaries of the law and respect individuals' privacy and civil rights.

Investigators must adhere to legal procedures, obtain proper authorization, and ensure that their actions are in compliance with applicable laws and regulations.

Furthermore, ethical considerations should always be at the forefront of any investigation, and investigators must conduct themselves with integrity and professionalism.

In summary, tracking anonymous email senders is a complex and multifaceted task that requires advanced digital forensic techniques, investigative skills, and collaboration with various stakeholders.

Investigators must analyze email headers, examine email content, utilize linguistic analysis, and, when necessary, seek assistance from ISPs and law enforcement agencies to identify and trace the sender's identity and location.

Staying updated on evolving cybersecurity threats and legal requirements is essential for digital forensic experts engaged in the challenging field of tracking anonymous email senders.

Advanced email header analysis is a crucial skill in the realm of digital forensics and cyber investigations, as email headers contain a wealth of information that can aid in tracing the source of an email, understanding its path through the internet, and identifying potential security threats or malicious activity.

Email headers, also known as message headers or SMTP headers, are an integral part of every email message, and they provide a detailed record of the email's journey from the sender to the recipient.

While the body of an email contains the message's content, the email header contains metadata and routing information that allows email servers and clients to process and deliver the message correctly.

An email header typically includes various fields, such as "From," "To," "Subject," "Date," and "Received," each of which provides essential information about the email.

Advanced email header analysis involves a thorough examination of these fields and the use of specialized tools and techniques to extract, interpret, and validate the information they contain.

One of the primary objectives of advanced email header analysis is to identify the source of the email, including the sender's IP address and the path the email took through various mail servers.

To accomplish this, investigators often start by accessing the email header information, which can usually be found within the email client's settings or by viewing the email's properties.

Once the email header information is obtained, advanced email header analysis tools and techniques are used to extract the IP addresses recorded in the "Received" fields.

These IP addresses represent the servers and intermediaries that handled the email during its transmission, and they are listed in reverse chronological order.

By analyzing the "Received" fields, investigators can trace the email's path from the recipient's email server back to the sender's originating server.

However, it's important to note that advanced users and malicious actors may attempt to hide their true identity by altering or falsifying the information in the email header.

Advanced email header analysis techniques can help investigators detect such manipulation and uncover inconsistencies within the header.

Moreover, advanced email header analysis involves checking the authenticity of the sender's domain and email address by performing DNS (Domain Name System) queries and reverse DNS lookups.

Investigators verify that the sender's domain has valid DNS records and that the email address is associated with the claimed domain.

This step helps identify phishing attempts or email spoofing, where attackers impersonate legitimate senders.

Another critical aspect of advanced email header analysis is the examination of the "Message-ID" field, which provides a unique identifier for the email message.

By scrutinizing the "Message-ID," investigators can verify the email's integrity and check for any signs of tampering or forgery.

Furthermore, advanced email header analysis includes the study of email authentication mechanisms, such as SPF (Sender Policy Framework), DKIM (DomainKeys Identified Mail), and DMARC (Domain-based Message Authentication, Reporting, and Conformance).

These protocols help ensure that emails are legitimate and have not been altered during transit.

Advanced email header analysis tools can validate the presence and correctness of these authentication mechanisms, providing insights into the email's authenticity.

In cases where email threats or malicious activity are suspected, advanced email header analysis is crucial for identifying signs of phishing, spam, or malware distribution.

By examining the email header's content and metadata, investigators can assess the legitimacy of the email's source and content.

Additionally, advanced email header analysis can help detect email-based attacks, such as spear-phishing, where attackers target specific individuals or organizations.

Advanced users may also employ anonymization techniques, such as Tor, to hide their IP addresses and obscure their true location.

In such cases, advanced email header analysis experts may need to collaborate with cybersecurity professionals to apply advanced network analysis and tracking methods to uncover the true source of the email.

Moreover, advanced email header analysis is instrumental in analyzing email headers from a large volume of messages, which is essential for cybersecurity professionals responsible for monitoring and responding to email threats on a broader scale.

In organizations, advanced email header analysis tools and automated systems can be employed to process and analyze email headers in real-time, allowing for rapid detection and response to suspicious email activity.

In summary, advanced email header analysis is an indispensable skill for digital forensics experts, cybersecurity professionals, and investigators tasked with tracing the source of emails, verifying their authenticity, and identifying potential security threats.

By examining email headers, extracting IP addresses, checking authentication mechanisms, and scrutinizing the metadata, advanced email header analysis provides valuable insights into the origins and legitimacy of email messages.

This skill is essential for uncovering email-based threats, phishing attempts, and malicious activity while also helping organizations protect their email communications and data.

Chapter 6: Machine Learning and OSINT

Leveraging machine learning for open-source intelligence (OSINT) has become increasingly important in the field of digital investigations and information gathering. Machine learning, a subset of artificial intelligence, enables computers to learn from data and make predictions or decisions without explicit programming. In the context of OSINT, machine learning algorithms can be applied to various aspects of the intelligence gathering process to automate tasks, improve accuracy, and extract valuable insights from vast amounts of publicly available data. One of the primary applications of machine learning in OSINT is text analysis. Machine learning models can be trained to process and understand text data from websites, social media platforms, news articles, and other online sources. These models can identify patterns, sentiments, and key information, making it easier for analysts to extract actionable intelligence. For example, sentiment analysis algorithms can automatically assess public sentiment towards a particular topic, product, or entity by analyzing social media posts and online discussions. Machine learning can also aid in entity recognition and extraction, which involves identifying and categorizing entities such as names, locations, dates, and organizations within text data. This capability is particularly valuable in OSINT investigations, where analysts need to identify relevant individuals, places, or events mentioned in online content. Furthermore, machine learning can enhance image analysis in OSINT. Computer vision algorithms, powered by machine learning, can process and categorize images found on the internet, identifying objects, people, or landmarks. This is especially useful when investigating individuals, tracking locations, or monitoring the spread of visual content across the web. Machine learning models can also be used to detect and flag potentially harmful or illegal content, such as images related to terrorism or child exploitation. Additionally, machine learning is invaluable in the analysis of social media data, where vast amounts of user-generated content are generated daily. Natural language processing (NLP) models can parse and understand the context of social media posts, comments, and messages, enabling analysts to uncover trends, track emerging threats, and detect patterns of interest. Machine learning can also play a significant role in OSINT by automating the collection of data. Web scraping and data extraction tasks can be streamlined through the use of machine learning-based scraping tools. These tools can adapt to changes in website structures and layouts, ensuring the continuous retrieval of relevant information from online sources. Moreover, machine learning algorithms can assist in the geolocation of data points in OSINT investigations. By analyzing contextual information from multiple sources, such as text data and metadata, machine learning models can estimate the geographic location associated with a particular piece of information or event. This is essential for tracking the movements of individuals or identifying the origin of news reports. Machine learning also has the potential to enhance link analysis in OSINT. Link analysis involves mapping connections between individuals, organizations, websites, and other entities to uncover relationships and networks of interest. Machine learning algorithms can assist in the automated identification of significant links and patterns within large datasets, aiding analysts in visualizing complex networks more effectively. Furthermore, machine learning-driven anomaly detection can be a valuable tool in OSINT investigations. By establishing baseline patterns and behaviors from historical data, machine learning models can identify deviations or anomalies that may indicate suspicious or noteworthy events. This can be particularly useful in monitoring online forums, websites, or social media platforms for unusual activities. Machine learning can also assist in tracking the evolution of disinformation campaigns and online propaganda. By analyzing the spread of false or misleading information across digital platforms, machine learning models can detect common themes, strategies, and sources behind such campaigns. This information can be vital for understanding and countering the dissemination of false narratives. However, it's essential to recognize that while machine learning offers significant advantages in OSINT, it is not without its challenges and limitations. The quality of training data plays a crucial role in the effectiveness of machine learning models. Biased or incomplete training data can lead to inaccurate predictions and unreliable results. Furthermore, the dynamic nature of online information requires machine learning models to adapt continuously. Data drift, changes in online platforms, and evolving tactics by threat actors can impact the performance of machine learning algorithms. Additionally, the ethical considerations surrounding the use of machine learning in OSINT must not be overlooked. Privacy concerns, the potential for algorithmic bias, and issues related to data protection and consent should be carefully considered when applying machine learning techniques in intelligence gathering. In summary, leveraging machine learning for open-source intelligence represents a powerful advancement in the field of digital investigations and information gathering. Machine learning algorithms can automate tasks, enhance text and image analysis, streamline data collection, and improve the overall efficiency and effectiveness of OSINT efforts.

However, it is essential for practitioners in this field to be aware of the challenges and ethical considerations associated with machine learning, and to continually adapt to the evolving landscape of online information and threats. Predictive analytics has emerged as a valuable tool in the realm of intelligence gathering, offering the capability to forecast future events and trends based on historical data and statistical models. In the context of intelligence, predictive analytics leverages a wide range of data sources, including open-source information, to provide insights that aid decision-making and strategy development. One of the primary applications of predictive analytics in intelligence gathering is the prediction of emerging threats and security risks. By analyzing historical data related to incidents, attacks, and geopolitical events, predictive models can identify patterns and trends that may indicate the likelihood of future security challenges. These insights enable intelligence agencies and organizations to proactively allocate resources, implement security measures, and respond to potential threats before they escalate. Moreover, predictive analytics can be instrumental in identifying vulnerabilities and weaknesses in critical infrastructure, such as transportation networks, energy grids, and communication systems. By assessing historical data on infrastructure failures, cyberattacks, and natural disasters, predictive models can highlight areas at higher risk, guiding efforts to fortify and protect these vital assets. Another significant use of predictive analytics in intelligence is the forecasting of political instability and social unrest. Historical data on protests, demonstrations, and political crises can be analyzed to identify factors and indicators associated with such events. Predictive models can then assess the likelihood of unrest in specific regions or countries, helping governments and organizations prepare for potential disruptions and instability. Furthermore, predictive analytics can enhance the efficiency of resource allocation in intelligence operations. For example, in the field of law enforcement, predictive models can analyze crime data to predict the likelihood of criminal activity in specific areas or neighborhoods. This information can guide the deployment of law enforcement personnel and resources to prevent and respond to criminal incidents more effectively. In the realm of cybersecurity, predictive analytics plays a crucial role in identifying and mitigating cyber threats. By analyzing historical data on cyberattacks, intrusion attempts, and malware infections, predictive models can identify evolving threat vectors and predict potential targets. This information enables organizations to strengthen their cybersecurity measures and proactively defend against emerging threats. Moreover, predictive analytics can be applied to financial intelligence gathering, particularly in the detection of fraud and financial crimes. Historical data on fraudulent transactions, money laundering, and suspicious financial activities can be analyzed to develop predictive models that flag potentially fraudulent transactions or activities in real-time. This proactive approach helps financial institutions and regulatory bodies prevent financial crimes and protect the integrity of the financial system. Another critical application of predictive analytics in intelligence is in the field of counterterrorism. Historical data on terrorist incidents, recruitment activities, and social media communications can be analyzed to identify patterns and trends associated with radicalization and terrorist threats. Predictive models can then assess the risk of individuals becoming involved in extremist activities, allowing law enforcement and intelligence agencies to focus their efforts on high-risk individuals. Furthermore, predictive analytics can assist in intelligence collection and analysis by automating the process of identifying relevant information from vast amounts of open-source data. Natural language processing (NLP) algorithms can extract and categorize text-based information from online sources, news articles, social media, and websites. This capability speeds up the process of data collection and enables analysts to focus their efforts on interpreting and analyzing the extracted information. However, it is essential to acknowledge that predictive analytics in intelligence gathering is not without its challenges and limitations. Data quality and availability are critical factors that can impact the accuracy of predictive models. Incomplete or biased data can lead to inaccurate predictions and unreliable insights. Moreover, the ethical implications of predictive analytics in intelligence must be carefully considered. Issues related to privacy, civil liberties, and the potential for algorithmic bias require careful oversight and regulation. Additionally, predictive analytics is not a crystal ball; it provides probabilities and forecasts based on historical data and models, and there will always be uncertainty in predicting future events. In summary, predictive analytics has become a valuable asset in intelligence gathering, offering the ability to forecast emerging threats, vulnerabilities, and social trends based on historical data and statistical analysis. Its applications span across various domains, including security, law enforcement, cybersecurity, and financial intelligence. However, the successful implementation of predictive analytics in intelligence relies on the quality of data, ethical considerations, and the recognition of its limitations in predicting complex and dynamic events in an ever-changing world.

Chapter 7: Exploiting IoT Devices for Intelligence

In the modern era, the proliferation of Internet of Things (IoT) devices has brought convenience and connectivity to our lives, but it has also introduced new security challenges that demand a comprehensive vulnerability assessment. IoT devices, ranging from smart thermostats to industrial sensors, are integrated into our homes, workplaces, and critical infrastructure, making them potential targets for cyberattacks. A thorough IoT vulnerability assessment is essential to identify weaknesses in these devices and mitigate the associated risks. One of the primary concerns in IoT vulnerability assessment is the sheer diversity of devices and their associated software and firmware. This diversity creates a complex landscape with a wide range of potential vulnerabilities, as different manufacturers may not prioritize security equally in their product development. Conducting an IoT vulnerability assessment begins with inventory management, where all IoT devices in a network or environment are identified and documented. This step is essential because it's challenging to secure devices if you don't know they exist. Once the inventory is established, the next phase involves assessing the devices for known vulnerabilities. This includes reviewing manufacturer security advisories, patching levels, and firmware updates. Devices with outdated firmware or unpatched vulnerabilities are prime targets for attackers, and addressing these issues is a critical part of the assessment. Another aspect of IoT vulnerability assessment is the analysis of communication protocols and network traffic. IoT devices often communicate with each other or with central servers, and the analysis of this traffic can reveal potential security weaknesses. This analysis involves monitoring network traffic for anomalies, unauthorized access attempts, or unusual data flows that may indicate a compromise. Furthermore, IoT devices may use various communication protocols, such as Bluetooth, Zigbee, Wi-Fi, or cellular networks, each with its own set of security considerations. Assessors need to be knowledgeable about these protocols to identify vulnerabilities specific to each. Physical security is also an essential aspect of IoT vulnerability assessment. Physical access to an IoT device can result in tampering or compromise. Assessors should evaluate the physical security measures in place, such as device enclosures, tamper-evident seals, or access controls. In some cases, it may be necessary to conduct physical penetration testing to assess the resilience of IoT devices to physical attacks. Authentication and authorization mechanisms are critical components of IoT security. Assessors need to examine how devices authenticate users or other devices and how they grant or deny access. Weak or improperly implemented authentication can lead to unauthorized access, putting data and device control at risk. Encryption is another vital aspect of IoT vulnerability assessment. Data transmitted between IoT devices or between devices and central servers should be encrypted to protect it from interception and eavesdropping. Assessors should verify that strong encryption algorithms and protocols are used and that cryptographic keys are properly managed. Device management and patching mechanisms are crucial for ongoing security. IoT devices should have mechanisms in place for applying updates and patches to address known vulnerabilities. Assessors need to evaluate the device management processes and ensure that devices can receive and apply updates securely. Vulnerability scanning and testing are core components of any IoT vulnerability assessment. Tools and techniques, such as vulnerability scanners and penetration testing, can help identify weaknesses in devices and networks. Regular scanning and testing should be part of an ongoing security program to address new vulnerabilities as they emerge. IoT devices often rely on cloud services or backend servers for data storage and processing. Assessors need to evaluate the security of these cloud services and the APIs used for communication. Misconfigured cloud settings or insecure APIs can expose sensitive data to attackers. Privacy concerns are significant in IoT vulnerability assessment. Many IoT devices collect and transmit data, often including personal or sensitive information. Assessors should review data handling practices and assess compliance with privacy regulations and standards. Intrusion detection and monitoring are essential for detecting suspicious or malicious activities. IoT environments should have intrusion detection systems (IDS) and security information and event management (SIEM) solutions in place. These systems can help assessors identify and respond to security incidents in real-time. Access controls and permissions are vital components of IoT security. Assessors should review access control lists, permissions, and user roles to ensure that only authorized individuals or devices can interact with IoT devices or systems. Unauthorized access can lead to data breaches or device manipulation. A significant concern in IoT vulnerability assessment is the potential for supply chain vulnerabilities. Devices may contain components or software from various suppliers, and weaknesses in any part of the supply chain can impact security. Assessors should examine the supply chain for potential risks and ensure that suppliers meet security standards. Security awareness and training are crucial for IoT device users and administrators. Assessors should evaluate the effectiveness of security training programs and user awareness initiatives. Human error is a common factor in security incidents, and education can help mitigate these risks. Finally, risk assessment and risk management are fundamental aspects of IoT vulnerability assessment. Assessors should prioritize vulnerabilities based on their potential impact and likelihood, allowing organizations to focus their resources on mitigating the most significant risks. In summary, IoT vulnerability assessment is a multifaceted process that involves identifying, evaluating, and mitigating security weaknesses in a diverse and interconnected ecosystem of devices. It requires a combination of technical expertise, comprehensive testing, and a thorough understanding of the IoT landscape. Effective vulnerability assessment can help organizations reduce the risk of IoT-related security incidents and protect their data, systems, and infrastructure.

In the era of the Internet of Things (IoT), data collection and analysis have become paramount in harnessing the full potential of interconnected devices. IoT devices, which range from smart sensors in industrial settings to wearable fitness trackers, generate a vast amount of data that can be leveraged to gain insights, improve efficiency, and drive innovation. However, the effective collection and analysis of IoT data come with unique challenges and opportunities that organizations must address to fully capitalize on this valuable resource. One of the primary challenges in IoT data collection is the sheer volume and diversity of data generated. IoT devices continuously produce data streams, such as sensor readings, location information, and device status updates, often in real-time. This influx of data can quickly overwhelm traditional data collection and storage systems. To address this challenge, organizations must implement scalable and efficient data collection infrastructure capable of handling large data volumes and streaming data. Moreover, IoT data is often generated at the edge, where devices are deployed, and then transmitted to central repositories or cloud platforms for analysis. Ensuring reliable data transmission and minimizing latency are critical considerations in IoT data collection. In addition to volume and velocity, the variety of IoT data is another key challenge. Data generated by IoT devices can come in diverse formats, including structured, semi-structured, and unstructured data. This data may include sensor readings, images, videos, geospatial information, and text data from various sources. As a result, organizations need to implement flexible data collection and processing methods that can accommodate this variety. Data quality and integrity are crucial in IoT data collection. Inaccurate or incomplete data can lead to incorrect insights and decisions. To address this challenge, organizations must establish data validation and cleansing processes to identify and rectify data anomalies or errors. Furthermore, data governance practices are essential to maintain data quality throughout its lifecycle. Another challenge in IoT data collection is data security and privacy. IoT devices often handle sensitive information, such as personal health data, industrial processes, or confidential business data. Organizations must implement robust security measures to protect data in transit and at rest, and ensure that data privacy regulations and compliance standards are met. IoT data analysis is the process of extracting meaningful insights and knowledge from the collected data. It involves a range of techniques and technologies, including data analytics, machine learning, and artificial intelligence. One of the primary objectives of IoT data analysis is to detect patterns, anomalies, and trends within the data. This can help organizations identify opportunities for optimization, predict equipment failures, or uncover valuable consumer insights. Descriptive analytics is the first step in IoT data analysis, providing a summary of historical data and enabling organizations to understand past trends and events. Diagnostic analytics delves deeper into data to identify the causes of past events or anomalies. Predictive analytics uses historical data to forecast future events, such as equipment failures or consumer behavior. Prescriptive analytics goes a step further by recommending actions based on predictive insights. Machine learning plays a significant role in IoT data analysis. Machine learning models can be trained to recognize patterns and make predictions based on historical data. For example, in industrial settings, machine learning algorithms can analyze sensor data to predict when equipment maintenance is required, reducing downtime and operational costs. In healthcare, machine learning can analyze patient data to identify early signs of disease or recommend personalized treatment plans. Furthermore, IoT data analysis can provide real-time insights and decision support. In applications like autonomous vehicles, sensor data is analyzed in real-time to make split-second decisions for navigation and safety. Similarly, in smart cities, real-time data analysis can optimize traffic flow, energy consumption, and emergency response. Geospatial analysis is another valuable aspect of IoT data analysis. Geospatial data, such as GPS coordinates, can be integrated with other IoT data to gain location-based insights. For example, in agriculture, geospatial analysis can optimize crop management by considering factors like soil quality, weather conditions, and crop health based on sensor data. Sentiment analysis is employed in IoT data analysis to gauge public opinion and consumer sentiment. By analyzing text data from social media, customer reviews, or chat logs, organizations can gain insights into how their products or services are perceived and make informed decisions based on this feedback. IoT data analysis can also be used for anomaly detection. By establishing normal patterns and behaviors from historical data, organizations can identify deviations that may indicate equipment malfunctions or security breaches. This proactive approach helps prevent costly failures and security incidents. Real-time monitoring and alerts are essential components of IoT data analysis. Organizations must have mechanisms in place to detect and respond to critical events or anomalies as they occur. This requires the integration of analytics engines with monitoring systems and alerting mechanisms. Data visualization is a vital aspect of IoT data analysis. Effective visualization tools and dashboards allow organizations to convey complex data insights in an easily understandable manner. Visualization aids in decision-making by providing clear and actionable information to stakeholders. In summary, IoT data collection and analysis are central to leveraging the potential of interconnected devices. While challenges related to data volume, variety, quality, security, and privacy must be addressed, the benefits of IoT data analysis are substantial. From predictive maintenance to real-time decision support, IoT data analysis empowers organizations to make data-driven decisions, optimize operations, and drive innovation in diverse industries and applications.

Chapter 8: OSINT Automation and Custom Tools

In the world of Open-Source Intelligence (OSINT), automation has become a crucial element in streamlining the collection and analysis of vast amounts of online data. Building custom OSINT automation scripts empowers analysts and investigators to efficiently gather information from various sources, extract valuable insights, and stay ahead in the ever-evolving digital landscape. Custom automation scripts provide the flexibility to tailor OSINT operations to specific needs and objectives. However, creating effective automation scripts requires a combination of technical skills, strategic planning, and a deep understanding of the OSINT domain. Before diving into script development, it's essential to define clear objectives and scope for your automation project. What information are you looking to collect? Which sources will you target? What analytical goals do you want to achieve? Answering these questions guides the development process and ensures that your automation efforts align with your OSINT objectives.

Choosing the right programming language for your automation scripts is a critical decision. Python, with its extensive libraries and community support, is a popular choice in the OSINT community. Other languages like JavaScript, Ruby, or even shell scripting may also be suitable, depending on your specific requirements. Once you've chosen a programming language, you'll need to set up your development environment, including any necessary libraries or packages for web scraping, data manipulation, and analysis. APIs (Application Programming Interfaces) are valuable resources for collecting data from online platforms in a structured and efficient manner. Many social media platforms, search engines, and websites offer APIs that allow you to access data programmatically. Integrating these APIs into your automation scripts can simplify data retrieval and ensure compliance with platform terms of service. However, some APIs may require authentication or have usage limitations, so it's essential to review the API documentation and terms before integration. Web scraping is another key component of OSINT automation. When APIs are unavailable or insufficient, web scraping allows you to extract data from websites directly. Tools like BeautifulSoup and Scrapy in Python make web scraping more accessible and efficient. Keep in mind that web scraping should be conducted ethically and within the bounds of the law. Respect robots.txt files and terms of service, and avoid overloading websites with excessive requests. To maintain the quality and integrity of collected data, data cleaning and preprocessing are essential steps in OSINT automation. Raw data often contains inconsistencies, duplicates, or irrelevant information that can affect the accuracy of your analysis. Automation scripts should include data cleaning routines to address these issues, such as removing duplicates, handling missing values, and standardizing data formats.

Once you have collected and cleaned your data, the next step is data analysis. Automation scripts can include analytical techniques to extract actionable insights from the gathered information. This could involve sentiment analysis of social media posts, geospatial mapping of locations, or identifying trends and patterns in large datasets. The choice of analysis methods depends on your OSINT objectives and the nature of the data you've collected. Visualization is a powerful tool in OSINT automation. Creating charts, graphs, and maps can help you present your findings effectively and make complex data more accessible to stakeholders. Visualization libraries like Matplotlib, Seaborn, or D3.js can be integrated into your scripts to generate compelling visual representations of your OSINT results. It's important to ensure that your automation scripts are designed with scalability and maintainability in mind. As your OSINT operations grow, you may need to collect data from an increasing number of sources or expand the scope of your analysis. Modular and well-documented scripts are easier to extend and adapt to evolving requirements. Additionally, consider incorporating error handling and logging mechanisms into your automation scripts to facilitate debugging and troubleshooting. Security is a paramount concern in OSINT automation. When building custom scripts, it's essential to follow best practices for securing sensitive information, such as API keys or authentication tokens. Avoid hardcoding credentials directly into your scripts, and instead use secure storage solutions or environment variables.

Furthermore, ensure that your automation processes adhere to privacy and legal regulations, both at the national and international levels. Collecting, processing, and analyzing data from online sources should be conducted within the bounds of the law and ethical guidelines. Documentation is often overlooked but is a critical aspect of OSINT automation. Comprehensive documentation ensures that your scripts can be understood and maintained by others in your organization or community. Include clear comments, explanations of script functionality, and examples of usage to make your scripts accessible and user-friendly. Collaboration within the OSINT community is highly beneficial. Sharing your automation scripts and techniques can contribute to the collective knowledge and capabilities of OSINT practitioners. Platforms like GitHub provide a collaborative environment where you can publish and contribute to open-source OSINT projects. Engaging with the community allows you to receive feedback, discover new tools, and stay informed about emerging trends in the field. In summary, building custom OSINT automation scripts is a powerful means of enhancing your information-gathering and analysis capabilities. Effective OSINT automation requires careful planning, technical proficiency, and a commitment to ethical and legal principles. By creating modular, scalable, and well-documented scripts, you can streamline your OSINT operations, gain valuable insights, and contribute to the broader OSINT community's knowledge and expertise.

In the realm of Open-Source Intelligence (OSINT), the ability to access and utilize data from various online sources is essential for investigators, analysts, and researchers. While manual data collection methods have their merits, integrating Application Programming Interfaces (APIs) into OSINT workflows can significantly enhance efficiency and access to valuable information. API integration allows OSINT practitioners to programmatically retrieve data from social media platforms, search engines, databases, and other online resources. This automation streamlines the data collection process, reduces human error, and enables real-time access to dynamic information. One of the key advantages of API integration in OSINT is the ability to access structured and organized data directly from online platforms. Many popular social media platforms, such as Twitter, Facebook, and Instagram, offer APIs that provide access to user profiles, posts, comments, and more. Search engines like Google and Bing also offer APIs for web and image search, news articles, and geographical data. These APIs enable OSINT professionals to gather data in a systematic and efficient manner, ensuring that information is up-to-date and reliable. Moreover, integrating APIs into OSINT workflows allows for comprehensive searches across multiple platforms simultaneously. This multidimensional approach can provide a more comprehensive view of a subject or topic, allowing for more informed analysis and decision-making. For example, an OSINT investigator tracking an individual's online presence may use APIs to gather data from various social media platforms and online forums simultaneously. This holistic approach can reveal a more complete picture of the individual's activities and affiliations. API integration also enables OSINT practitioners to automate repetitive data collection tasks, saving time and effort. For instance, monitoring a specific hashtag on Twitter for relevant posts can be a time-consuming process if done manually.

By integrating the Twitter API, OSINT analysts can set up automated searches and receive real-time notifications when new posts matching their criteria are published. This automation ensures that critical information is not missed and allows investigators to focus on analysis rather than data collection. Another advantage of API integration is the ability to access historical data archives. Many APIs provide access to past posts, comments, and interactions, allowing OSINT professionals to analyze trends, patterns, and historical context. For instance, an OSINT researcher studying a social media campaign's impact can use API access to retrieve and analyze posts from previous months or years. Additionally, APIs often offer advanced search and filtering capabilities, allowing OSINT practitioners to refine their queries and extract specific information. For example, the Twitter API allows users to search for tweets containing specific keywords, hashtags, and user mentions within a specified timeframe. This level of granularity enables analysts to focus on the most relevant data for their investigations. Despite the numerous benefits of API integration in OSINT, there are challenges and considerations that practitioners must address. First and foremost, APIs are subject to rate limits and usage restrictions imposed by the platform providers. Exceeding these limits can result in temporary or permanent suspension of API access. OSINT professionals must carefully monitor their API usage to ensure compliance with the platform's terms of service. Moreover, API providers may change their terms, pricing models, or access policies, impacting the availability and functionality of the APIs.

OSINT practitioners need to stay informed about any updates or changes to the APIs they rely on to avoid disruptions in their workflows. Security and privacy considerations are also paramount when integrating APIs into OSINT processes. API requests often require authentication through API keys or access tokens, which must be stored and managed securely. Leaked or compromised API keys can lead to unauthorized access to sensitive data, so robust security practices are crucial. Furthermore, OSINT professionals must respect privacy regulations and ethical guidelines when collecting and using data obtained through APIs. Some API providers impose restrictions on data usage, such as prohibiting the collection of personally identifiable information without consent. OSINT practitioners must be aware of these restrictions and ensure that their data collection and analysis processes align with legal and ethical standards. In summary, API integration is a powerful tool in the OSINT practitioner's toolkit, offering the ability to access structured and real-time data from a variety of online sources. The advantages of automation, comprehensive searches, historical data access, and advanced filtering make API integration invaluable for efficient and effective OSINT operations. However, practitioners must navigate challenges related to rate limits, changing API policies, security, and privacy to maximize the benefits of API-driven OSINT. By leveraging APIs responsibly and staying informed about updates and best practices, OSINT professionals can enhance their capabilities and stay ahead in the evolving landscape of online intelligence gathering.

Chapter 9: Advanced Cryptocurrency Investigations

In the realm of Open-Source Intelligence (OSINT), the tracking and analysis of cryptocurrency transactions have become increasingly vital for investigators and analysts. Cryptocurrencies, such as Bitcoin, Ethereum, and others, offer a degree of anonymity and decentralization that can make traditional financial investigations challenging. However, with advanced crypto transaction analysis techniques, OSINT practitioners can uncover valuable insights and trace the flow of digital assets. To effectively analyze cryptocurrency transactions, it's crucial to understand the fundamental principles of blockchain technology. Blockchains are decentralized ledgers that record all transactions across a network of computers. Each transaction is grouped into a block, and these blocks are linked together, forming a chain. This transparent and immutable ledger is the foundation of cryptocurrencies, as it ensures the integrity and security of transactions. One of the first steps in advanced crypto transaction analysis is obtaining the relevant transaction data. Blockchain explorers, such as Blockchair, Etherscan, and Blockchain.info, provide searchable databases of cryptocurrency transactions, allowing users to access transaction histories and associated wallet addresses. These platforms offer a user-friendly interface for querying blockchain data, making it accessible to both novice and experienced analysts. Once transaction data is obtained, the next step is to identify the cryptocurrency wallets involved. Each wallet has a unique address, often represented as a long string of alphanumeric characters. By examining the sender and receiver addresses in a transaction, analysts can link transactions to specific wallets. This wallet-level analysis forms the basis for tracing the movement of digital assets. To enhance crypto transaction analysis, it's crucial to understand the concepts of inputs and outputs. In a cryptocurrency transaction, inputs represent the sources of funds, while outputs are the destinations. Analyzing the inputs and outputs of a transaction can reveal important information about the flow of funds. For example, if multiple inputs are combined into a single output, it may indicate a consolidation of funds or a change in ownership. Advanced crypto transaction analysis also involves identifying patterns in transaction behavior. For instance, mixing services or coin tumblers are often used to obscure the origin of funds by mixing them with those of other users. Identifying such mixing patterns can be challenging but is essential for tracking the flow of assets. Additionally, some cryptocurrencies, like Monero, offer enhanced privacy features that make transaction analysis more complex. These privacy coins use techniques like ring signatures and confidential transactions to obfuscate sender and receiver addresses and transaction amounts. As a result, tracing transactions on privacy-focused blockchains requires specialized knowledge and tools. Advanced crypto transaction analysis extends beyond identifying wallet addresses and patterns. It also involves tracking the movement of funds across multiple transactions and addresses. This process often requires the use of specialized software and databases that can link wallets and transactions across the blockchain. Chain analysis tools, like Chainalysis and CipherTrace, provide comprehensive insights into cryptocurrency flows, wallet clustering, and suspicious activities. They enable OSINT practitioners to identify illicit transactions, money laundering, and connections to darknet markets. Another essential aspect of advanced crypto transaction analysis is the use of heuristic techniques.

Heuristic analysis involves making educated guesses or assumptions based on available data. In crypto transaction analysis, heuristics can help identify linked wallets or transactions that may not be immediately obvious. For example, heuristic techniques can uncover hidden relationships between wallets by analyzing common spending patterns or shared inputs. The use of heuristics requires a deep understanding of blockchain data and the ability to make informed judgments based on available evidence. Analyzing cryptocurrency transactions also involves monitoring and analyzing the behavior of known illicit entities. Darknet marketplaces, ransomware groups, and cybercriminal organizations often use cryptocurrencies for illegal activities. By tracking their transactions and wallet addresses, OSINT practitioners can identify patterns and connections within the crypto ecosystem. Additionally, collaboration with law enforcement agencies and other organizations can provide access to databases of known illicit wallet addresses and entities. These resources aid in the identification and tracking of suspicious cryptocurrency activities. Advanced crypto transaction analysis also encompasses the use of graph analysis techniques. Graph analysis involves visualizing the relationships between wallets and transactions as a network of nodes and edges. This approach allows analysts to identify clusters of related wallets, visualize fund flows, and uncover hidden connections. Graph analysis can be particularly effective when dealing with complex cryptocurrency investigations involving multiple parties and transactions. Moreover, the integration of blockchain data with other sources of OSINT, such as social media profiles or online forums, can provide valuable context and attribution. For example, linking a cryptocurrency wallet to a social media account can help identify the wallet owner and provide insights into their activities and affiliations. However, it's essential to exercise caution when attempting to de-anonymize individuals, as privacy and legal considerations must be respected. In summary, advanced crypto transaction analysis is a crucial skill for OSINT practitioners seeking to navigate the complex world of cryptocurrency investigations. Understanding blockchain fundamentals, identifying wallet addresses, analyzing transaction inputs and outputs, and recognizing patterns are foundational aspects of this discipline. Additionally, leveraging specialized tools, heuristics, and graph analysis techniques can enhance the effectiveness of crypto transaction analysis. Collaboration with law enforcement and access to databases of known illicit entities further supports investigations in the cryptocurrency space. By continuously developing expertise in advanced crypto transaction analysis, OSINT professionals can uncover valuable insights, trace the movement of digital assets, and contribute to efforts to combat illicit activities within the crypto ecosystem.

In the realm of Open-Source Intelligence (OSINT) and cryptocurrency investigations, one of the most challenging aspects is the investigation of privacy coins. Privacy coins, also known as anonymous cryptocurrencies, are digital currencies designed to offer enhanced privacy and anonymity to users. These cryptocurrencies aim to provide a level of transactional privacy that traditional cryptocurrencies like Bitcoin do not. While privacy coins offer legitimate privacy benefits, they have also been associated with illicit activities, making them a subject of interest for OSINT practitioners. The investigation of privacy coins involves understanding their underlying technology and the privacy features they offer. One of the most well-known privacy coins is Monero, which uses advanced cryptographic techniques to obfuscate transaction details, such as sender addresses and transaction amounts. To investigate privacy coins effectively, it's crucial to grasp how these privacy mechanisms work and how they impact transaction analysis. Unlike transparent blockchains like Bitcoin, privacy coin transactions are not easily traceable on public block explorers. This poses a challenge for investigators, as traditional methods of tracking transactions and addresses may not be applicable. To navigate these challenges, OSINT practitioners must employ specialized tools and techniques tailored to privacy coins. One of the primary privacy features in many privacy coins is ring signatures. Ring signatures combine multiple signatures into a single transaction, making it challenging to determine which participant in the ring actually initiated the transaction. This anonymity feature makes it difficult to attribute transactions to specific users. Additionally, privacy coins often employ stealth addresses, which generate unique, one-time addresses for each transaction. These addresses prevent observers from linking multiple transactions to the same recipient. When investigating privacy coin transactions, OSINT practitioners must consider these privacy-enhancing features and their implications for tracking. To investigate privacy coin transactions, OSINT practitioners often use specialized blockchain explorers and analysis tools designed for privacy coins. For example, Monero users have access to block explorers like XMRchain, which are tailored to Monero's blockchain and provide insights into transactions and wallet balances. These tools allow investigators to explore the blockchain while respecting user privacy. One of the challenges of investigating privacy coin transactions is the need for access to accurate and up-to-date data. Privacy coin block explorers and analysis tools may not always be as widely available or feature-rich as those for transparent blockchains. As a result,

OSINT practitioners may need to rely on a combination of tools and data sources to gather the necessary information. Additionally, privacy coin transactions often involve multiple layers of encryption and obfuscation, making it challenging to trace the flow of funds. While privacy coins like Monero have made strides in enhancing user privacy, they have also faced scrutiny from regulators and law enforcement agencies. Some exchanges and businesses have delisted privacy coins to comply with anti-money laundering (AML) and know your customer (KYC) regulations. This has implications for OSINT investigations, as it may limit the availability of data for tracking privacy coin transactions. To address these challenges, OSINT practitioners may need to collaborate with blockchain forensics experts, law enforcement agencies, or cryptocurrency exchanges to access relevant data. Another aspect of investigating privacy coins involves monitoring for illicit activities and patterns. Privacy coins have been associated with darknet marketplaces, ransomware payments, and other illegal transactions. OSINT practitioners may need to focus on identifying and tracking suspicious wallet addresses and patterns of behavior within the privacy coin ecosystem. This can involve monitoring known darknet marketplaces and forums for discussions related to privacy coin usage. Moreover, advanced crypto transaction analysis techniques, such as graph analysis, can be applied to uncover connections between wallets and transactions. These methods may help identify entities or individuals engaged in illicit activities using privacy coins. Privacy coin investigations also require a strong understanding of legal and ethical considerations. While privacy coins offer enhanced privacy to users, they may also be used for illegal purposes. Investigators must balance the need to track and monitor privacy coin transactions with respecting user privacy and adhering to legal standards. Privacy coin investigations should be conducted within the bounds of applicable laws and regulations. Moreover, OSINT practitioners should be cautious when attempting to de-anonymize users, as privacy coin transactions are designed to protect user identities. In summary, investigating privacy coins presents unique challenges and considerations for OSINT practitioners. Privacy coin technologies, such as ring signatures and stealth addresses, make transaction analysis more challenging compared to transparent blockchains. To navigate these challenges, OSINT professionals should use specialized tools and explore collaborations with blockchain forensics experts and law enforcement agencies. Monitoring for illicit activities, understanding legal and ethical boundaries, and staying informed about privacy coin developments are essential aspects of privacy coin investigations. Overall, investigating privacy coins requires a combination of technical expertise, adaptability, and a commitment to upholding privacy and security standards.

Chapter 10: Real-world Intelligence Operations

Covert Open-Source Intelligence (OSINT) operations represent a specialized and discreet approach to gathering intelligence and information. In contrast to traditional OSINT methods, which often involve openly available data sources and techniques, covert operations require a more clandestine and covert approach. Covert OSINT operations are typically employed in situations where overt methods would be ineffective, too conspicuous, or could jeopardize the mission's success. These operations may be conducted by intelligence agencies, law enforcement, private investigators, or corporate entities to gather sensitive information discreetly. One of the key characteristics of covert OSINT operations is the emphasis on secrecy and anonymity. Operatives involved in covert OSINT must take extensive measures to conceal their identities, activities, and affiliations. This often involves the use of aliases, encrypted communication channels, and elaborate cover stories. Operatives may need to assume false identities and backgrounds to access specific information or infiltrate targeted groups or organizations. Additionally, the use of specialized equipment, such as encrypted smartphones and secure communication tools, is common in covert operations to protect operational security. Covert OSINT operations require careful planning and risk assessment. Operatives must consider the potential legal, ethical, and operational risks associated with their activities. Depending on the nature of the operation, operatives may need to obtain legal clearances, permissions, or warrants to collect certain types of information. Ethical considerations are also paramount, as covert operations must adhere to strict ethical guidelines to protect the privacy and rights of individuals and organizations. Operatives involved in covert OSINT must also be highly skilled in information gathering techniques, counter-surveillance, and digital tradecraft. These skills are essential for navigating the challenges of gathering intelligence while remaining undetected. The use of open-source information and publicly available data is a core component of covert OSINT operations. Operatives leverage the internet, social media, online forums, and other digital resources to collect information without raising suspicion. However, they must do so in a way that does not leave a digital footprint that could be traced back to their true identities. Advanced search techniques, data analysis, and information synthesis are essential skills for operatives to effectively collect and make sense of data from diverse sources. Operatives may also employ techniques such as deep web research, which involves accessing hidden online resources not indexed by traditional search engines. These hidden resources can contain valuable information that is not readily available to the public. Another critical aspect of covert OSINT operations is the creation of cover stories and personas. Operatives must develop believable backstories and identities that align with their mission objectives. These cover stories help operatives gain access to restricted areas, organizations, or individuals without raising suspicion. The creation of credible cover stories requires a deep understanding of human psychology and the ability to adapt to various social and cultural contexts. In many cases, operatives may need to establish long-term relationships or infiltrate groups over an extended period, posing additional challenges and risks. Covert OSINT operations often involve the use of human intelligence (HUMINT) techniques. This may include recruiting and handling human assets who can provide insider information or access to restricted areas. Operatives must build trust with their assets while maintaining the utmost discretion to protect both the asset's safety and the operation's success. Effective communication and rapport-building skills are crucial in managing HUMINT sources. Additionally, operatives may need to employ surveillance and counter-surveillance tactics to monitor targets discreetly and detect any potential threats or risks. The use of surveillance technology, such as hidden cameras and tracking devices, may be necessary to collect valuable information without direct contact with the target. Operatives must also be well-versed in operational security (OPSEC) principles to minimize the risk of detection. This includes safeguarding communication, avoiding predictable patterns of behavior, and taking precautions to protect sensitive information. While covert OSINT operations can yield valuable intelligence, they are not without risks and ethical considerations. Operatives must constantly assess the potential impact of their activities on individuals and organizations. It is crucial to balance the need for information with ethical guidelines and legal constraints. Covert OSINT operations require meticulous planning, rigorous training, and a commitment to ethical conduct to achieve their objectives effectively. Operatives must operate in the shadows, employing a combination of technical skills, psychological acumen, and operational security to collect valuable intelligence while remaining hidden. By carefully managing risks, adhering to ethical principles, and staying adaptable, covert OSINT operations can provide valuable insights and support various security and intelligence objectives. In summary, covert Open-Source Intelligence operations represent a specialized and discreet approach to gathering information. These operations require secrecy, anonymity, and careful planning to minimize risks and achieve mission success. Operatives involved in covert OSINT must employ a wide range of skills, from information gathering techniques and digital tradecraft to HUMINT and surveillance tactics. Ethical considerations and legal constraints are paramount in conducting covert operations, emphasizing the importance of responsible and ethical intelligence gathering practices. Despite the challenges and risks, covert OSINT operations play a significant role in supporting intelligence, security, and investigative efforts. Intelligence gathering in high-stakes environments represents a unique and demanding aspect of the intelligence field. These environments are characterized by elevated risks, sensitive information, and critical decision-making. High-stakes intelligence operations often involve national security, law enforcement, counterterrorism, corporate security, or diplomatic missions. The success of intelligence gathering in such contexts can have profound consequences for individuals, organizations, and nations. One of the defining features of high-stakes environments is the heightened level of secrecy and classification associated with the information being sought. Operatives conducting intelligence gathering in these situations typically handle highly classified or sensitive data that, if compromised, could lead to severe repercussions. This necessitates strict adherence to security protocols and clearances to ensure that only authorized personnel have access to the information. The objectives of intelligence gathering in high-stakes environments can vary widely, from preventing terrorist attacks and uncovering espionage to safeguarding trade secrets and protecting critical infrastructure. These diverse goals require tailored intelligence strategies and approaches. Operatives in high-stakes environments often collaborate with counterparts in other intelligence agencies, law enforcement agencies, or private sector organizations to pool resources and expertise. Such collaborations can enhance the breadth and depth of intelligence gathering efforts. Intelligence operatives working in high-stakes environments must possess a high degree of situational awareness and adaptability. The rapidly changing nature of threats and risks means that intelligence strategies must be flexible and responsive. Operatives must continuously monitor evolving threats, vulnerabilities, and opportunities to gather timely and actionable intelligence. To effectively gather intelligence in high-stakes environments, operatives employ a range of techniques, including human intelligence (HUMINT), signals intelligence (SIGINT), and open-source intelligence (OSINT). HUMINT involves the recruitment and handling of human assets who can provide valuable insider information. This approach often requires building trust and rapport with sources while safeguarding their identities and safety. SIGINT involves the interception and analysis of electronic communications, such as phone calls, emails, and radio transmissions. In high-stakes environments, SIGINT can be crucial for uncovering covert operations, tracking threats, and monitoring adversaries. OSINT, on the other hand, relies on publicly available information to gather intelligence. In high-stakes environments, OSINT can be used to analyze online discussions, monitor social media activity, and assess open-source data related to potential threats or targets. Operatives conducting OSINT must be adept at data analysis and identifying trends and patterns. Technical skills are often paramount, as intelligence operatives in high-stakes environments may need to use advanced tools and technologies to collect, analyze, and disseminate intelligence. Operational security (OPSEC) is a critical consideration in high-stakes intelligence gathering. Operatives must take extensive precautions to protect their identities and activities from detection by adversaries or hostile actors. This includes using secure communication channels, adopting pseudonyms, and avoiding predictable patterns of behavior. Furthermore, the use of encryption and other cybersecurity measures is essential to safeguard sensitive information. Ethical considerations are central to intelligence gathering in high-stakes environments. Operatives must adhere to strict ethical guidelines and legal standards to ensure that their actions are justified and legal. Respecting human rights, privacy, and due process is paramount, even when dealing with sensitive intelligence activities. The consequences of unethical or unlawful intelligence gathering can be severe, both in terms of legal liability and damage to reputation. Intelligence operatives in high-stakes environments often face significant psychological and emotional challenges. The nature of their work can be mentally taxing, requiring resilience and coping mechanisms to manage stress and exposure to distressing information. Regular debriefings, psychological support, and ethical guidance are essential components of ensuring the well-being of operatives. Additionally, operatives may need to undergo extensive training in subjects such as risk assessment, crisis management, and cultural sensitivity to navigate complex and potentially dangerous environments. The dissemination of intelligence gathered in high-stakes environments is a critical aspect of the process. Timely and accurate reporting to decision-makers is essential for informed decision-making and threat mitigation. Operatives must ensure that intelligence is conveyed in a clear, concise, and actionable manner to support effective responses. The importance of intelligence gathering in high-stakes environments extends beyond national security and law enforcement. Private sector organizations, including multinational corporations, also engage in intelligence gathering to protect their assets, trade secrets, and personnel. These organizations often have their own security and intelligence units focused on safeguarding their interests. In summary, intelligence gathering in high-stakes environments is a complex and multifaceted endeavor. It demands a combination of technical skills, ethical principles, operational security measures, and adaptability. Operatives in these environments play a vital role in protecting national security, preventing threats, and safeguarding critical assets. Their work requires constant vigilance, a commitment to legality and ethics, and a dedication to the highest standards of professionalism. Intelligence gathering in high-stakes environments is a dynamic field that continues to evolve in response to emerging threats and challenges, making it a crucial element of contemporary security and intelligence efforts.

BOOK 4
MASTERING OSINT INVESTIGATIONS
CUTTING-EDGE STRATEGIES AND TOOLS

ROB BOTWRIGHT

Chapter 1: OSINT in the Era of Big Data

Harnessing big data for open-source intelligence (OSINT) represents a paradigm shift in the field of intelligence gathering. The proliferation of digital technologies and the internet have led to an unprecedented volume of data being generated daily. This data explosion has opened up new opportunities and challenges for OSINT practitioners. Big data in the context of OSINT refers to the vast and diverse array of digital information available from sources such as social media, websites, forums, and online databases. This data encompasses text, images, videos, geospatial information, and more, making it a rich source of intelligence. The sheer volume of big data can be overwhelming, but it also holds immense potential for uncovering hidden insights, trends, and patterns. Harnessing big data effectively requires specialized tools, techniques, and strategies tailored to the unique characteristics of this information landscape. One of the key advantages of big data in OSINT is its ability to provide a real-time and near-real-time view of events and developments. Social media platforms, for example, offer a continuous stream of user-generated content that can be analyzed to gain insights into breaking news, public sentiment, and emerging trends. OSINT practitioners can monitor hashtags, keywords, and trending topics to identify critical information as it unfolds. In high-stakes environments, such as national security or crisis management, real-time OSINT analysis of big data can be a game-changer. Another significant advantage of big data is its potential for geospatial analysis. Many online services and applications collect location-based data, allowing OSINT analysts to track movements, identify hotspots of activity, and assess the geographical spread of events. This geospatial intelligence can be invaluable for monitoring security threats, disaster response, and geopolitical analysis. However, the vastness of big data poses challenges in terms of data collection, storage, and processing. Traditional OSINT methods and tools may struggle to cope with the scale and velocity of big data. As a result, OSINT practitioners need to adopt advanced technologies and analytics to harness the full potential of this information source. Machine learning and artificial intelligence (AI) are indispensable tools in big data OSINT. These technologies enable automated data collection, classification, sentiment analysis, image recognition, and natural language processing at a scale that would be impossible for human analysts alone. Machine learning models can sift through vast datasets to identify relevant information, anomalies, and patterns, thereby reducing the time and effort required for analysis. Moreover, AI-driven tools can provide predictive analytics, helping OSINT practitioners anticipate events and trends based on historical data. The fusion of big data and AI has given rise to the concept of predictive OSINT, where algorithms are used to forecast developments and threats. The ethical implications of big data OSINT are profound and must be carefully considered. As OSINT practitioners delve into the public and semi-public spheres of the internet to collect information, they often encounter sensitive and private data. Respecting privacy rights and adhering to ethical guidelines are paramount in this context. Moreover, the potential for misinformation and fake data in big data sources necessitates rigorous verification and validation processes. False or misleading information can have serious consequences, particularly in critical decision-making scenarios. The legal aspects of big data OSINT are complex and subject to evolving regulations. OSINT practitioners must be aware of privacy laws, data protection regulations, and intellectual property rights that may apply when collecting, storing, and disseminating big data. Violating these legal boundaries can result in legal liabilities and reputational damage. To effectively harness big data for OSINT, organizations and agencies need to invest in advanced analytics platforms and technologies. These platforms can aggregate data from multiple sources, perform real-time analysis, and generate actionable intelligence reports. Moreover, they can provide visualization tools that allow OSINT analysts to explore data visually, uncovering insights that may not be apparent through traditional text-based analysis. The use of open-source big data tools and platforms, such as Hadoop, Spark, and Elasticsearch, has become commonplace in OSINT operations. These technologies provide the scalability and flexibility needed to handle the immense volumes of data encountered in big data OSINT. Collaboration and information sharing among OSINT practitioners have become essential in the big data era. Given the global nature of online data, threats and opportunities often transcend borders. International cooperation and coordination can enhance the effectiveness of OSINT efforts, enabling the sharing of insights and expertise. Big data OSINT has a wide range of applications across various domains. In the field of national security, it can be used to monitor terrorist activities, assess geopolitical developments, and track emerging threats. In corporate intelligence, big data OSINT can help organizations protect their assets, monitor competitors, and anticipate market trends. Humanitarian organizations can leverage big data OSINT for disaster response, assessing the impact of natural disasters and coordinating relief efforts. Journalists and investigative reporters use big data OSINT to uncover stories, expose corruption, and shed light on critical issues. In summary, harnessing big data for open-source intelligence is a transformative development in the field of intelligence gathering. It offers unprecedented opportunities to gain insights, monitor events in real time, and predict future developments. However, the challenges of data volume, velocity, and veracity require OSINT practitioners to adopt advanced technologies, ethical practices, and legal compliance measures. The fusion of big data and artificial intelligence is shaping the future of OSINT, enabling predictive analytics and enhanced decision support. As the digital landscape continues to evolve, so too will the methodologies and techniques used in big data OSINT, making it a dynamic and essential component of contemporary intelligence efforts. Big data analytics has emerged as a powerful tool for intelligence agencies and organizations seeking to extract valuable insights from vast and complex datasets. In the realm of intelligence gathering, big data analytics offers the capability to sift through massive amounts of information to identify patterns, trends, and anomalies. The term "big data" refers to datasets that are too large and dynamic to be effectively managed and analyzed using traditional data processing tools and methods. These datasets often consist of structured and unstructured data from a multitude of sources, including social media, sensors, internet of things (IoT) devices, and more. The field of intelligence has been revolutionized by the application of big data analytics, enabling agencies to enhance their situational awareness, make data-driven decisions, and respond proactively to emerging threats. One of the key advantages of big data analytics in intelligence is its ability to provide real-time or near-real-time insights. This timeliness is crucial for intelligence agencies to stay ahead of rapidly evolving threats and situations. By continuously monitoring data streams, such as social media feeds or sensor data, analysts can detect and respond to emerging events in a timely manner. Furthermore, big data analytics can help intelligence agencies identify potential threats, anomalies, or trends that might have otherwise gone unnoticed. This proactive approach allows agencies to take preemptive action and prevent security breaches or incidents. Big data analytics is particularly valuable in the context of open-source intelligence (OSINT), where publicly available information is analyzed to gather intelligence. With the vast amount of online data generated daily, OSINT analysts rely on big data analytics tools to search, collect, and analyze information from diverse sources, including websites, forums, and social media platforms. These tools can automatically scan and process vast amounts of text, images, and videos to identify relevant information and connections. Another critical application of big data analytics in intelligence is in the field of cybersecurity. Intelligence agencies and organizations face an ongoing battle against cyber threats and attacks. Big data analytics enables the monitoring of network traffic, the detection of unusual behavior or patterns indicative of cyberattacks, and the identification of vulnerabilities in real time. This proactive cybersecurity approach is vital to safeguard sensitive data and infrastructure from malicious actors. Machine learning and artificial intelligence (AI) play a significant role in enhancing the capabilities of big data analytics for intelligence. These technologies enable the development of predictive models that can anticipate and respond to threats. Machine learning algorithms can analyze historical data to identify patterns associated with specific threats or attacks, allowing organizations to take preventive measures. AI-driven chatbots and virtual assistants can also assist analysts in finding relevant information quickly and efficiently. Moreover, natural language processing (NLP) algorithms can be used to extract valuable insights from unstructured text data, such as news articles or social media posts. Despite the immense potential of big data analytics in intelligence, there are several challenges that must be addressed. One of the primary challenges is data privacy and protection. Intelligence agencies often deal with sensitive and classified information, and the use of big data analytics raises concerns about data breaches and unauthorized access. Strict data governance and encryption measures are essential to mitigate these risks. Additionally, the sheer volume of data can overwhelm intelligence analysts, leading to information overload. To address this challenge, agencies must implement efficient data filtering and prioritization mechanisms to ensure that analysts focus on the most relevant and critical information. Interoperability and integration of various data sources and tools also pose challenges. Intelligence agencies often have a multitude of data repositories, software solutions, and databases. Ensuring that these systems can work together seamlessly and share information is crucial for effective intelligence operations. Furthermore, the skills and training of analysts are critical in leveraging big data analytics effectively. Agencies must invest in training programs to ensure that analysts have the necessary skills to work with advanced analytics tools and interpret the results accurately. In summary, big data analytics has become a game-changer in the field of intelligence gathering. It empowers agencies and organizations to harness the vast amount of data generated daily to enhance their situational awareness, make data-driven decisions, and respond proactively to emerging threats. The application of machine learning and artificial intelligence further enhances the capabilities of big data analytics, enabling predictive and proactive approaches to intelligence and cybersecurity. However, addressing challenges related to data privacy, information overload, interoperability, and analyst training is essential for maximizing the benefits of big data analytics in intelligence.

Chapter 2: Advanced Social Media Profiling

Advanced behavioral analysis on social media represents a cutting-edge approach to understanding human behavior in the digital age. As people increasingly use social media platforms to express their thoughts, emotions, and actions, these platforms have become a treasure trove of valuable data for researchers, businesses, and intelligence agencies. Traditional methods of behavioral analysis have evolved to encompass the unique characteristics and challenges posed by online social interactions. One of the fundamental aspects of advanced behavioral analysis on social media is the study of human emotions and sentiment. Researchers and organizations can analyze the language, tone, and content of social media posts to gain insights into the emotional states of individuals and the collective sentiment of user communities. Sentiment analysis algorithms can automatically classify posts as positive, negative, or neutral, providing a snapshot of public opinion on various topics and events. Understanding sentiment is invaluable for businesses seeking to gauge customer satisfaction, political campaigns monitoring public perception, and intelligence agencies assessing public sentiment in regions of interest. Another key dimension of advanced behavioral analysis on social media is the study of social networks and connections. Social network analysis (SNA) techniques allow researchers to map and analyze the relationships between users, identifying influential individuals, communities, and information flow patterns. By visualizing social networks, analysts can uncover hidden connections, track the spread of information or misinformation, and identify potential influencers or disruptors. This analysis is especially relevant in the context of intelligence and security, where identifying the key players in online extremist networks or tracking the dissemination of false information is crucial. Advanced behavioral analysis also delves into the study of online personas and identity. On social media, users often project specific identities or personas, which may differ from their real-life selves. Researchers can employ techniques such as text analysis, image analysis, and pattern recognition to understand how individuals construct and maintain online identities. This knowledge is valuable for marketing and advertising, as it enables businesses to tailor their messaging to specific user personas. In intelligence and security, understanding online personas is essential for tracking and profiling potential threats. A significant challenge in advanced behavioral analysis on social media is the sheer volume of data generated daily. Social media platforms produce an overwhelming amount of content in the form of text, images, videos, and multimedia. Handling and processing this data necessitates advanced computational techniques, including natural language processing (NLP), machine learning, and data mining. NLP algorithms can parse and extract meaning from text data, enabling the identification of keywords, topics, and themes within social media posts. Machine learning models can categorize and classify posts, while data mining techniques can uncover hidden patterns or anomalies in large datasets. The integration of AI-driven chatbots and virtual assistants further enhances the efficiency of data processing and analysis. Ethical considerations play a crucial role in advanced behavioral analysis on social media. While the analysis of publicly available data is generally permissible, concerns arise when dealing with user data that may be sensitive or personally identifiable. Respecting user privacy and adhering to data protection regulations is essential.

Moreover, the potential for bias in algorithms and analysis methods is a concern. Bias can lead to skewed results and reinforce stereotypes or inequalities. Addressing bias in advanced behavioral analysis requires rigorous testing, validation, and transparency in methodologies. In addition to ethical considerations, legal boundaries must be observed when conducting advanced behavioral analysis on social media. Data collection, storage, and analysis must comply with relevant laws and regulations. For intelligence agencies and law enforcement, strict adherence to legal frameworks is crucial to avoid infringing on civil liberties and privacy rights. Advanced behavioral analysis on social media has a wide range of applications across diverse domains. In marketing and advertising, businesses use social media analysis to understand consumer preferences, target specific demographics, and measure the effectiveness of marketing campaigns. In political campaigns, social media analysis is employed to gauge public sentiment, identify key issues, and assess the impact of campaign messaging. In healthcare, researchers use behavioral analysis to monitor public health trends, detect disease outbreaks, and identify areas requiring intervention. In intelligence and security, advanced behavioral analysis on social media aids in threat detection, monitoring extremist activities, and tracking the dissemination of propaganda or disinformation. As social media continues to evolve, so too will the techniques and methodologies used in advanced behavioral analysis. The integration of emerging technologies, such as augmented reality and virtual reality, may provide new avenues for understanding online behavior. Moreover, as social media platforms introduce new features and functionalities, analysts must adapt their approaches to capture the evolving landscape of digital interactions. In summary, advanced behavioral analysis on social media is a dynamic and evolving field with significant implications for research, business, and security. By leveraging the vast amounts of data generated on social media platforms, analysts can gain valuable insights into human behavior, sentiment, and social networks. However, ethical considerations, legal boundaries, and the challenges of handling big data are critical factors that must be addressed in the pursuit of advanced behavioral analysis on social media. Targeted profiling techniques represent a critical aspect of modern intelligence gathering and investigation. In today's digital age, where vast amounts of information are readily available online, the ability to profile individuals and entities accurately is invaluable. Profiling is the process of creating detailed descriptions or profiles of specific individuals, organizations, or subjects of interest based on available information. These profiles can encompass a wide range of attributes, including demographics, behaviors, affiliations, and activities. One of the primary objectives of targeted profiling is to gain a comprehensive understanding of the subject's background, motivations, and potential threats or opportunities. Effective profiling can inform decision-making, risk assessment, and the development of appropriate strategies and actions. The first step in targeted profiling is to identify the subject of interest. This could be a person, a company, a criminal organization, a political group, or any entity that requires investigation or analysis. Once the subject is identified, the profiler begins collecting information from various sources. These sources may include publicly available data, social media profiles, online publications, news articles, financial records, and more. The profiler must employ a diverse set of research methods and tools to gather as much relevant information as possible. Open-source intelligence (OSINT) is a key component of targeted profiling, as it involves collecting and analyzing publicly available information from the internet. OSINT sources can provide valuable insights into a subject's online presence, activities, interests, and connections. Social media platforms, for example, often contain a wealth of information about individuals, including their interests, relationships, and recent activities. However, it's essential to approach social media profiling with caution, respecting privacy boundaries and ethical considerations. Profiling techniques may vary depending on the nature of the subject and the goals of the investigation. In some cases, profiling focuses on individuals or groups with malicious intent, such as cybercriminals, terrorists, or other threat actors. Profiling these subjects often involves identifying patterns of behavior, recognizing indicators of intent, and assessing the level of risk they pose. For example, in cybersecurity, profiling can help identify potential threats and vulnerabilities in a network by analyzing the behavior and characteristics of hackers or malware. In other instances, profiling may be used for marketing and advertising purposes, where businesses aim to understand customer preferences, buying behavior, and demographics. Profiling can help tailor marketing campaigns to specific customer segments and improve the effectiveness of advertising efforts. Regardless of the context, ethical considerations must always be at the forefront of profiling activities. Respecting privacy, data protection laws, and individual rights is essential. Profiling should never involve illegal or intrusive activities, such as hacking or unauthorized access to private information. Furthermore, profiling should be conducted with transparency and accountability, ensuring that individuals understand how their data is being used and have the option to opt out or request corrections. One of the challenges in targeted profiling is the volume and diversity of available data. With the proliferation of the internet and digital communication, the amount of information that can be accessed and analyzed is overwhelming. Professionals engaged in profiling must have the skills to sift through vast datasets, filter out irrelevant information, and focus on key insights. Additionally, the accuracy of profiling depends on the quality and reliability of the data sources. False or misleading information can lead to incorrect conclusions and potentially harmful actions. To mitigate this risk, profilers should cross-reference information from multiple sources and verify the authenticity of data whenever possible. Advanced technologies, such as machine learning and natural language processing, can aid in automating data collection and analysis processes. These technologies can help identify patterns, trends, and anomalies in data, making profiling more efficient and accurate. Machine learning algorithms can also assist in predictive profiling, where the goal is to anticipate future behaviors or actions based on historical data. Another aspect of targeted profiling is the development of behavioral profiles. Behavioral profiling seeks to understand and predict an individual's actions, choices, and responses based on their past behavior and psychological characteristics. This approach is often used in criminal investigations, where profilers aim to create profiles of potential suspects or offenders. Behavioral profiling can help law enforcement agencies prioritize leads, narrow down suspect lists, and allocate resources more effectively. While behavioral profiling can be a powerful tool, it's essential to recognize its limitations. Profiling, whether based on behavior or demographics, is not a foolproof method of prediction. Human behavior is influenced by numerous factors, including personal experiences, emotions, and external events. Therefore, profilers should approach their work with humility and an understanding of the inherent uncertainties. In summary, targeted profiling techniques are integral to intelligence gathering, investigation, marketing, and various other domains. Profiling involves creating detailed descriptions or profiles of subjects based on available information, and it can serve a wide range of purposes. Profiling should always be conducted ethically, with respect for privacy and legal boundaries. The challenge lies in handling the vast and diverse datasets available today, requiring advanced skills and technologies. Behavioral profiling adds an additional layer of complexity by aiming to predict future actions based on past behavior. While profiling is a valuable tool, it's essential to recognize its limitations and uncertainties in understanding human behavior and decision-making.

Chapter 3: Augmented Reality and OSINT

Augmented reality (AR) applications have begun to play a significant role in the field of intelligence gathering, revolutionizing the way information is collected and analyzed. AR technology overlays digital information, such as images, data, or 3D models, onto the real-world environment, enhancing the user's perception and understanding of their surroundings. In the context of intelligence gathering, AR offers several advantages, including real-time data visualization, enhanced situational awareness, and improved decision-making. One of the key uses of AR in intelligence gathering is in the field of geospatial intelligence (GEOINT). AR applications can provide GEOINT analysts with the ability to visualize geographical data, such as terrain maps, satellite imagery, and infrastructure details, in a real-world context. By wearing AR glasses or using AR-equipped devices, analysts can superimpose these data layers onto their field of view, allowing for more accurate navigation and on-the-fly analysis. This capability is particularly valuable for military and law enforcement personnel operating in complex and dynamic environments. In addition to GEOINT, AR can also be applied to human intelligence (HUMINT) operations. AR-equipped devices can facilitate discreet and real-time communication between field agents and intelligence officers. Agents in the field can use AR glasses or headsets to transmit live audio, video, and text data to their handlers, who can then provide immediate guidance and support. This seamless communication enhances the safety and effectiveness of intelligence-gathering missions. Furthermore, AR can assist in the identification and tracking of individuals of interest. Facial recognition technology, when integrated with AR, allows for the real-time identification of persons in a crowd or public space. This capability is invaluable for law enforcement agencies and counterterrorism units in identifying potential threats or persons of interest in real-time situations. Beyond physical surveillance, AR can also be applied to cyber intelligence and cybersecurity. AR applications can provide cybersecurity analysts with a visual representation of network traffic, system vulnerabilities, and potential threats. By visualizing complex cyber data in an immersive AR environment, analysts can quickly identify anomalies and potential security breaches, enabling faster response times and more effective threat mitigation. Moreover, AR can assist in training and simulation exercises for intelligence personnel. AR-based training scenarios can replicate real-world intelligence-gathering situations, allowing trainees to practice and improve their skills in a safe and controlled environment. This immersive training approach can help intelligence professionals develop the necessary expertise to handle complex and high-stakes operations. Another application of AR in intelligence gathering is in the field of open-source intelligence (OSINT). AR can be used to enhance OSINT analysts' ability to process and analyze vast amounts of online data. AR-equipped devices can provide analysts with a real-time feed of social media posts, news articles, and other online information relevant to their investigations. By visualizing this data in an AR environment, analysts can quickly identify trends, emerging threats, and critical insights. Furthermore, AR can aid in the interpretation of data collected from remote sensing platforms, such as drones or satellites. AR overlays can provide real-time information about the environment, weather conditions, and potential obstacles, assisting remote operators in making informed decisions during intelligence-gathering missions. As with any technology, the use of AR in intelligence gathering raises important ethical and privacy considerations. The collection and analysis of data, especially in public spaces, must be conducted within the bounds of legal and ethical frameworks. Furthermore, the potential for misuse or abuse of AR technology in intelligence operations must be carefully monitored and regulated. Privacy concerns regarding facial recognition and the capture of personal data must be addressed transparently and responsibly. In summary, AR applications have the potential to transform intelligence gathering by providing real-time data visualization, enhanced communication, and improved situational awareness. Whether in the fields of geospatial intelligence, human intelligence, cybersecurity, or open-source intelligence, AR technology offers valuable tools for intelligence professionals. However, the ethical and privacy implications of AR use in intelligence operations must be carefully considered and balanced with the benefits it offers. As technology continues to evolve, intelligence agencies and organizations must adapt their practices and policies to ensure responsible and effective use of AR in the pursuit of national security and public safety. Geospatial augmented reality (GeoAR) has emerged as a powerful tool in the realm of open-source intelligence (OSINT), revolutionizing the way analysts gather and interpret geospatial data. This technology combines the capabilities of augmented reality with geospatial information, allowing OSINT professionals to overlay digital maps, satellite imagery, and location-based data onto the physical world. GeoAR has proven to be invaluable in a variety of OSINT applications, from military and law enforcement operations to disaster response and urban planning. One of the primary advantages of GeoAR is its ability to provide real-time situational awareness in the field. Analysts equipped with GeoAR devices can access up-to-date geospatial data, such as maps, terrain information, and infrastructure details, directly within their field of vision. This real-time visualization enhances decision-making, navigation, and the assessment of on-the-ground situations. In military operations, for example, GeoAR can offer soldiers and commanders a comprehensive view of the battlefield, including the positions of friendly and enemy forces, key landmarks, and potential threats. The integration of GeoAR with tactical maps and mission-critical data can significantly improve mission success rates and troop safety. For law enforcement agencies, GeoAR aids in crime scene analysis, suspect tracking, and search-and-rescue operations. GeoAR devices can overlay maps with crime data, witness testimonies, and real-time GPS coordinates, helping officers make informed decisions in high-pressure situations. Moreover, GeoAR can assist in disaster response efforts by providing emergency responders with real-time information about affected areas, road closures, and the location of critical infrastructure. This technology allows responders to coordinate their efforts more effectively, ultimately saving lives and minimizing damage. Beyond military, law enforcement, and disaster response, GeoAR has applications in urban planning and development. City planners and architects can use GeoAR to visualize proposed building projects within the context of existing urban landscapes. By overlaying 3D models of new structures onto city streets, planners can assess their impact on traffic flow, sunlight exposure, and overall city aesthetics. GeoAR can also be a valuable tool in environmental monitoring and conservation efforts. Researchers and scientists can use it to track wildlife movements, study habitat changes, and assess the impact of climate change on ecosystems. One of the key features of

GeoAR is its ability to enhance collaboration among OSINT professionals. In multi-agency operations or international missions, GeoAR can provide a shared augmented reality environment where analysts from different organizations or countries can collaborate in real time. This collaborative approach can lead to more comprehensive intelligence gathering and a better understanding of complex situations. Furthermore, GeoAR can facilitate data sharing and communication between field operatives and intelligence officers. Field agents wearing GeoAR devices can transmit live video feeds, images, and annotations to remote analysts, allowing for immediate feedback and guidance. This seamless communication enhances the effectiveness and safety of intelligence-gathering missions. Despite its many advantages, the adoption of GeoAR in OSINT is not without challenges. One significant challenge is the integration of diverse geospatial data sources into GeoAR platforms. These platforms must be capable of processing data from satellites, drones, aerial imagery, and terrestrial sensors to provide a holistic view of the environment. Data accuracy and consistency are also crucial, as discrepancies in geospatial data can lead to misinterpretations and errors in decision-making. Another challenge is the potential for information overload. With the vast amount of geospatial data available today, analysts may face difficulties in selecting and prioritizing the most relevant information. To address this, GeoAR systems must incorporate advanced filtering and data management features. Ethical considerations are another important aspect of GeoAR in OSINT. Privacy concerns arise when GeoAR devices are used to capture images or video in public spaces. Analysts and operators must adhere to strict ethical guidelines and legal regulations regarding data collection and privacy rights. Additionally, there is the risk of misuse or abuse of GeoAR technology, such as the tracking of individuals without their consent or the unintentional exposure of sensitive information. To mitigate these risks, GeoAR users must undergo thorough training and be aware of ethical best practices. In summary, geospatial augmented reality is transforming the field of open-source intelligence by providing real-time visualization, enhanced collaboration, and improved decision-making capabilities. Its applications span a wide range of domains, from military and law enforcement to disaster response, urban planning, and environmental conservation. However, the successful adoption of GeoAR in OSINT requires addressing challenges related to data integration, information overload, ethics, and privacy. As technology continues to evolve, GeoAR will likely become an even more indispensable tool for OSINT professionals seeking to make sense of the complex geospatial landscape.

Chapter 4: Cybersecurity Threat Hunting

Proactive threat detection strategies have become increasingly vital in today's fast-paced and interconnected digital landscape. In a world where cyberattacks and security breaches are a constant threat, organizations and individuals alike must take proactive measures to safeguard their digital assets. Traditional security approaches, such as firewalls and antivirus software, are essential but no longer sufficient on their own. To effectively defend against evolving threats, a proactive mindset is necessary. Proactive threat detection involves actively seeking out vulnerabilities, identifying potential threats, and responding before an attack occurs. This approach requires a comprehensive understanding of the threat landscape and a commitment to continuous monitoring and improvement. One fundamental aspect of proactive threat detection is vulnerability assessment. This process involves regularly scanning systems, networks, and applications for weaknesses or misconfigurations that could be exploited by attackers. By identifying vulnerabilities early, organizations can address them before cybercriminals have the opportunity to exploit them. Another key component of proactive threat detection is intrusion detection and prevention systems (IDPS). These systems monitor network traffic and system activity in real-time, looking for suspicious behavior or known attack patterns. When anomalies are detected, IDPS can take automated actions to block or mitigate the threat, reducing the risk of a successful attack. Continuous monitoring is a critical element of proactive threat detection. It involves the constant surveillance of an organization's digital environment, looking for signs of unauthorized access, data exfiltration, or other malicious activity. This proactive approach enables organizations to detect and respond to threats as they emerge, rather than after the damage is done. Threat intelligence plays a vital role in proactive threat detection. It involves gathering and analyzing information about current and emerging threats, including tactics, techniques, and indicators of compromise (IOCs). Armed with this intelligence, organizations can adjust their security measures to better protect against specific threats. Machine learning and artificial intelligence (AI) are increasingly being employed in proactive threat detection. These technologies can analyze vast amounts of data to identify patterns and anomalies that may be indicative of a threat. Machine learning models can continuously learn and adapt to new attack techniques, making them valuable tools in staying ahead of cybercriminals. Behavioral analytics is another proactive approach to threat detection. It focuses on understanding normal user and system behavior, allowing organizations to detect deviations from the norm that could indicate an attack. By identifying unusual or suspicious behavior, organizations can respond quickly and effectively. Red teaming and penetration testing are proactive techniques used to assess an organization's security posture. In these exercises, security professionals simulate real-world attacks to identify vulnerabilities and weaknesses. The results of these tests can inform security improvements and help organizations better prepare for potential threats. Threat hunting is an active and ongoing process of searching for signs of compromise within an organization's environment. Security analysts proactively seek out indicators of an intrusion, even when there is no specific alert or alarm. This proactive approach can uncover threats that may have gone undetected by automated systems. Cyber hygiene and employee training are crucial aspects of proactive threat detection. Many security breaches occur due to human error or negligence, such as clicking on phishing emails or using weak passwords. By educating employees about security best practices and enforcing good cyber hygiene, organizations can reduce the risk of insider threats and common attack vectors. The proactive threat detection strategies mentioned above are not standalone measures; they work best when integrated into a holistic security framework. Organizations should adopt a layered security approach that combines various tools, technologies, and practices to create a robust defense against threats. Additionally, regular security audits and assessments are essential to evaluate the effectiveness of proactive measures and identify areas for improvement. In summary, proactive threat detection is a proactive approach to cybersecurity that focuses on identifying and mitigating threats before they can cause harm. It involves a combination of vulnerability assessment, intrusion detection, continuous monitoring, threat intelligence, advanced technologies, and best practices. By adopting a proactive mindset and implementing these strategies, organizations can significantly enhance their security posture and reduce the risk of falling victim to cyberattacks. Advanced threat intelligence sharing represents a critical component of modern cybersecurity. In today's interconnected digital landscape, cyber threats are constantly evolving and growing in sophistication. To effectively defend against these threats, organizations must collaborate and share intelligence. Traditional cybersecurity measures, such as firewalls and antivirus software, are necessary but no longer sufficient. They are like pieces of armor, but without intelligence, they are blind to the enemy's tactics. This is where threat intelligence sharing comes into play. It involves the exchange of information about current and emerging threats among organizations, government agencies, and security researchers. The goal is to provide a collective defense against cyber adversaries. Advanced threat intelligence sharing goes beyond the basic sharing of indicators of compromise (IOCs) or malware signatures. It encompasses a wide range of information, including threat actor profiles, tactics, techniques, and procedures (TTPs), and insights into the motivations and goals of cyber adversaries. This comprehensive intelligence enables organizations to better understand the threat landscape and proactively defend against attacks. Threat intelligence sharing can take various forms, including formal information sharing partnerships, industry-specific information sharing and analysis centers (ISACs), and informal peer-to-peer sharing among trusted organizations. Formal information sharing partnerships often involve government agencies, law enforcement, and critical infrastructure providers. These partnerships enable the sharing of classified and sensitive intelligence to protect national security and critical infrastructure. Industry-specific ISACs are organizations established to facilitate threat intelligence sharing within a particular sector, such as finance, healthcare, or energy. Members of these ISACs share sector-specific threat information to improve collective cybersecurity. Informal peer-to-peer sharing occurs when organizations voluntarily exchange threat intelligence with trusted peers and partners. This type of sharing can be more flexible and tailored to the specific needs and trust relationships of the organizations involved. Advanced threat intelligence sharing is not without its challenges. One significant challenge is the need for effective anonymization and privacy protection when sharing sensitive data. Organizations must strike a balance between sharing valuable intelligence and safeguarding sensitive information. Legal and regulatory considerations also play a role in shaping threat intelligence sharing practices. Data protection laws, privacy regulations, and liability concerns can impact how and what information is shared. Moreover, there is the challenge of information overload. With the vast amount of threat data available, organizations may struggle to filter, prioritize, and act on the most relevant intelligence. To address this, advanced threat intelligence sharing initiatives must incorporate automated analysis and intelligence-driven decision-making processes. Interoperability and standardization are crucial for effective threat intelligence sharing. To facilitate seamless data exchange, organizations and technology providers should adhere to industry standards and open protocols. Additionally, advanced threat intelligence sharing must involve continuous learning and adaptation. Threat actors constantly evolve their tactics, and intelligence sharing communities must stay ahead of the curve. This requires ongoing collaboration, threat hunting, and the development of new intelligence sources. Machine learning and artificial intelligence (AI) are increasingly used in threat intelligence sharing to analyze and categorize large volumes of data. These technologies can identify patterns and anomalies that human analysts might miss. Furthermore, AI can automate the dissemination of intelligence, ensuring that relevant information reaches the right people in a timely manner. A key benefit of advanced threat intelligence sharing is the ability to detect and respond to threats more effectively. By leveraging collective intelligence, organizations can identify attacks earlier in their lifecycle and take proactive measures to mitigate them. This proactive approach reduces the likelihood of successful breaches and minimizes the impact of cyberattacks. In addition to threat detection and response, advanced threat intelligence sharing can inform strategic decision-making. By understanding the tactics and motivations of threat actors, organizations can make informed investments in cybersecurity defenses and prioritize resources. Furthermore, threat intelligence sharing can enhance incident response capabilities. When an organization experiences a security incident, access to shared threat intelligence can expedite the investigation and containment of the threat. It provides context and insights that help incident responders take the appropriate actions. In summary, advanced threat intelligence sharing is a critical component of modern cybersecurity. It involves the exchange of comprehensive threat information among organizations, government agencies, and security researchers. While challenges such as privacy concerns and information overload exist, the benefits of collective defense, early threat detection, and informed decision-making outweigh these challenges. As cyber threats continue to evolve, advanced threat intelligence sharing will remain essential in the ongoing battle to protect digital assets and critical infrastructure.

Chapter 5: The Future of Artificial Intelligence in OSINT

AI-powered predictive analysis stands at the forefront of technological advancements in various industries. In today's data-driven world, organizations are seeking ways to harness the power of artificial intelligence and machine learning to gain valuable insights into future trends and outcomes. Predictive analysis, with its ability to forecast and anticipate events, is revolutionizing decision-making processes. AI, as the driving force behind predictive analysis, enables computers to analyze vast datasets, identify patterns, and make predictions with remarkable accuracy. The key to AI-powered predictive analysis lies in its ability to extract valuable information from historical data and apply it to future scenarios. By examining past trends and behaviors, AI models can identify hidden correlations and generate forecasts that guide decision-makers in a multitude of domains. One of the key applications of AI-powered predictive analysis is in financial markets and investment strategies. Machine learning algorithms analyze historical market data, news sentiment, and economic indicators to make predictions about stock prices, currency exchange rates, and investment opportunities. These predictions assist traders, investors, and financial institutions in making informed decisions and managing risks effectively. In the healthcare sector, AI-powered predictive analysis has the potential to revolutionize patient care and disease management. By analyzing patient records, genomic data, and medical research, AI models can predict disease outbreaks, identify high-risk patients, and recommend personalized treatment plans. This technology holds the promise of early disease detection and more effective healthcare interventions. AI-driven predictive maintenance is transforming industries that rely on machinery and equipment. By monitoring the performance of machines and analyzing sensor data, predictive analysis algorithms can forecast equipment failures and recommend maintenance actions before breakdowns occur. This not only reduces downtime and maintenance costs but also enhances operational efficiency. The retail sector benefits from AI-powered predictive analysis through demand forecasting and inventory management. Machine learning models analyze sales data, consumer behavior, and external factors to predict product demand accurately. Retailers can optimize their inventory levels, reduce overstock and understock situations, and improve customer satisfaction by ensuring the availability of products. AI-powered predictive analysis is also playing a significant role in improving energy efficiency and sustainability. Smart grids and IoT devices collect vast amounts of data, which AI models analyze to predict energy consumption patterns and optimize energy distribution. This contributes to reduced energy waste and a more sustainable approach to resource management. In the field of marketing and customer relationship management, AI-driven predictive analysis helps businesses tailor their marketing strategies. By analyzing customer data, purchase history, and online behavior, AI models can predict customer preferences and recommend personalized marketing campaigns. This leads to higher customer engagement and increased sales. The insurance industry utilizes AI-powered predictive analysis to assess risk and set insurance premiums more accurately. By analyzing historical data and identifying risk factors, AI models can predict the likelihood of accidents, natural disasters, or health-related events. This enables insurance companies to offer customized policies and pricing to their customers. AI-driven predictive analysis extends its benefits to transportation and logistics by optimizing route planning and supply chain management. Machine learning algorithms analyze real-time traffic data, weather conditions, and historical transportation patterns to predict the most efficient routes and delivery schedules. This results in cost savings and faster delivery times. The field of agriculture benefits from AI-powered predictive analysis in precision farming. By analyzing soil data, weather forecasts, and crop history, AI models can predict optimal planting times, irrigation schedules, and crop yields. This technology assists farmers in maximizing their productivity and minimizing resource usage. Human resources departments utilize AI-powered predictive analysis for talent acquisition and employee retention. By analyzing candidate resumes, interview performance, and employee engagement data, AI models can predict which candidates are the best fit for job openings and which employees are at risk of leaving the company. Predictive analysis helps organizations make informed decisions about hiring and employee development. In the realm of cybersecurity, AI-powered predictive analysis is a powerful tool for threat detection and prevention. Machine learning algorithms analyze network traffic, user behavior, and historical attack patterns to predict and identify potential security threats. This proactive approach enhances organizations' ability to defend against cyberattacks. AI-powered predictive analysis is also making strides in the field of weather forecasting. By analyzing meteorological data, satellite images, and climate trends, AI models can generate more accurate and timely weather predictions. This is particularly crucial for disaster preparedness and agriculture planning. The implementation of AI-powered predictive analysis does come with its challenges. One significant challenge is the need for high-quality data. AI models rely on historical data to make predictions, so the accuracy of those predictions is directly related to the quality and quantity of available data. Additionally, the interpretability of AI models can be a challenge, as complex algorithms may generate predictions that are difficult to explain or understand. This can be a concern in industries where decision-making transparency is essential. Ethical considerations, such as data privacy and bias, also require careful attention when implementing AI-powered predictive analysis. Ensuring that algorithms are fair and unbiased is crucial to avoid reinforcing existing inequalities or making discriminatory decisions. In summary, AI-powered predictive analysis is a transformative technology that has applications across various industries. By leveraging the capabilities of artificial intelligence and machine learning, organizations can make more informed decisions, optimize operations, and enhance their competitiveness. While challenges exist, the benefits of predictive analysis are driving its widespread adoption, shaping the future of data-driven decision-making.

Automated OSINT data collection with AI is a game-changer in the world of open-source intelligence. In an era where information is abundant but time is scarce, the ability to gather data efficiently and effectively is paramount. AI-powered automation streamlines the process of collecting vast amounts of data from diverse sources, allowing analysts to focus on analysis rather than manual data collection. Traditional OSINT data collection methods often involve manually searching websites, social media platforms, and other online sources for relevant information. This process can be time-consuming and prone to human error. AI-powered automation, on the other hand, uses machine learning algorithms to perform these tasks at scale and with a high degree of accuracy. One of the key benefits of automated OSINT data collection is speed. AI can process data much faster than humans, enabling organizations to gather real-time or near-real-time information about evolving situations. This speed is particularly crucial in situations where timely intelligence is critical, such as cybersecurity incidents or crisis response. Another advantage of AI-powered automation is the ability to monitor a wide range of sources simultaneously. AI algorithms can scan websites, social media platforms, news articles, and even dark web forums simultaneously, ensuring that no relevant information is missed. This comprehensive approach to data collection enhances the breadth and depth of OSINT analysis. Furthermore, AI can be trained to recognize and filter out irrelevant or redundant information, reducing the volume of data analysts need to sift through. This not only saves time but also improves the quality of the data that reaches analysts' desks. AI-powered OSINT data collection is not limited to text-based information. It can also analyze multimedia content, such as images and videos, to extract valuable insights. For example, AI algorithms can identify objects, locations, and individuals in images, helping analysts understand the context of visual content. Additionally, AI can analyze the sentiment of social media posts and news articles, providing insights into public opinion and sentiment trends. The integration of natural language processing (NLP) technology into AI-powered OSINT data collection further enhances its capabilities. NLP enables AI to understand and interpret human language, making it possible to analyze unstructured text data, such as social media posts and chat messages. This allows organizations to gain valuable insights from sources that were previously challenging to process. In addition to speed and comprehensiveness, AI-powered OSINT data collection offers scalability. Organizations can adjust the scope and scale of their data collection efforts to match their specific needs and objectives. Whether it's monitoring a single social media account or tracking mentions of a brand across the entire internet, AI can adapt to the task at hand. Moreover, AI can assist in identifying trends and anomalies in large datasets, enabling organizations to detect emerging issues or threats. For example, in the field of cybersecurity, AI can analyze network traffic data to identify patterns indicative of a potential breach or attack. This proactive approach to threat detection can help organizations mitigate risks before they escalate. However, AI-powered OSINT data collection is not without its challenges. One significant challenge is the need for data privacy and ethical considerations. As AI collects and analyzes vast amounts of data, organizations must ensure that they comply with privacy regulations and protect individuals' sensitive information. Bias in AI algorithms is another concern. AI models can inherit biases present in the data they are trained on, leading to biased results in data collection and analysis. To mitigate this, organizations must implement measures to address bias and ensure fairness. Furthermore, the ever-evolving nature of online platforms and sources requires continuous adaptation of AI algorithms. New websites, social media platforms, and communication channels emerge regularly, making it essential to keep AI algorithms up-to-date and capable of accessing the latest data sources. Interoperability is another challenge, as AI-powered OSINT data collection systems may need to integrate with existing tools and databases. Effective collaboration and information sharing among organizations also become crucial in the context of AI-powered OSINT data collection. To make the most of AI-powered OSINT data collection, organizations should adopt a holistic approach that combines automation with human expertise. While AI can efficiently collect and process data, human analysts provide critical context, interpretation, and domain expertise. Collaboration between AI and human analysts ensures that the insights derived from automated data collection are accurate, actionable, and aligned with organizational goals. In summary, automated OSINT data collection with AI is a transformative technology that enhances the speed, comprehensiveness, and scalability of open-source intelligence efforts. It allows organizations to gather and analyze vast amounts of data from diverse sources, providing valuable insights for decision-making and risk mitigation. While challenges exist, the benefits of AI-powered OSINT data collection make it an essential tool in today's information-rich and fast-paced world.

Chapter 6: Quantum Computing and OSINT

Quantum cryptography represents a revolutionary paradigm shift in the field of secure communication and intelligence operations. This cutting-edge technology leverages the principles of quantum mechanics to provide a level of security that is theoretically unbreakable by classical computing. In traditional cryptography, security relies on mathematical algorithms and computational complexity to protect sensitive information. However, the advent of quantum computers threatens to undermine the security of many classical encryption methods through their ability to solve complex mathematical problems quickly. Quantum cryptography, on the other hand, harnesses the unique properties of quantum particles, such as photons, to ensure the absolute security of data transmission. One of the fundamental concepts in quantum cryptography is the phenomenon of quantum entanglement. Entangled particles, like photons, are linked in such a way that the state of one particle instantly influences the state of the other, regardless of the physical distance separating them. This property allows for the creation of quantum keys, which form the basis of secure communication in quantum cryptography. Quantum key distribution (QKD) protocols, such as the well-known BBM92 protocol, enable two parties to exchange cryptographic keys with the assurance that any eavesdropping attempt will be detectable. In a QKD exchange, Alice sends a stream of entangled photons to Bob, who measures their properties and communicates his results to Alice. If the photons' properties have been intercepted or tampered with in any way, the disturbance caused by the eavesdropping attempt will be evident to Alice and Bob, alerting them to a potential security breach. This property of QKD makes it theoretically impossible for an eavesdropper to intercept the quantum key without detection, providing an unprecedented level of security for intelligence operations. Another aspect of quantum cryptography that enhances security is the no-cloning theorem. This theorem states that it is impossible to create an identical copy of an arbitrary unknown quantum state. In the context of cryptography, it means that an eavesdropper cannot intercept a quantum key and create a duplicate without altering the original key in a detectable manner. This property makes quantum keys inherently resistant to replication and theft. Quantum cryptography also addresses the challenge of secure key distribution over long distances. Quantum key distribution systems, such as those based on satellite communication, have been developed to enable secure communication between parties separated by thousands of kilometers. Satellites equipped with quantum technology can transmit entangled photons between ground stations, allowing for secure key exchange across vast geographical areas. The use of quantum satellites in intelligence operations provides a means of secure communication that is immune to interception, even by adversaries with advanced computing capabilities. Furthermore, quantum cryptography offers the possibility of information-theoretic security, which means that the security of a cryptographic system is based on fundamental physical principles rather than computational complexity. This level of security is particularly appealing for intelligence agencies dealing with highly sensitive information. However, it's important to note that practical quantum cryptography systems face technical challenges and limitations. One of the main challenges is the susceptibility of quantum signals to environmental factors, such as noise and signal loss. These factors can degrade the quality of quantum key distribution and require the development of error correction techniques to maintain security. Additionally, the deployment of quantum key distribution networks on a global scale presents logistical and infrastructure challenges. Despite these challenges, quantum cryptography holds great promise for intelligence operations in an era of increasing cyber threats and advanced adversaries. The ability to establish secure communication channels that are immune to classical and quantum computing attacks is a significant advantage for intelligence agencies. Quantum-resistant encryption algorithms, designed to withstand attacks from quantum computers, are also being developed to complement existing quantum cryptography systems. Incorporating both quantum key distribution and quantum-resistant algorithms into intelligence operations can provide a robust and future-proof security framework. Quantum cryptography's potential applications in intelligence operations extend beyond secure communication. Quantum-enabled sensors and detectors can enhance intelligence gathering by detecting and measuring physical quantities with unprecedented precision. For example, quantum sensors can be used for the detection of magnetic fields, gravitational waves, and electromagnetic signals, enabling intelligence agencies to gather valuable data for a wide range of purposes. Quantum-enhanced imaging techniques, such as quantum lidar and quantum-enhanced cameras, can also play a role in intelligence operations by providing high-resolution imaging capabilities that surpass classical technologies. Furthermore, quantum computing itself has the potential to revolutionize intelligence analysis. Quantum algorithms, such as Shor's algorithm and Grover's algorithm, can significantly speed up certain calculations and optimization problems. These algorithms have implications for code-breaking, cryptanalysis, and pattern recognition tasks that are central to intelligence analysis. Quantum computing, when fully realized, could provide intelligence agencies with unprecedented computational power for processing and analyzing vast amounts of data. In summary, quantum cryptography is poised to become a cornerstone of secure communication and intelligence operations in the modern age. Its ability to provide provably secure communication channels, coupled with its potential applications in sensing and computation, positions quantum cryptography as a critical tool for intelligence agencies seeking to protect sensitive information and gain a strategic advantage in an evolving landscape of cyber threats and technological advancements.

Quantum computing represents a significant advancement in the field of computational technology. Its potential to revolutionize various industries, including encryption, has garnered attention and concern alike. At its core, quantum computing operates on the principles of quantum mechanics, allowing it to perform calculations at speeds far beyond the capabilities of classical computers. This increase in computational power raises questions about the impact of quantum computing on encryption, a cornerstone of modern information security. To understand this impact, it is essential to delve into the basics of encryption and the vulnerabilities that quantum computing may exploit. Encryption is the process of converting plaintext data into a scrambled form known as ciphertext, making it unreadable to unauthorized users. To perform this transformation, encryption algorithms use mathematical keys that act as the instructions for both encryption and decryption. The security of encrypted data relies on the difficulty of reversing this process without the correct key. In classical computing, the security of encryption methods primarily depends on the complexity of mathematical problems that underpin them. For example, the widely used RSA encryption algorithm relies on the difficulty of factoring the product of two large prime numbers. This factoring problem is believed to be computationally hard, making it impractical for classical computers to break RSA encryption by brute force. However, quantum computers introduce a paradigm shift in computational capabilities. One of the most well-known quantum algorithms, Shor's algorithm, has the potential to efficiently factor large numbers, rendering RSA encryption and other related methods vulnerable. Shor's algorithm leverages quantum parallelism and the properties of quantum superposition to explore multiple possibilities simultaneously, making it exponentially faster than classical factoring algorithms. This means that, with a sufficiently powerful quantum computer, cryptographic keys generated using classical encryption algorithms could be deciphered relatively quickly. While Shor's algorithm poses a threat to classical public-key encryption methods like RSA and ECC (Elliptic Curve Cryptography), it's important to note that not all encryption is equally vulnerable to quantum attacks. Symmetric encryption algorithms, which use the same key for both encryption and decryption, are generally considered more robust against quantum threats. Quantum computers may still have the potential to attack symmetric encryption, but the impact is less clear-cut compared to public-key encryption. To address the vulnerabilities posed by quantum computing, the field of post-quantum cryptography has emerged. Post-quantum cryptography seeks to develop encryption methods that are resistant to attacks by quantum computers. These methods are designed to maintain data security even in a world where powerful quantum computers exist. Several promising post-quantum encryption techniques are being actively researched and evaluated for their practicality and security. These include lattice-based cryptography, code-based cryptography, multivariate polynomial cryptography, and more. Each approach leverages different mathematical structures and problems that are believed to be hard for both classical and quantum computers. For example, lattice-based cryptography relies on the complexity of lattice problems, which involve finding the shortest vector in a lattice of points. This problem is considered challenging even for quantum computers, making lattice-based encryption a potential candidate for post-quantum security. Another approach is code-based cryptography, which is based on the difficulty of decoding certain linear error-correcting codes. The security of these methods rests on the assumption that quantum computers cannot efficiently solve the underlying mathematical problems. As quantum computing continues to advance, it is crucial for organizations and governments to prepare for the post-quantum era of encryption. This involves developing and implementing encryption methods that can withstand quantum attacks. Furthermore, the transition to post-quantum cryptography must be carefully managed to ensure a smooth migration without compromising security. It's worth noting that while quantum computing has the potential to break existing encryption methods, the timeline for achieving practical, large-scale quantum computers remains uncertain. Quantum technologies are still in their infancy, and building stable, error-corrected quantum computers is a formidable engineering challenge. However, the potential risks posed by quantum computing to data security have prompted proactive measures. For example, the National Institute of Standards and Technology (NIST) in the United States has been actively soliciting and evaluating proposals for post-quantum encryption standards. NIST aims to standardize encryption algorithms that can resist quantum attacks, providing a clear roadmap for secure communication in the future. In summary, the impact of quantum computing on encryption is a topic of ongoing research and concern. While quantum computers have the potential to break widely used encryption methods, the development of post-quantum cryptography offers hope for maintaining data security in the face of this new computational paradigm. Organizations and governments must stay vigilant, prepare for the post-quantum era, and collaborate on developing robust encryption solutions that can withstand the challenges posed by quantum computing.

Chapter 7: OSINT for Counter-Terrorism

Combating terrorism is a critical global priority that involves a multifaceted approach to counter threats from extremist organizations. Open Source Intelligence, or OSINT, plays a significant role in the efforts to track, monitor, and combat terrorism worldwide. OSINT provides valuable tools and techniques for collecting and analyzing information from publicly available sources, aiding both governmental and non-governmental organizations in their counterterrorism efforts. One of the primary advantages of OSINT in combating terrorism is its ability to access a wide range of open sources, including news reports, social media, websites, and publicly available government documents. This extensive pool of information allows intelligence analysts to gain insights into the activities, motivations, and networks of terrorist organizations. In the digital age, terrorists often use the internet and social media platforms to disseminate propaganda, communicate with sympathizers, and plan attacks. OSINT specialists can monitor these online channels to identify and track terrorist individuals and groups, ultimately disrupting their activities. OSINT techniques include monitoring jihadist forums, tracking social media accounts, and analyzing online publications to detect early warning signs of radicalization and potential threats. Another critical aspect of OSINT in counterterrorism is geospatial intelligence, which involves analyzing geographic information to understand the spatial aspects of terrorist activities. Geospatial OSINT can help identify potential terrorist hotspots, track the movement of extremist fighters, and assess the security risks in specific regions. This information is invaluable for law enforcement and intelligence agencies in their efforts to prevent terrorist attacks and protect national security. The collaborative nature of OSINT also enhances counterterrorism efforts, as information can be shared and analyzed by multiple agencies and organizations. This sharing of open-source data facilitates a more comprehensive and holistic understanding of the threat landscape. Moreover, OSINT enables international collaboration, allowing countries to work together to combat terrorism on a global scale. Through OSINT, governments can access publicly available information from foreign sources, which can be particularly useful in tracking the activities of transnational terrorist organizations. In addition to monitoring extremist content and online activities, OSINT can be instrumental in tracking financial transactions related to terrorism. Terrorist organizations require funds to operate, and they often resort to illicit financial activities to raise and move money. OSINT can help identify suspicious financial transactions and connections, aiding in the disruption of terrorist financing networks. One of the notable advantages of OSINT in combating terrorism is its ability to provide real-time information and situational awareness. In a rapidly evolving threat environment, timely access to relevant data is crucial for making informed decisions and responding effectively to potential threats. For example, during a terrorist attack or crisis situation, OSINT can provide on-the-ground information, eyewitness accounts, and updates from social media that help authorities assess the situation and respond appropriately. Furthermore, OSINT can contribute to the identification and tracking of foreign fighters who travel to conflict zones to join terrorist organizations. By monitoring travel records, visa applications, and open-source information, intelligence agencies can identify individuals who may pose a threat upon their return to their home countries. This proactive approach can help prevent terrorist attacks and mitigate the risks associated with returning foreign fighters. However, it's essential to acknowledge that OSINT has its limitations in combating terrorism. While OSINT can provide valuable insights, it relies on publicly available information, which may not encompass all relevant data. Terrorist organizations often operate in secrecy, using encrypted communication channels and avoiding public exposure. These clandestine activities are less susceptible to OSINT analysis, necessitating the use of other intelligence disciplines, such as human intelligence (HUMINT) and signals intelligence (SIGINT). Additionally, the ethical considerations of OSINT should not be overlooked. Collecting and analyzing open-source information must be conducted within the boundaries of legal and ethical frameworks, respecting individuals' privacy rights and adhering to data protection regulations. The responsible use of OSINT is crucial to maintain public trust and uphold democratic values while combating terrorism. In summary, OSINT is a valuable tool in the fight against terrorism, providing intelligence agencies and law enforcement with critical information from publicly available sources. Its ability to monitor online activities, track financial transactions, and provide real-time situational awareness enhances counterterrorism efforts. However, OSINT is just one component of a comprehensive counterterrorism strategy, and it must be used in conjunction with other intelligence disciplines and ethical considerations to effectively combat the evolving threat of terrorism in the modern world. Identifying radicalization patterns online is a crucial aspect of countering extremism and preventing acts of terrorism. In today's digital age, the internet and social media platforms have become significant channels for the dissemination of extremist ideologies and recruitment of individuals into radicalized groups. To effectively combat this threat, it is essential to recognize the signs and patterns of radicalization that manifest in online spaces. Radicalization refers to the process by which an individual adopts extremist beliefs and ideologies, often leading to the willingness to engage in acts of violence to achieve political, religious, or ideological goals. Online platforms provide a fertile ground for the spread of extremist content, enabling like-minded individuals to connect, share propaganda, and reinforce each other's beliefs. One of the key challenges in identifying radicalization patterns online is the sheer volume of content and the diversity of platforms where extremist materials can be found. Extremist groups and individuals often operate across multiple online spaces, making it essential for analysts and law enforcement agencies to monitor various channels. Common platforms used for radicalization include social media networks, messaging apps, discussion forums, and video-sharing websites. Radicalization patterns may vary depending on the specific ideology and goals of the extremist group, but several common indicators can help identify individuals who are becoming radicalized. One such indicator is the consumption of extremist propaganda and content. Individuals on the path to radicalization often consume a steady diet of extremist materials, which may include videos, articles, speeches, and social media posts that promote violence and hatred. Monitoring an individual's online activity for the repeated consumption and sharing of such content can be a red flag. Another indicator is the engagement with like-minded individuals and groups. Radicalization often occurs within echo chambers, where individuals reinforce each other's beliefs and become isolated from opposing viewpoints. Individuals who regularly interact with extremist social media accounts, join extremist forums, or participate in closed chat groups may be in the process of radicalization. Expressions of extreme or violent views in online discussions are also significant indicators. These may include advocating for violence against specific groups, praising terrorist acts, or expressing a desire to join extremist organizations. Tracking such expressions of radical beliefs can help identify individuals who pose a potential threat. Changes in behavior and personal life can be observed as individuals become more radicalized online. They may withdraw from their offline social circles, exhibit increased hostility towards certain communities, and demonstrate a willingness to act on their extremist beliefs. These behavioral changes can provide valuable insights into an individual's radicalization process. Online recruitment efforts by extremist groups are another critical element to consider. Radicalization often involves recruitment, where individuals are persuaded to join extremist organizations or take part in violent activities. Tracking recruitment attempts, whether through direct messages, social media posts, or online forums, can help identify individuals who are being targeted for radicalization. In addition to tracking individual indicators, it is essential to analyze the broader online environment. This includes monitoring the online presence of extremist groups and tracking their activities. Identifying trends in the dissemination of extremist content, shifts in messaging tactics, and the emergence of new recruitment strategies can inform counter-radicalization efforts. The role of algorithms and artificial intelligence (AI) in identifying radicalization patterns online has also grown in importance. AI-powered tools can assist in the analysis of vast amounts of online content, flagging potential radicalization indicators and trends. However, the use of AI in this context raises ethical considerations, as it requires balancing the need for security with protecting individuals' privacy and free expression rights. While technology can aid in the identification of radicalization patterns online, human analysts play a crucial role in interpreting the data and making informed assessments. This involves not only identifying potential threats but also assessing the level of risk posed by individuals on the path to radicalization. Effective counter-radicalization efforts require a multidisciplinary approach involving intelligence agencies, law enforcement, social services, mental health professionals, and community organizations. Preventing radicalization and extremism is not solely a law enforcement matter; it involves addressing the underlying factors that drive individuals toward extremist ideologies. These factors can include social isolation, economic disenfranchisement, exposure to hate speech, and a sense of identity and belonging within extremist groups. Community engagement and intervention programs that provide support and alternative pathways for individuals at risk of radicalization are essential components of a comprehensive strategy. Furthermore, education and awareness campaigns can help individuals recognize the signs of radicalization in their peers and encourage reporting to relevant authorities or organizations. In summary, identifying radicalization patterns online is a critical task in the fight against extremism and terrorism. Monitoring the consumption of extremist content, changes in behavior, engagement with extremist groups, and recruitment efforts are essential aspects of this effort. Effective counter-radicalization strategies require a combination of technology, human analysis, community engagement, and support programs to address the root causes of radicalization and prevent individuals from being drawn into extremist ideologies.

Chapter 8: Ethical Hacking and OSINT Synergy

Ethical hacking, also known as white-hat hacking, is a valuable approach to enhance Open Source Intelligence (OSINT) capabilities. It involves authorized and legal attempts to identify vulnerabilities and weaknesses in computer systems, networks, and online platforms. The ethical hacker, often referred to as a penetration tester, mimics the tactics of malicious hackers to uncover security flaws before they can be exploited by cybercriminals. Ethical hacking can be a powerful tool in the OSINT arsenal, as it allows professionals to assess the security posture of target organizations and individuals. One key aspect of ethical hacking for OSINT enhancement is vulnerability assessment. Ethical hackers systematically scan and probe digital assets to discover vulnerabilities that might be exploited by malicious actors.

By identifying weaknesses in an organization's infrastructure, OSINT practitioners can better understand potential points of entry for attackers. These vulnerabilities could range from unpatched software to misconfigured security settings, and their discovery is essential for strengthening defenses. Another critical role of ethical hacking in OSINT is in testing the effectiveness of privacy protection measures. Individuals and organizations often rely on various privacy tools and techniques to safeguard their online presence. Ethical hackers can evaluate the effectiveness of these measures by attempting to collect information that might be considered private or sensitive. By doing so, they help individuals and organizations identify gaps in their privacy strategies and take corrective action. Social engineering assessments are another vital aspect of ethical hacking for OSINT. Social engineering involves manipulating individuals into divulging confidential information or taking specific actions. Ethical hackers employ social engineering techniques to evaluate the susceptibility of employees or individuals to such attacks. The results of these assessments can inform OSINT practitioners about the potential risks posed by social engineering tactics and help them develop countermeasures. Penetration testing is a core component of ethical hacking that assesses an organization's ability to withstand real-world attacks. Ethical hackers simulate attack scenarios to determine whether systems and networks can resist intrusion attempts. This process can uncover vulnerabilities that might not be apparent through other assessment methods and provide a realistic view of an organization's security posture. In the context of OSINT, penetration testing can be used to gauge the resilience of online profiles, websites, and digital infrastructure against targeted attacks.

The concept of "red teaming" is an extension of ethical hacking that involves the creation of adversarial scenarios to challenge an organization's security measures. Red team exercises are valuable for assessing an organization's readiness to respond to sophisticated threats. For OSINT practitioners, red teaming can help identify potential weak points in their online presence and evaluate their ability to detect and respond to attacks. Collaboration between ethical hackers and OSINT professionals can be highly beneficial. Ethical hackers possess technical expertise in assessing vulnerabilities and conducting security assessments. When working in conjunction with OSINT practitioners, they can provide valuable insights into the security implications of OSINT activities. By understanding the potential risks and vulnerabilities associated with OSINT gathering, professionals can take proactive steps to mitigate them. It is crucial to note that ethical hacking should always be conducted within a legal and ethical framework. Permission and consent must be obtained from the target organization or individual before any testing or assessments take place. Ethical hackers should adhere to strict codes of conduct and respect privacy and confidentiality. Ethical hacking for OSINT enhancement also aligns with responsible disclosure practices, whereby vulnerabilities discovered during assessments are reported to the affected parties and addressed promptly. Engaging with ethical hackers can be seen as a proactive approach to improving an organization's security posture. Rather than waiting for cyberattacks to occur, organizations can take proactive measures to identify and rectify vulnerabilities before they can be exploited. This approach aligns with the principles of risk management and cybersecurity best practices. In the context of OSINT, ethical hacking can be a powerful tool for individuals and organizations looking to protect their digital footprints and sensitive information.

By proactively assessing vulnerabilities, testing privacy measures, and simulating real-world attacks, OSINT practitioners can better understand their online risks and take steps to enhance their security. In summary, ethical hacking plays a significant role in enhancing OSINT capabilities by identifying vulnerabilities, testing privacy measures, and simulating real-world attacks. Collaboration between ethical hackers and OSINT practitioners can provide valuable insights into an organization's security posture and improve its overall resilience to cyber threats. Coordinated ethical hacking and intelligence gathering represent a strategic approach to enhancing an organization's cybersecurity and intelligence capabilities. This integrated approach combines the expertise of ethical hackers and intelligence professionals to identify threats, vulnerabilities, and relevant intelligence for decision-making. Coordinated efforts bridge the gap between proactive cybersecurity and effective intelligence collection. Ethical hackers play a pivotal role in identifying vulnerabilities within an organization's digital infrastructure and assessing its security posture. Their technical skills and knowledge of hacking techniques enable them to simulate real-world cyberattacks to uncover weaknesses before malicious actors can exploit them. By collaborating with intelligence professionals, ethical hackers can align their activities with the organization's broader threat landscape and intelligence needs. Intelligence professionals are responsible for collecting, analyzing, and disseminating information that supports informed decision-making. Their focus extends beyond technical vulnerabilities to encompass a wide range of threats, including geopolitical, competitive, and socio-cultural factors. Intelligence professionals identify emerging trends, assess the intentions of potential adversaries, and provide early warnings of impending threats. When combined with ethical hacking efforts, intelligence gathering becomes more targeted, context-aware, and actionable.

A coordinated approach ensures that cybersecurity measures are aligned with the organization's broader intelligence objectives. The fusion of cyber threat intelligence with ethical hacking activities enhances the organization's ability to detect, respond to, and mitigate cyber threats effectively. This synergy enables organizations to prioritize their cybersecurity efforts based on intelligence-driven insights. For example, if intelligence suggests that a specific threat actor is targeting the organization's industry, ethical hackers can focus on identifying vulnerabilities relevant to that actor's tactics, techniques, and procedures (TTPs). Ethical hackers can also emulate these TTPs during their assessments to gauge the organization's preparedness against the specific threat. Conversely, intelligence professionals benefit from the technical insights provided by ethical hackers. These insights include the identification of zero-day vulnerabilities, novel attack vectors, and indicators of compromise (IoCs). By analyzing the technical aspects of cyber threats, intelligence professionals can develop more accurate threat profiles, improve attribution capabilities, and provide timely warnings to decision-makers. The synergy between ethical hacking and intelligence gathering extends beyond technical assessments. Ethical hackers can assist intelligence professionals by conducting open source intelligence (OSINT) operations to collect information on potential threat actors. This may involve monitoring dark web forums, tracking hacker groups, or identifying digital footprints associated with malicious activities.

Ethical hackers are skilled in tracing digital breadcrumbs left by threat actors, which can contribute to the intelligence collection process. Furthermore, ethical hackers can actively engage with threat actors in online forums, posing as potential recruits or collaborators to gather intelligence on their operations and intentions. Coordinated efforts between ethical hackers and intelligence professionals can also enhance the organization's incident response capabilities. When a security incident occurs, the insights gained from intelligence gathering and ethical hacking assessments can expedite the identification of the attack's source, scope, and impact. This, in turn, enables a more effective and targeted incident response, reducing the time to contain and mitigate the threat. Moreover, the intelligence-driven approach can aid in attributing cyberattacks to specific threat actors or state-sponsored entities, facilitating the pursuit of legal action or diplomatic responses. In addition to enhancing technical cybersecurity measures, coordinated efforts also extend to the human element of security. Security awareness and training programs benefit from intelligence insights on emerging social engineering tactics and psychological manipulation techniques employed by threat actors. Ethical hackers can conduct simulated phishing campaigns, tailored to mimic the tactics observed in the threat landscape, to assess the organization's resilience to social engineering attacks. The gathered intelligence on successful phishing attempts and employee susceptibility informs targeted training and awareness programs. Coordinated ethical hacking and intelligence gathering activities are not limited to traditional organizations.

Government agencies, critical infrastructure operators, and law enforcement agencies also leverage this approach to strengthen their cybersecurity and intelligence capabilities. For instance, national cybersecurity agencies collaborate with intelligence organizations to assess the security of critical infrastructure, identify potential vulnerabilities, and analyze cyber threats. By adopting a coordinated approach, these entities enhance their preparedness and resilience against cyberattacks with national security implications. International collaboration is also essential, as cyber threats often transcend borders. Information sharing and coordinated efforts between nations facilitate the identification and attribution of cybercriminals and state-sponsored threat actors. Ethical hacking activities play a crucial role in supporting law enforcement agencies in their efforts to combat cybercrime. In summary, coordinated ethical hacking and intelligence gathering represent a holistic and strategic approach to cybersecurity and intelligence. This synergy leverages the technical expertise of ethical hackers and the intelligence analysis capabilities of professionals to enhance an organization's overall resilience to cyber threats. The fusion of technical assessments, threat intelligence, and human-centric security measures creates a robust defense against the evolving threat landscape.

Chapter 9: Deep Learning and Natural Language Processing

Advanced sentiment analysis with deep learning represents a significant leap in the field of natural language processing (NLP). Traditional sentiment analysis techniques primarily rely on rule-based or machine learning approaches, which have limitations in handling the nuances and complexities of human language. Deep learning, specifically neural networks, has revolutionized sentiment analysis by allowing machines to understand context, sarcasm, and subtle emotions in text. The core concept of deep learning in sentiment analysis is the use of artificial neural networks, which are inspired by the structure and function of the human brain. These networks consist of interconnected layers of artificial neurons that can process and analyze data in a hierarchical manner. One of the most popular types of neural networks used in sentiment analysis is the recurrent neural network (RNN). RNNs are designed to handle sequential data, making them well-suited for tasks like text analysis, where the order of words and context matter. However, traditional RNNs have limitations in capturing long-term dependencies in text, which can lead to issues in understanding sentiment in longer documents or complex sentences. To address this limitation, a more advanced variant of RNNs called long short-term memory networks (LSTMs) has gained prominence. LSTMs are equipped with memory cells that can capture and store information over longer sequences, making them more effective in understanding context in sentiment analysis. Another breakthrough in deep learning for sentiment analysis is the use of transformers, particularly the Bidirectional Encoder Representations from Transformers (BERT) model. BERT revolutionized NLP by pre-training on a massive corpus of text, enabling it to learn context and semantics effectively. BERT's bidirectional nature allows it to understand words in the context of both their preceding and following words, leading to more accurate sentiment analysis. With deep learning models like BERT, sentiment analysis can move beyond classifying text as merely positive, negative, or neutral. These models can provide fine-grained sentiment analysis by identifying emotions such as joy, sadness, anger, and surprise. Emotion detection is crucial in applications like brand monitoring, customer feedback analysis, and market sentiment analysis. Deep learning models for sentiment analysis require substantial computational resources and training data. Pre-trained models like BERT are available, but fine-tuning them on domain-specific data is often necessary to achieve optimal results. Transfer learning, which involves taking a pre-trained model and fine-tuning it for a specific task, significantly reduces the amount of labeled data required for sentiment analysis. This approach is particularly valuable for organizations with limited resources for data annotation. The quality of sentiment analysis heavily depends on the quality of the training data and the diversity of the data sources. Ensuring that the training dataset represents a wide range of language styles, domains, and cultural contexts is essential to develop robust sentiment analysis models. Data preprocessing plays a crucial role in preparing text data for deep learning models. Tasks like tokenization, text normalization, and handling of special characters are necessary to ensure the model's effectiveness. Additionally, techniques such as word embeddings and subword embeddings are employed to represent words in a numerical format that neural networks can process. Word embeddings, like Word2Vec and GloVe, map words to high-dimensional vectors based on their co-occurrence patterns in a large corpus of text. Subword embeddings, like FastText, capture morphological and subword information, making them suitable for handling out-of-vocabulary words. Sentiment analysis models often incorporate attention mechanisms that allow them to focus on the most informative parts of the text. Attention mechanisms assign different weights to different words in a sentence, enabling the model to weigh the importance of each word in the sentiment prediction. This attention mechanism is particularly valuable when dealing with long documents or complex sentences. In addition to text, advanced sentiment analysis can incorporate other modalities, such as images, audio, and video. Multimodal sentiment analysis considers information from various sources to provide a more comprehensive understanding of sentiment. For example, analyzing facial expressions in videos or audio cues in customer service calls can complement text-based sentiment analysis. Emotion recognition from speech and facial expressions can provide insights into customers' emotional states during interactions, leading to better customer service and product development. Deep learning models are also being applied to contextual sentiment analysis, which considers the sentiment expressed in the context of a conversation or a thread of messages. This is crucial in applications like social media monitoring, where understanding the sentiment of a single message without considering the surrounding conversation can lead to misinterpretations. Contextual sentiment analysis models, often based on transformers, take into account the entire conversation to provide a more accurate sentiment analysis. Deep learning models for sentiment analysis are not only used for understanding customer sentiment but also for various applications in finance, politics, and healthcare. In financial markets, sentiment analysis can help predict stock price movements by analyzing news articles, social media posts, and financial reports. In politics, sentiment analysis of public opinion can inform election strategies and policy decisions. In healthcare, sentiment analysis of patient reviews and feedback can improve the quality of healthcare services. Despite the remarkable progress in advanced sentiment analysis with deep learning, challenges remain. One major challenge is the potential bias in sentiment analysis models, which can lead to unfair or discriminatory outcomes. Bias can be introduced through biased training data or the limitations of pre-trained models.

Natural Language Processing (NLP) techniques play a crucial role in Multilingual Open-Source Intelligence (OSINT), enabling analysts to extract valuable information from diverse language sources. The growth of the internet has made it essential to monitor and analyze content in multiple languages, as international events and threats often transcend linguistic boundaries. Multilingual OSINT involves collecting, processing, and analyzing information from various sources, including news articles, social media posts, and government reports, in languages from around the world. One of the primary challenges in Multilingual OSINT is language diversity, as there are thousands of languages spoken globally. NLP techniques provide solutions to overcome language barriers and make sense of the vast amount of multilingual data available. Machine translation is a fundamental NLP technique used in Multilingual OSINT to automatically translate text from one language to another. Services like Google Translate and DeepL have made significant advancements in providing accurate translations, but they are not always perfect, especially for languages with complex grammar or idiomatic expressions. Analysts must be aware of the potential for translation errors and context loss when relying on machine translation for critical information. Transliteration is another NLP technique that converts text from one script to another, typically from non-Latin scripts to the Latin script. This is essential when dealing with languages that use different writing systems, such as Arabic, Cyrillic, or Chinese. Transliteration helps ensure that text in these scripts can be processed and analyzed alongside content in Latin-based languages. Language identification is a critical NLP task in Multilingual OSINT, as it helps determine the language of a given document or text snippet. This information is crucial for routing content to analysts who are proficient in the respective language and for ensuring that multilingual data is appropriately handled. Language identification algorithms use statistical models and patterns in the text to make accurate language predictions. Sentiment analysis is another NLP application used in Multilingual OSINT, as it helps assess public sentiment, opinions, and emotions expressed in various languages. Understanding sentiment in different languages can provide valuable insights into the public's reaction to events, products, or political developments. However, sentiment analysis models must be trained and fine-tuned for each language to achieve accurate results. Named Entity Recognition (NER) is an essential NLP technique for identifying and categorizing entities such as names of people, organizations, locations, and dates in text. In Multilingual OSINT, NER helps extract and organize information about key entities mentioned in diverse language sources. NER systems need language-specific models to perform effectively across multiple languages. Language-specific resources, such as dictionaries and language models, are indispensable for accurate Multilingual OSINT analysis. These resources help improve the quality of machine translation, sentiment analysis, and other NLP tasks by providing language-specific context and vocabulary. Developing and maintaining a repository of language resources is essential for organizations engaged in Multilingual OSINT. Cross-lingual information retrieval is a technique that allows analysts to retrieve relevant documents in one language based on queries in another language. For example, an English-speaking analyst might need to find relevant Arabic news articles about a specific event. Cross-lingual information retrieval systems use NLP techniques to bridge the language gap and retrieve documents that match the query's intent. Machine learning models are at the heart of many NLP techniques used in Multilingual OSINT. These models require training data in each language of interest to perform well. Collecting and annotating training data for multiple languages can be resource-intensive, but it is essential for building accurate and robust NLP systems. Open-source NLP libraries and frameworks, such as spaCy, NLTK, and Hugging Face Transformers, provide valuable tools for developing Multilingual OSINT applications. These libraries offer pre-trained models and resources for a wide range of languages, reducing the effort required to build language-specific NLP solutions. Multilingual OSINT analysts must consider cultural nuances and local context when interpreting information in different languages. The meaning of certain words, phrases, or symbols can vary significantly between cultures and regions, leading to potential misunderstandings. Cultural sensitivity and domain expertise are essential for accurate analysis. Multilingual OSINT also involves monitoring social media platforms in various languages to track emerging trends, news, and public sentiment. Social media data streams in multiple languages provide valuable real-time insights, but they also pose challenges in terms of data volume and language-specific content moderation. Multilingual OSINT teams often employ a combination of automated NLP tools and human analysts who are proficient in the languages under scrutiny. The human element is crucial for context-sensitive analysis and verifying the accuracy of automated NLP outputs. Machine learning techniques, such as neural machine translation and cross-lingual transfer learning, continue to advance Multilingual OSINT capabilities. These techniques aim to improve the quality of machine translation, sentiment analysis, and other NLP tasks by leveraging large multilingual datasets and sophisticated models. Ethical considerations are paramount in Multilingual OSINT, particularly when handling information in languages associated with marginalized or vulnerable communities. Respect for privacy, cultural sensitivity, and responsible information sharing are essential principles that guide ethical Multilingual OSINT practices. Multilingual OSINT analysts should stay informed about the latest developments in NLP and machine learning, as these technologies evolve rapidly. Continuous training and collaboration with experts from diverse linguistic backgrounds help ensure the effectiveness of Multilingual OSINT efforts. In summary, NLP techniques are indispensable in Multilingual OSINT for overcoming language barriers, extracting valuable information, and gaining insights from diverse language sources. Machine translation, sentiment analysis, NER, and other NLP applications empower analysts to navigate the complexities of a multilingual digital landscape effectively. However, these techniques must be used judiciously, with cultural sensitivity and ethical considerations at the forefront, to ensure responsible and accurate Multilingual OSINT analysis.

Chapter 10: OSINT in the Age of Disinformation

In today's interconnected world, the spread of disinformation campaigns has become a pervasive and concerning issue. Disinformation refers to the deliberate spread of false or misleading information with the intent to deceive, manipulate public opinion, or achieve specific political or social objectives. Detecting and countering disinformation campaigns is essential to maintain the integrity of information ecosystems and protect the public from misinformation. Disinformation can take many forms, including fabricated news stories, manipulated images and videos, and deceptive social media posts. These campaigns often exploit existing societal divisions, amplify existing biases, and undermine trust in reliable sources of information. The consequences of successful disinformation campaigns can be far-reaching, influencing public opinion, elections, and even public health decisions. Detecting disinformation campaigns requires a multifaceted approach that combines technological tools, human expertise, and collaborative efforts from various stakeholders. One key element in detecting disinformation is the use of advanced data analytics and machine learning algorithms. These algorithms can analyze vast amounts of data from social media, news sources, and online forums to identify patterns and anomalies associated with disinformation campaigns. Natural Language Processing (NLP) techniques are particularly useful in analyzing text-based content to identify deceptive or manipulative language patterns. However, it's important to note that while technology plays a significant role in detection, human analysts are still crucial in verifying the findings and understanding the context. Social media platforms and tech companies also play a pivotal role in the detection and mitigation of disinformation campaigns. They have implemented various measures, such as content moderation algorithms and fact-checking initiatives, to identify and label misleading or false information. Additionally, they often collaborate with third-party organizations and experts to assess and respond to disinformation threats effectively. Collaboration is a fundamental aspect of countering disinformation. Government agencies, civil society organizations, and media outlets must work together to share information, insights, and best practices in identifying and countering disinformation campaigns. Transparency and information sharing are critical to developing a comprehensive understanding of the disinformation landscape. Education and media literacy programs are essential components of countering disinformation at its root. By equipping individuals with the skills to critically evaluate information sources and discern reliable news from false information, we can empower the public to resist the influence of disinformation campaigns. Media literacy programs should be tailored to different age groups and demographics to address their specific vulnerabilities to disinformation. Fact-checking organizations play a crucial role in countering disinformation by independently verifying the accuracy of claims made in public discourse. They assess the credibility of information sources and provide the public with accurate information to counter false narratives. Fact-checkers also play a vital role in holding public figures and institutions accountable for spreading false information. The spread of disinformation often relies on the virality of content on social media platforms. To counter this, social media companies have implemented measures to reduce the reach of false information and promote credible sources. These measures include algorithms that deprioritize misleading content, warnings on potentially false information, and efforts to identify and remove bot accounts that amplify disinformation. It's important for users to report suspicious content and accounts to social media platforms to aid in their efforts to combat disinformation. Media organizations and journalists play a central role in countering disinformation by upholding journalistic principles and providing accurate, well-sourced reporting. They must remain vigilant in verifying information before publishing stories and providing context to help the public better understand complex issues. Media outlets should also be transparent about their sources and methodologies, fostering trust with their audiences. Engaging with the audience through fact-checking articles, reader feedback, and open discussions can help build a sense of community and credibility. Government agencies have a role in countering disinformation, particularly when it threatens national security or the democratic process. They can provide resources and support for efforts to detect and counter disinformation campaigns, while also promoting transparency and accountability in government actions. However, government involvement in countering disinformation should be carefully balanced with respect for free speech and the protection of civil liberties. Disinformation campaigns often target vulnerable communities, exploiting existing fears and biases. Countering this requires a nuanced understanding of the specific vulnerabilities and needs of these communities. Community organizations, advocacy groups, and researchers can play a crucial role in reaching and educating these communities about disinformation and its impact. Combating disinformation also involves addressing the economic incentives that drive the spread of false information. Some individuals and organizations profit from disinformation by generating clicks, views, and engagement on their content. Efforts to reduce these economic incentives can help mitigate the spread of false information. In some cases, legal measures may be necessary to hold individuals and entities accountable for intentionally spreading disinformation that harms society. These measures must be carefully crafted to protect free speech while discouraging the deliberate spread of false information. Public awareness campaigns can be effective in countering disinformation by informing the public about the tactics and strategies used by disinformation campaigns. These campaigns can educate individuals on how to spot disinformation and encourage responsible information sharing. Promoting critical thinking and skepticism in the face of sensational or polarizing content is key to reducing the impact of disinformation. Ultimately, countering disinformation is an ongoing challenge that requires the collective efforts of individuals, technology companies, media organizations, governments, and civil society. It requires a commitment to upholding the principles of accuracy, transparency, and accountability in the information ecosystem. By working together and remaining vigilant, we can mitigate the harmful effects of disinformation and protect the integrity of public discourse and democratic processes. In an age of digital information overload, the prevalence of misinformation has become a significant concern for individuals and society as a whole. Misinformation refers to false or inaccurate information that is unintentionally spread, often due to errors, misunderstandings, or misinterpretations. It can lead to confusion, fear, and misguided decision-making, making it crucial for individuals to develop effective OSINT strategies for misinformation awareness. One fundamental aspect of combating misinformation is understanding its sources and drivers. Misinformation can originate from various places, including social media, news outlets, online forums, and even well-intentioned individuals who inadvertently share false information. Identifying the sources of misinformation is essential for determining its credibility and reliability. Fact-checking organizations play a vital role in verifying the accuracy of information and debunking false claims. By referring to trusted fact-checkers, individuals can quickly assess whether a piece of information is accurate or misleading. Misinformation often thrives in environments where sensationalism and confirmation bias are prevalent. Confirmation bias refers to the tendency of individuals to seek out and interpret information in ways that confirm their pre-existing beliefs or opinions. To counter this bias, it is essential to promote critical thinking and skepticism when encountering new information. This involves questioning the source, evaluating the evidence provided, and considering alternative viewpoints. Misinformation can spread rapidly on social media platforms, where information is disseminated quickly, and the lines between fact and opinion are often blurred. One effective OSINT strategy for misinformation awareness is to evaluate the credibility of the source. Is the information coming from a reputable news outlet, an expert in the field, or a credible organization? Checking the source's track record for accuracy and reliability can help individuals assess the information's trustworthiness. It's also crucial to be cautious of information that lacks clear attribution or relies on anonymous sources. Misinformation often thrives in the absence of transparency and accountability. Another vital aspect of OSINT strategies for misinformation awareness is cross-referencing information. Before accepting a piece of information as true, individuals should seek multiple sources that corroborate the same facts. This practice helps confirm the accuracy of information and reduces the likelihood of falling victim to misinformation. Additionally, individuals should be aware of the potential for misinformation to be perpetuated by echo chambers. Echo chambers are online communities where individuals are exposed only to information that aligns with their existing beliefs. Being aware of these dynamics can help individuals recognize when they are in an echo chamber and seek out diverse perspectives. Misinformation can take various forms, from false statistics and fabricated stories to manipulated images and videos. Visual content, in particular, can be misleading, as it may be altered or taken out of context. As part of their OSINT strategies for misinformation awareness, individuals should develop media literacy skills. This includes the ability to analyze visual content critically, looking for signs of manipulation or distortion.

Tools and techniques for reverse image search and video verification can also aid in confirming the authenticity of visual content. Misinformation can sometimes be deliberately spread for various reasons, including political agendas, financial gain, or malicious intent. Conspiracy theories, in particular, are a common source of misinformation, often driven by distrust in authorities and institutions. To counter such narratives, individuals should engage in open, respectful dialogue and share credible information to debunk baseless claims. Misinformation can also emerge during crises and emergencies when accurate information is essential for public safety. In such situations, it is crucial for individuals to rely on official sources and trusted news outlets for updates. Avoiding the rapid sharing of unverified information can prevent the spread of rumors and false claims during critical moments. Misinformation awareness should extend beyond individual efforts to collective responsibility. Communities, schools, and organizations can play a role in promoting media literacy and critical thinking skills. Education campaigns that teach individuals how to evaluate information sources and fact-check claims can empower people to become more discerning consumers of information. Fact-checking initiatives, both independent and institutional, should be supported and encouraged to combat the spread of misinformation. While OSINT strategies for misinformation awareness are essential, it's equally important to recognize that misinformation can be challenging to eradicate entirely. In some cases, individuals may continue to believe false information even after it has been debunked. This persistence is known as the "backfire effect" and highlights the need for ongoing efforts to address misinformation at its root. Ultimately, misinformation awareness is a continuous process that requires vigilance, critical thinking, and an openness to learning. By arming themselves with the necessary skills and knowledge, individuals can navigate the digital information landscape more effectively and contribute to the fight against misinformation. Misinformation is a complex issue with social, psychological, and technological dimensions. It thrives in an environment where information is abundant and easily disseminated, making it crucial for individuals to take proactive steps to verify information and promote accurate, reliable sources. In an era where misinformation can have real-world consequences, misinformation awareness is not just a personal responsibility but a societal imperative.

Conclusion

In the ever-evolving landscape of online investigations and intelligence gathering, the journey from novice to expert is a transformative one. This book bundle, "Advanced OSINT Strategies," has taken you on a comprehensive exploration of the field, from laying the foundations of OSINT mastery to mastering cutting-edge strategies and tools.

In "Foundations of OSINT Mastery: A Beginner's Guide," you embarked on your OSINT journey, building a solid understanding of the fundamentals. You learned to navigate the vast realm of online information, uncovering the importance of digital footprints, and exploring various OSINT information sources. As you progressed through internet search techniques, social media investigations, and website analysis, you began honing your skills as an OSINT practitioner. Along the way, you developed a strong ethical framework and learned to safeguard your privacy in this digital age.

Moving on to "Navigating the Digital Shadows: Intermediate OSINT Techniques," you delved deeper into the world of online investigations. You expanded your expertise with advanced search queries, explored the mysteries of the deep web and dark web, and honed your geospatial intelligence skills. The book empowered you with techniques for advanced social media analysis, email tracing, and open-source analysis tools. You automated your OSINT workflows and ventured into the realm of cyber threat intelligence, setting the stage for your journey into expert-level intelligence gathering.

"Advanced OSINT Arsenal: Expert-Level Intelligence Gathering" elevated your skills to new heights. You delved into topics such as analyzing cryptocurrencies and blockchain, exploiting IoT devices for intelligence, and employing advanced data scraping and automation techniques. The book equipped you with the knowledge to tackle real-world intelligence operations and provided insights into the role of OSINT in countering terrorism. You also explored the integration of ethical hacking with OSINT, showcasing the synergy between these fields.

Finally, in "Mastering OSINT Investigations: Cutting-Edge Strategies and Tools," you reached the pinnacle of your OSINT journey. You uncovered the potential of big data, artificial intelligence, and quantum computing in the OSINT realm. The book emphasized the importance of OSINT in combating disinformation and securing our digital world. You ventured into the dark corners of hidden markets and forums, honed your skills in tracking cryptocurrencies on the dark web, and learned advanced geospatial analysis techniques. You were also introduced to the world of IoT vulnerability assessment and data collection and analysis.

As you conclude your journey through "Advanced OSINT Strategies," you now possess a comprehensive set of skills and strategies that span from beginner to expert levels. The knowledge you've gained empowers you to navigate the complex web of online information, protect your privacy, and contribute to the pursuit of truth and security in the digital age.

Remember that OSINT is an ever-evolving field, and continual learning and adaptation are key to staying at the forefront of online investigations and intelligence gathering.

Whether you're an aspiring OSINT practitioner or a seasoned expert, the journey to mastery is one of curiosity, dedication, and relentless pursuit of knowledge.

We hope this book bundle has been a valuable resource in your quest to become an OSINT master. As you embark on your future endeavors in this dynamic field, may you continue to explore, innovate, and make a positive impact in the world of online investigations and intelligence gathering.
Top of Form

www.ingramcontent.com/pod-product-compliance
Lightning Source LLC
Chambersburg PA
CBHW070935050326
40689CB00014B/3210